To My Adopted
Grandma
Gail

MY BOOK IS MY STORY

My
Angel.

2013

MY BOOK IS MY STORY

Surrendering My Journey to the Holy Spirit

LA VIRGIL-MALDONADO

authorHOUSE®

AuthorHouse™
1663 Liberty Drive
Bloomington, IN 47403
www.authorhouse.com
Phone: 1-800-839-8640

Published by AuthorHouse   04/02/2013

ISBN: 978-1-4772-7880-2 (sc)
ISBN: 978-1-4772-7877-2 (e)

Library of Congress Control Number: 2012919094

Any people depicted in stock imagery provided by Thinkstock are models, and such images are being used for illustrative purposes only.
Certain stock imagery © Thinkstock.

This book is printed on acid-free paper.

Because of the dynamic nature of the Internet, any web addresses or links contained in this book may have changed since publication and may no longer be valid. The views expressed in this work are solely those of the author and do not necessarily reflect the views of the publisher, and the publisher hereby disclaims any responsibility for them.

This book is in more of a coffee table format verses being a novel. So feel free to read the chapters as the Spirit leads you.

Please make note that as I was editing often the words became twisted and sometimes appeared as a foreign language. However with His strength I was able to finish for someone out there needs to hear His whosoever message and that the Trinity is love beyond our comprehension of measure.

ABOUT THE AUTHOR

www.hismultimediaintl.com

Fondly known in the Industry as "LA" or "LA Virgil" she is the definition of a truly multifaceted seasoned Artist. She performs tasks as Music and Media Publicist, Creative Consultant, A.S.C.A.P Songwriter and Publisher, Producer of International film Documentaries, Published Journalist, Television Producer, Artistic Marketing Agent, Event Producer, Community Activist and Creative Pioneer. She was once referred to as the Mother Teresa of Bermuda's creative talent. She has pioneered not for the fame or fortune but has shed tears over us in the Creative Industry recognizing, believing and empowering ourselves!

LA is comfortable working behind the scenes inspiring others to pursue their dreams . . . . Her motto is "Keep it Real . . . ." She has brokered deals with several labels and films for various artists to have distribution throughout Europe and the world.

In addition she has written, arranged, collaborated and produced numerous songs. Some of which have been featured on Television and Film.

She was Awarded "Woman of the Year 2010/2011" by the National Association of Professional Women for excellence and dedication and is quite proud of the cherry wood plaque. In addition to all of this she has a music award in her name in Bermuda, the "LA Virgil Artist of the Year Award" with the UMA which is for those artists who show extreme dedication to their craft.

Her most recent attribute to her extensive roaster is an enlightening thirty minute television show "The Light Switch" which she produces for her company. This airs in Philadelphia on

Comcast 66 and Verizon 29 with Philly Cam. LA keeps her pulse on various community programs including homeless musicians, anti violence, women in transition, women and children in shelters and is Answering whatever Call God dials for her.

DEDICATION

I dedicate this to my Parents; **Leslie and Idell Virgil**, my Aunts; **Estlyn Harvey** and **Eleanor Joell**, my Husband, my Life coaches, my sincere friends and every person who has believed in me, encouraged my heart, empowered my soul and those who befriended me before leaving this planet earth.

Six weeks to the day before submitting this manuscript I lost my neighbor, friend and prayer warrior partner of the last three years **"Ms. Renee Harris."** I could hear her saying "You go L!" I never knew the true meaning of having a neighbor in America until God placed me with her. I didn't know the reason as to why I was so driven to purchase this house but now I do for it was to experience an unconditional friendship. The night before she passed we "cut up" over the phone and out of nowhere I said, "Ms. Renee, please don't leave me" and she said, "Come on L, why would you say that?" I responded with, "Well I guess it's because the neighbor on the other side of my wall Mrs. G passed after she was given an oxygen tank and went on a cruise; now you just returned from our church cruise and have one." She went on to explain about her breathing and I said I could identify with that and gave her my smoking story. She knew that I had my health struggles for I had temporarily lost much of my sight due to a lupus flare up and she witnessed what others never saw. She was there when I gave the first publishers an outline and my money and then I couldn't contact the publishing consultant. I wanted to give up but she said, "Press on L you have come too far and this is for God's glory!" We then prayed after a few giggles and her last words to me was the scripture that I recite throughout this book. Her final words to me on that Tuesday night were "L always say I will live and not die and proclaim His works."

The next morning less than twenty four hours after we spoke I watched her being carried out on a stretcher on our shared concrete landing and all I could do was scream "Ms. Renee, Ms. Renee." She had passed. On that Sunday morning in the wee hours she visited me and all I could do was weep and say "I don't want to sit next to anyone else in church, I don't want to ride with anyone else. Who will I pray and share with without ever hearing it?" She smiled and whispered in my ear "L you have a husband and you can still pray with me. It will be okay, I'm fine now!" Then she disappeared and I awoke feeling this unexplainable peace. I immediately called my other best friend, my Mother who calmly said, "I was wondering if she was going to visit you since you two were so close." I also want to thank **Pop Barlow** and **Jo Jo Sharon** for always encouraging me and being **real**! May you all rest in peace.

CONTENTS

Brain Tumor Race 4 Hope Team worn but not broken

CD Credits as Publicist and Producer of children on client Hubert Smith's
Bermuda Santa Claus

Friend Diane and son Conner

Godson Raphael

In Canada with Dad n Jo

My #1 support team Mom, Aunt El, Dad n Aunt Es

Spiritual Advisor Carvin Haggins

the Maldonado family

with cuz Lez

with my Mom n Momettes

You Better Recognize It's Double Digits!!

Can you believe it, it's a new decade, a new season and a time to truly recognize the reason why each and every one of us is here. It's double digits meaning put in double the effort, double the love, double the sharing, double the result and double the vision of HIS light.

It is time to do less talk and more walk for God is so good. Let me just share some of my journey over the years. Read this book and walk with me and make a decision after having conversations about light and darkness. You will see and feel for yourself where the greatest power resides. You decide if there is more to our lives than what we can physically see. If you are like me no one can just tell you stories about something. So when your inner gut reacts and you feel something is not right with the picture, than just maybe there is more to the story. Therefore you begin paying closer attention to certain things that totally passed you by because you were unaware. However once your three eyes are opened and that light bulb turns on you will see all the dust, all the webs and all the parasitic bugs. You see stuff that you would have stumbled over if you kept walking in the direction of darkness. Hey, all I know is that experience can be a teacher, a deliverer or on the flip side something that can either protect us or keep us in bondage. In this game called life it is more than just the choices we make but the moves that we decide to take!

We can remain stuck or move forward and be grateful that we have been placed on this planet earth for a reason, not just to take up space. Well I've said more than a mouthful but hopefully once you've read this you will have drank more than a sip of the most awesome power and love that abides within us and around us. Just thinking of it illuminates me and maybe that's the glow that others see, true genuine love and light. If you are truly ready to take this ride, put on your seatbelts because we are going to experience smooth, bumpy and jerky movements but don't worry you will land safely that I can promise. However I cannot promise that you will depart from this as the same inner self; for after all we will land in several destinations so once you've seen, once you've heard and once you've experienced the rest is up to you. Okay partner, Mr. Holy Spirit

I believe it's clear and we are ready for take off!!

Living in a State of Emergency

I realize that due to my medical conditions I often feel in my mind that I'm in a state of emergency but this journey is training and teaching me to understand the true application of what it means to put your trust in God. The only emergency should be the second coming and am I ready. But I have this seed inside me that says to finish but enjoy the moments along the way, making memories! As a result I take a lot of pictures and record to leave that legacy. You know you hear the many clichés of it's all in Gods time and this is so true. If I were to receive what I have now back then I couldn't because my life was filled with just stuff. Only now I'm beginning to understand that when your path is so cluttered you can't see your way clearly. You have to be willing to submit and clear those weeds and distractions out of your comfort zone. It is almost as if we become comfortable with hoarding things, people and places in our space, our home, our temple our bodies. As a result we can't detect what is good and that which is not needed so we begin to rely on something outside of ourselves.

Truthfully we don't have it all together as we portray to others. In our quiet time we know we must seek and often we get caught up filling our spaces with material things, people, clubs, bars, pets, religion, gym, churches etc. We are needy creatures let's face it we all want something; we all need someone or some external. I don't care if you are a loner, so am I but we immerse our souls into something. We are all striving for that "GREATER!" For me that space filler is the Holy Spirit. This is my partner through and out.

While I'm living in my state of emergency I'm learning to release it to the universe, to God and let Him totally have His way. I'm enjoying my journey with my partner and letting the Spirit just guide me. I've met interesting people, traveled to different places and spaces all because of my friend. So this book is a journey of how you can survive through terminal illness and other degenerating diseases that have been pronounced over your life. Like my Dad always says the word can't is not an option. So journey along with me and embrace your 'shoop' sections because once you have that tight relationship with Christ you can do ALL things. I know I am, just watch! I got married and have a stepson when they told me at the hospital that if I didn't go back on chemo for my brain cancer I would die, That was several years ago.

FROM THE BEGINNING

Back in the day at Aunt Es   Baby LA

I'm here lying in bed next to my mother and she's telling me about how it all began and here it is. When I was entering this earth my Mom had toxemia which is poison? The doctors told her that either one of us would die. She immediately started praying that we both would live. She then had a ruptured membrane and they said I would be blind and she passed all of this green stuff so they thought I would be blind from that. I was born bluish due to lack of oxygen because Mom was told by the nurses to hold back because they wanted to perform a C Section after her being in labor for EIGHTEEN hours but I ended up coming out naturally. Even though I was a blue baby God protected me from the beginning! I was born in prayer with my praying Mom and my Prayer Warrior Evangelist Grandmother who was abroad on an assignment from the Father at the time. I cried right away they didn't even have to spank me and the doctors said that I was a miracle. So from the day I was born the word "**miracle**" were pronounced over my life. I was due on the 23rd of December but I entered January the 2nd. I was the first baby born in my country that year having arrived just before 3 a.m. Now oddly enough my brother was due on January 2nd and arrived December 23rd so we switched dates from the beginning!

BELIEVE YOU CAN FLY

It's like R. Kelly's song "I believe I can fly, I can touch the sky, I believe I can soar, I believe. If I can see it I can do it." I'm here listening to Gerald Levert and Yolanda Adams version and God reminded me that anything I want, the desires of my heart can be fulfilled if I just follow him and trust in Him. All the visions my partner, the Holy Spirit has led me through are not by chance but to open my eyes and see the Light. Now look at that I typed in the word "Light" and right after that they said the word 'Light' on Music choice in the song "Since Jesus Came'" by Tonex and Kirk Franklin.

"Look I may not have all the answers but I do know about my life and what has happened to me and I became so free when love and light lifted me." For me it was when I truly gave my life to Christ. It was almost as if the door of hope had been swung wide open. It's no way I can survive all of my conditions such as cancer in three places, systemic lupus, not being able to talk, walk, or beating cocaine cold turkey. I snorted so much coke that my nose has no filters so any little dust goes straight to my throat and I cough but I'm being healed.

"It's all because of you Lord. You called me to be a fisher of men, to proclaim to a world seeking for answers that you, only Lord God Jehovah sits on the throne. It is you and you only that have saved my soul from despair! It is you and you only that gets me up in the morning to write these words. Lord Jesus I love you and accept you truly as my Lord and Savior. I will continually allow the Holy Spirit to guide and protect me because we are simply spiritual beings having an earthly experience! When my partner, Mr. Holy Spirit says to go left I will follow and not chose my own mind and go right. I will submit to you and lean not on my own understanding for you know the plans that you have for me and they are plans like you said in Jeremiah 29:11 not to harm me but to prosper me for my hope is in You and You alone."

I encourage you to not only read but feed on this book. Let it be a source of true encouragement and relief. Allow your spirit to be free as you read some of my testimonies and daily encounters with the Trinity. Let it lift you from sorrow to joy for as you are led you will realize that you will worry less and in my life hurry less for I have a shepherd that will never leave me nor forsake me. So fly and soar because once you accept this as your truth it becomes so clear and peaceful. A peace that passes all understanding. In the midst of any storm you will still sing praises.

CAN WE TALK?

Well I'm finally sitting down writing my thoughts and literally I said, "Ok God it's you and me let's do this thing." I had collected audio tapes for the past few years of my conversations with God.

My Mother heard me once and said it sounded like I was preaching but the reality is I'm talking with God more often, whether it is in the shower or while sitting on the throne. Every day I ask the Holy Spirit to order my steps. There is no sugarcoating in this book so if you are ready for some real talk and a real walk then you'll enjoy this ride. Now put on your seat belt, buckle up and get ready to enter a journey that takes you into real life and discover how Jesus still does real down to earth work. Today I consider myself a "Keep it Real Christian."

The conversations with Him get deep just like the lyrics He has given me in countless songs. I classify myself as a Christian outside the box! You see Jesus who is my number one boo lived a life outside of the box. He did not live his life within the religious constraints of that time. He broke the mold per say . . . Come on Holy Spirit guide me to write this book so that lives may be changed by spreading and absorbing your words and lessons throughout our journey.

I admire that Jesus did not serve God like everyone else for there was no formality but yet there was reverence and respect! I am a Jesus follower and like a stranger said to me on the train once while I was traveling and sort of struggling with my bag. He came and helped me and I told him that I was so thankful and he softly said he was just doing what Jesus would do. I try and I do say try because none of us are perfect to live the life as my Lord and Savior would. Jesus showed love to all, despite their race, culture or circumstance.

It did not matter with him and today we must recognize that although we are different we are still one species, that being human beings. We are one group of beings on this planet earth. Therefore requesting the ordering of steps on a daily is something that I strongly suggest for each one of us.

This morning I received a forward about a letter from Satan and how he loves it when we cuss people out or do things that destroy our lives like drugs, alcohol or gambling. Later I put on the Word station to Pastor Michael Freeman and I heard him saying how demons walk beside us and this is why we cuss people out. Well yesterday I got so upset with this cable company that shut off my internet in the middle of something important so I called my fiancé and used a cuss word in my delivery which he repeated and was shocked because I make it a habit of trying not to cuss. Even his son asks us if he can use a bad word.

Later during the day I listened to my voicemail and I heard on a message where my baby was cussing to his brother. Last night I discussed the subject and he said, "Oh I was mad but you cuss." I said to him that I was mad and he said, "Well so was I and that is why I was cussing." Yeah right that's not what I heard, it sounded like general conversation but the point is that we cannot allow Satan's friends to walk beside us rather than Jesus; we would end up doing all sorts of unthinkable things and then justify our actions. Just like me and my sweetie cussing. I remember that now as I'm writing, (thank you Holy Spirit after all this is your book for the people I'm only the instrument).

I watched Joyce Meyer talk about putting on the armor of God because we fight not against flesh and blood but against principalities. In Eph 6 the meaning to me is for us to be conscious and walk with Jesus at all times. I guess that is what the song meant by having that line A TALK WITH Jesus telling Him your problems. Trust me it doesn't hurt to have your hand in the hand of the Man that calmed the sea.

When I quit chemo I would have these brief but intense seizures were I would lose my speech and the only name I could call was Jesus! Every time; His name alone broke me out of these demonic chains. I tested and proved God and Jesus certainly is the name above all names. I remember having seizures every 5 minutes and my father had to sleep with me to keep check on me.(gosh I love my Dad and Mom and Aunts off course) My Aunt was sleeping in the room that was only separated by French doors and even she just kept hearing that name, the name above all others, Jesus.

I was in the recording studio having seizures trying to lay down vocals for a song God gave me about truth and all I could say after each seizure was Jesus. This happened so much that the engineer would look at me when I became silent in my frozen mode and say Jesus? And he is not a Christian, well not yet.

The same thing happened at a club when I was on the dance floor. This guy who I hadn't seen in years came up to me and as we started to talk I began to have this frozen seizure so I just stared at him. He said, "Oh man I need what she must be drinking, she's messed right up" and proceeded to ask the bartender for whatever it was that I was drinking. Now truth is told I was drinking a virgin Shirley temple so Lord knows what they gave him. Anyhoo he came back to dance with me, saying look I have what you have and began to get his groove on. Well all I could say to break out of my seizure silence was "Jesus, thank you Jesus, Jesus, thank you Jesus" and I repeated this until I was out of the trapped silent mode. Now imagine the look on this guy's face as he started to dance with me. The look was priceless and I bet you today he is a Christian. Talk about planting a seed in action! I know he will never forget that night for he saw firsthand the presence of Christ as there was the display of strength and humility which was released into the atmosphere. Jesus rocks!

'Shoop' Sections

Everybody has a 'shoop' section or sections in their life's journey, we can't escape it. Often we can't rely on others or ourselves, some answers can only come from our Creator. This is an excerpt from what I wrote on face book. This is a section that I wish to share not to expose but to assist others in their healing for I just know there is someone out there with some of these issues who can identify. This chapter is only a synopsis and actually can be a book on its own; you know it's a stand-alone piece. Sort of like that part of a song that could be a separate song that spins into other areas. I pray that this will heal a soul. Thank you partner, Mr. Holy Spirit for prompting me to do this, now let me take a breath and exhale and deliver my 'shoop' experience.

STAY FOCUSED AND FIGHT FOR PURPOSE!

Sometimes we get caught up, shaken up and broken up but all things work together for the good of those that love the Lord. Worship is an intimate relationship with our Savior. That is who Jesus Christ is a true Savior for there is no man, woman, child or thing that can save us from ourselves. God is a jealous God and I can understand Him getting angry with us, His creations. He created us for His purpose and plan so when we attach ourselves to other people, places, positions, and possessions we hurt Him. What separates us from others is the fact that we believe and trust in a higher power that is so solid that there is no other for us!

This morning I woke up with the spirit of fear, darkness all over me. I keep getting this cold and I know what it is every time I get better than when I go out around people out I get re-infected. It's that systemic lupus kicking in were your auto immune system is down. Now I can tell everyone else what to do but I need to follow my own advice and stick to my concoctions and rest when I'm weary! Last week I could just about walk and move without feeling some pain and God had me lay hands on myself and be strengthened in Him for when I went to the hospital and saw my history it was no joke, I could see why they term me as a 'miracle patient.' It finally reset my mind and accept that they say I have the diagnosis of cancer. The C term is something that I try and stay away from, but the lupus I seem to identify with more. When I left the C place, I asked my partner which direction I should take for I was excited to be walking without all the discomfort. I guess the Bermudian term would be 'serves me right' since I wanted to overdo it and walk everywhere. Anyhoo I was directed to this particular train station and when I walked in, it instantly brought back memories and my appetite kicked in. Before I tell you how was my 'purpose' encounter I want to point out how God directs our lives if we just obey and how God works in the littlest of things to bring us to our purpose.

I went to the other building for advanced medicine to take care of some things where I bumped into an unexpected fellow church member and we exchanged a few words. While I was there I went and got some information for my Aunt's illness and the staff went the extra mile and gave me this web link. When I was leaving this lady asked if she could help me which led to a conversation. I waited for her to finish assisting some other patients and one in particular was very mean to her. My partner, Mr. Holy Spirit had me wait so that I could say to this very sophisticated lady that God had placed her in that position to assist others for He knew that with her loving demeanor she could be able to handle people's attitudes. She responded by telling me that it was nothing but the grace of God and to Him she gives ALL the glory. Now was I expecting that not at all so I said, "Are you a Christian? And she graciously said to me, "I guess we are both family!" Now this lady was an older classy white woman and yeah God took me by surprise. My spirits were lifted by seeing the church member who I've always admired and now this Angel. The church member and this lady both have the same spirit now I'm thinking about it. This is the spirit of Christ. Wow Holy Spirit what a revelation! Is that how people view me when they say I'm an inspiration?

Alright getting back to the path; I left the building and was a bit hungry so I walked to the various food vendors outside but nothing caught my attention so I said to myself that I could wait until I got closer to home. I could have walked my usual route but my partner let me go a different way so I could be amongst the students and then I bumped into a guy on crutches looking for the sports medicine building. I told him where I thought it was and we exchanged conversation and walked our separate ways and then I looked back and told him to go to the hospital for they should know and he thanked me. Okay then I walked past my usual subway entrance and asked my partner where to go and I ended up at 30th Street station. I looked around and the place was packed but I decided I would treat myself and get a hard shell taco. When I walked past the tables I noticed this frail white woman and my partner told me that is where I was to sit when I got my food. So in my natural I said okay if she is still sitting there by herself when I get my food I'll sit there. You see I already gave permission for my life and my day to be directed by my partner, Mr. Holy Spirit. Therefore all the twists and turns were to prepare me for this assignment. I already was armored and empowered by the two Christian family members I had passed earlier. So I was equipped and ready!

I purchased my food and came and asked her if she minded if I sat at her table and she said no with a welcoming smile. Now remember I went to the hospital for two conditions but the main appointment was for my cancerous brain tumor. This lady who I could not have possibly known in the natural said that she comes to the city to get shots because she has a blockage in her brain's blood vessels and as a result has severe headaches. I didn't even know this condition existed let alone they had a medical treatment for it. Anyhoo the lady and I exchanged conversation and in that I learned about her family and challenges. For example she faced the strong possibility of being laid off from her job and she was a single mother of three with her youngest having autism. Her oldest son had his girlfriend move in and they weren't contributing and in the midst of that she couldn't get various disability benefits because she was working. She said she knew others who were getting over and using the system and didn't have as many challenges as she had. She wanted to work to be an example to her children to show them that if you want to succeed in life you have to work hard at it and not just collect from the government. She also told me about various festivals and events and some I was quite interested in. I told her how I was feeling sorry for myself and that you always hear the saying that somebody else may have a worse story and here she was. My heart went out to her and at the end of our meal I asked her if it was alright for me to pray for her and she said yes. I didn't care who was looking for it was a JUST US MOMENT.

I placed my hands over hers and started to pray and when I was finished I could see tears in her eyes. I gave her a card so that she could stay in contact and I wrote down her number. She looked at the card and said I have a problem with this and I said what. She pointed to the word Christ and I said really, why? She then told me how she was married to this religious Christian man and how bad he treated her and her children behind closed doors and they eventually divorced. Shortly after that she went to a church for comfort and there was a group of women at the church talking and laughing about how she was dressed. What they didn't know was that she was standing right behind them and when they realized that she was there they tried to smile at her and utter a few nice words but it was too late! That was eight years ago and she never stepped foot back into a church or dealt directly with Christ again. I hugged her and told her that Jesus never left her all she had to do was call on Him. I reminded her that Jesus was scorned by the church and went to those considered different because He was different so He could relate. She was so happy and smiled and said, "So you are a hugger too!" And I said, "Yes I am" and she replied, "That is so nice because many people aren't."

Well the bottom line is that I was sent on assignment that day to represent Christ and give her that warm hug and remind her of His love. Deep huh? Now that I'm writing this I must check on her for that was almost a week ago, let me go and find that number, I'll talk to you guys latter . . . I must share with her the scripture that got me out of my funk this morning Psalms 18:16 "He reached down from high and took hold of me and drew me out of the deep waters" marinate on that visual every time you feel low. Peace out!

FINDING PEACE IN THE PIECES

I was in meditation this morning and I could really see how that lyric my partner gave me "You answer my questions before I ask" in the song or "You Chose me Before I Chose You" is practical and on point. This morning I was saying to myself that they really didn't talk about life after death in the Old Testament and then out of nowhere my eyes fell on a notation that mentioned how David's use of the word "awake' implied that he knew there was life after death. It then went on to point out various scriptures that let it be known that in that era although they did not know completely about resurrection they knew only in part and as a result understood the concept partially. I went on and studied the verses that my partner, Mr. Holy Spirit had directed me to. I look at life when things occur that we can't understand things like sudden deaths, tragedies, theft, fraud etc. We only see that part but we must rely on our Maker that He knows more than just that part. If I honestly knew that I would have to paddle through brain cancer, systemic lupus with my heart being painfully affected, not being able to stand or walk just to get to my appointed husband; do you honestly think I would have volunteered for all of this?

Let's keep it real heck no! But God knew and still does that I can only comprehend in part and sometimes He allows me to peak into all the parts. Now within my own life I will try and put the pieces together because that's what we as humans do but I'm learning to just leave the broken pieces where they are and when my guide, my partner instructs me to place the pieces over here and there and I follow! Believe it or not I'm learning and experiencing peace in mending the pieces!

I WILL CONTINUE TO PROCLAIM HIS WORKS

I always say if my God were not to do another thing I will still sing his praises and bless His Holy name. We were discussing the other night how the simplest of things we take for granted. There was a transition stage in my journey where I couldn't walk, talk, or put my clothes on for myself but God propelled me to make it and I have the best support team. I mean we were laughing at how one of my Aunts was literally holding onto the wall crying her head off and saying, "Thank You Jesus." They were praying over the apartment I was in because every time I was in there I would have these seizures that would take my speech and the only words I could say were "Thank you Jesus". My other Aunt who is a nontraditional Christian told me to plead the blood of Jesus in my mind and when I did there was this battle. It became a game were I said, "Oh Satan you aren't going to have me." It was the hardest thing to get through that barrier reef in my head. I would look in the mirror when I was able to break through the barrier in my brain and say "Jesus!" I sounded like a babbling baby but once I got that name out I watched my face change.

Then I was able to speak so everyone around me knew when I was going through and all I could say was "thank you Jesus." One night I had seizure after seizure and slept with my father and my Aunt was in the nearby room because my Mom was away and all I could say every five minutes was "thank you Jesus." I said it so much that my Aunt heard it throughout her sleep. Another time I was in the studio recording this song for my cousin and I had seizure after seizure. I had seven seizures to the point that the engineer would look at me and he would know and say "ok it's a thank you Jesus moment" and I would laugh. Another associate of mine always says he remembers me being so sick and just laughing every time I came out of the seizures. I was telling my Godmother the other night how the last time I was home they had to put my contrast needle in my foot because all the other veins had collapsed and I foresaw this, I knew it would be feet time and asked Lord will we get through this?

You see there was a time only a few years ago when my body shut down again from heartache and I had to transition because God knew that these would be the testimonies that would change and encourage others. I tell you I know what it is like to have people put on my clothes because I couldn't respond. They would make statements like 'oh just put that on,' like I didn't hear but in my head I heard it all and would say, "Please don't I am still alive in here hello . . . ." You see a sense of humor will bring you through. And as I'm writing this I 'm crying because I love the Lord so much for He has brought me through so much that there are no words, no expressions to say thank you because He didn't have to bring me through. I have to stop right now and have a worship moment.

My St. David's Days

God is a God of order right down to the little details. For example when I was growing up I knew I had St. David's blood in me and a part of me always wanted to stay there weekends with my friends but my Mom wouldn't let me. However when I grew up I got involved with the same woman who years prior I felt compelled to help because she was in a bike accident. I was working at a bank and had heard about this female soccer star having her leg mangled in a crash. My heart felt her pain. This lady I worked with said she was looking for someone to give $5000 to from her club so I suggested the soccer star. Later I felt the former star's spirit of despair and told my friends to send her cards or go and visit her as she was laid up for months overseas. I didn't know her and wanted nothing from her but I did know that another human being was going through and felt empathy and compassion.

Now check this; years later I end up in a relationship and marrying this same woman who just happened to be from St. David's so I moved there with her family.

I will publicly cherish my St. David's and St. George's crew for the rest of my life for they were such a part of my journey. I remember having a seizure and than watching my boy B smoking a joint inside his mouth, just puffing away and we laughed so much. Wendy and I still have a giggle over that night every time I'm home. Now that I'm thinking about it Wendy was the one that named me weed burner when we attended Warwick Academy and that's another story. In St. David's we were family and would fish, cook and party together. The key phrase was we were one. One time I had a seizure in the bed and Mama Leta and Bo came running in trying rescue me, I could see them now all out of breath and frantic! I used to love sitting, talking and eating with them. They had so much knowledge and wisdom. Mama Leta became a grandmother figure since mine had already passed. I still remember all of her stories and our exercise walks. Lord rest her soul! As I'm writing I'm crying because I miss all of those who have passed on in my Eastern Parish circle. We would party at Mt Airy, the Cricket clubs, attend cruises and camp together. I recall when the boats came in at the dock and how the Hon. Nelson Bascome came in with his crew with a boat load of fish. Well Byrd, and others lit the half barrel pot while others gathered vegetables and we had a feast. We experienced so much together including the murder of my boy Red, several sudden deaths, births, a waterside burial and so many laughs that the thread will forever be there. The stories I can tell are a movie in itself which will make you laugh, cry and feel such pride of what it is was like living in an island. Now don't steal the idea DB!

To the Burchalls, Lambes, Paces, Minors, Foggos, Richardsons, Pitchers and Foxes. You represent true family, my extended family therefore continue to pass on those special values of true love over possessions to the next generations.

THE POWER OF A PRAYING FAMILY

You know how some families are known for certain characteristics like being loud, flashy, health nuts, drinkers, smokers, sex addicts, money grabbers, cons, gamblers, religious and the list goes on. Well my family especially on my Mom's side is known for prayer! My Great-Grandma was a prophetess and the mantle was passed onto my Grandmother who was known as an island prayer warrior even for our government and she passed the prayer warrior mantle on to us. And I'm being corrected as I write that she didn't pass the mantle God passed the mantle. Sorry about that but He is our creator. This morning I've been ministering to my cousin who is going through one of those life or death where the rubber meets the road situations. He says my testimonies are comforting to him and he will read them to his wife who is on life support. You know many are called but few are chosen and I didn't understand that cliché until now. I recall years ago in one of my cocaine snorting sessions I called my Mother about 4 a.m. saying "Mom I sold my soul for your life."

You see my Mom was very sick during my college days but to say that verbally was unthinkable so my Mom immediately told me to get a Bible and open it and wherever the pages landed I was to read it. I turned to where it said "Before you were born you were chosen." Now imagine the scene, you have about six people sitting in a circle snorting our buns of and some believe it or not were actually moving objects with their minds and bodies off the ground! I mean this drug was deep and it sat in the middle of a table in a huge pile in this plush city apartment.

Now here I come and move things as well by getting the phone and making that call. Then on top of that while in the midst of everyone's high session I asked the hosts of the

house for a Bible and where do I put the Bible smack there in the center of the table next to the pile of cocaine! I realize decades later that God was in the mix and I was the instrument He used to change the atmosphere by planting Himself smack in the middle of the "get high" session and He began by planting seeds. Every time after that incident when I got high I always had the Bible and began reading it. Now some may say that's sacrilegious but you know what, people didn't want to get high next to a Bible and others kept asking me to read scriptures and you know what God was definitely in the midst no doubt! Man God was always there even when I was abusing Him. Lord I'm so sorry but you know my spirit was obedient to that inner voice in order to get the Bible and be seen as a weirdo in that setting. I would even see dark shadows bouncing off the walls and I knew even in that state to pray for protection from the flying demons.

Ironically my hubby just sent me a text pertaining to a scripture that stated that through our testimonies many will come to know and acknowledge the Lord. Wow that gave me more of a reason to want to live. I just have to ask for the strength and protection to walk in God's timing. My spiritual friend gave me a lesson about timing and I want to say "Lord I love you so much and I want to just take this moment right now to say thank you for all that you have done and all that you are going to do. Lord I stand on your word that you are not a man that you should lie. I ask that the Angels go before me and surround me and my family. You didn't have to let me live but you chose me before I chose you just like the song you gave me says." The power of a praying family manifests miracles in not just our immediate family and friend's lives but also in countless observers. Thank you God for placing me in such a family. Like I said to my cousin that although our walks may vary our paths are the same and this equates to the motto He gave me 'We Are One.' That's right one spirit, one mind, one soul . . . um it's a deepie I tell you. And you know what, this lady who I prayed that God would reveal her colors showed herself again in the most painful of times. They say humans reveal who they really are under pressure. We may appear kind, generous and loving on the outside with our deeds but God knows our hearts. God is like a giant spotlight and always reveals truth because He is all truth!

THE JOURNEY BEGINS . . .

It's difficult for me to wrap my brain around the lead up to events but I have to share what happened. I was already having seizures and being treated for adult epilepsy. One Sunday I went to a football game and when this girl with long dreads asked me the time or something I went to answer her but couldn't. My speech became locked inside so she looked at me strangely and walked off. I told my then girlfriend what happened and we moved on to sitting by one of my favorite families, the Caiseys. Back then everyone was alive and you've never experienced laughter at a sports event until you've hung with Nell, Snipe and crew. Rest in peace Bees and Alshae.

When we went home I called for my regular physician but another doctor answered saying Dr E.B was away. I told him what happened and that I knew deep inside that something was really wrong. I was crying telling him I was scared and embarrassed and I needed to see someone. He responded rudely, "What is it that you possibly want me to do I'm not you're your physician." Where was the comfort, the empathy Dr. Butter? I remember feeling suicidal after I spoke with him for no one could understand what pain and fear I was feeling. What I didn't know at the time was that God did and that feeling I had was the Holy Spirit forewarning me and preparing me for the greatest change in my life. I wrote an article on what it's like to lose your speech and have your words locked inside but for some reason it was never printed it.

A month later when I was working overtime at my job at the Registrar of Companies the unexplainable happened. Sometimes on my way out I would often chat with Frank the custodian. and one evening he said to me, "Hey what is that huge lump on your neck?" I asked him what was he talking about and then I placed my hand on the back of my neck and it felt like an egg. On my way home on the bus this lady said, "Miss do you realize what's on the back of your neck, you really need to get that checked out." I responded with a quiet thank you. This thing hadn't been on my neck all day but I do remember what occurred the night before. There had been a sighting that was unexplainable in one part of the Island earlier that evening that some close to me had seen and reported to NASA. Later that night whist in a deep sleep I had a dream where I had an outer body experience in this huge lab like facility in the sky. The next day I returned to work and started having silent seizures with a voice in my head saying, "You can't tell them because they won't believe you."

I was scheduled for a meeting and my direct boss Mrs. Thomas understood that I wasn't feeling well and excused me. However my co worker made the remark, "Hey I have the flu do you think she will let me off the hook?" All I could do was look at him and laid my head back on the desk. Later I went to the hospital where I sat with my Mom for hours in the emergency room. They were letting all sorts of patients go before me who had visible bleeding wounds. My Mom who was a nurse demanded that I have a Cat Scan and what they saw was a huge dark mass. They asked me did I have chocolate at lunch and I told them, "No shrimp." The next thing I knew they were rushing me upstairs to a room and that is where I remained for days with tubes attached. I dwindled to 90 lbs and my main Doctor EB was there at the hospital making his rounds and was told that I was there but he never came to see me. I'm yet to ask him why? During that time he was running for political office and it took my Aunt Eleanor to call her boss the Hon. Nelson Bascome to contact my doctor and pretend that it was a political matter rather than medical. When he had him on the phone he read him the riot act saying I was a special person to him so therefore he needed to give me a referral to leave the country to go overseas for further observation. Now we will make note that this same doctor received his reinstated medical practice papers by my Mom going to her friend, a top doctor who was in a high position

to make such decisions. Also I used to hang out with the same doctor before he relocated to Bermuda. Therefore I wasn't amused to say the least. Right up until his untimely death while in his presence I would always tell people how Nelson Bascome saved my life. He was so humble and would just smile and say, "Stop that it was God's plan." Those fans who were there always looked at us dazed because they never knew the story.

While in the hospital I would have seizure after seizure and the doctors in Bermuda tried their best to figure out what was wrong with me. Trust and believe I had every test there was. They said maybe it was a stroke, maybe damage due to prolonged cocaine use, maybe it was this maybe it was that and the list goes on. After my referral papers were signed by Dr. EB, I was assigned a private nurse and I remember sitting outside in my wheelchair talking to my GF asking her to come with me because I was scared. But her Mom stated that she didn't want her to miss out on her $4000 bonus from her job for having a perfect attendance. Now remember the chain of empathy events. Several years prior to knowing her I suggested that she receive the $5000 from my former co-worker's private club which she did and this was a help to her and her mom when they were in need. In order to survive in this life I've learned forgiveness and that not everyone is wired to be compassionate or empathic. As the saying goes "some people just forget." That doesn't make her or Dr. EB bad people, just well you fill in your own blank_____! However when you become a follower of Christ we do take on His characteristics, and compassion and empathy are on top of the list. Therefore my tolerance level of those that profess to be Christians is much less. I'm not judging I'm just keeping it real.

My Aunt Estlyn and the private nurse flew with me to Boston with my tubes and drips attached. The nurse was excited and talked so much about her friends in Boston who she hadn't seen in years so I excused her. I figured just because I was in distress why not fulfill another's desire. Seeing her smile and hearing her heartfelt thank you was a spark to my spirit. She said, "Are you sure, are you really sure? If you need me call me." I told her that my Aunt and I would be fine. As we headed off for the hospital in a taxi I laid my head on my Aunt's chest and cried. Even writing this I have to take breaks because I'm shedding tears of the outpouring of love I had received.

As I laid on my earthly Angel's (Aunt Es) chest I could literally feel my spirit escaping but I was holding on with thoughts of how much I loved my family and all those that depended on me for hope. Prior to getting sick I had been at the top of my media game and had developed quite a following with my newspaper column, was one of the producers of a top television series, commercials, songwriting, music conferences and shows etc. You name it I was in it. Now I was laying here helpless with so many whys, so many emotions but never any fear. Strangely enough I felt a peace almost as if someone else was with me.

Prior to my leaving a loved one had made a profound statement to me knowing that I was dying and was about to face a life or death decision. I know they did this out of love because they have always supported my choices. They said, "Les you know you can't get to heaven being in love with a woman!"

At Lahey Clinic the doctors told me that I definitely had a brain tumor and they could not promise me that it wasn't cancerous. However they did give me a choice of either going in through my nose or my head. I thought briefly about that statement and asked if I could have a few minutes to absorb all of this. I mean brain tumor, cancer none of these were on my radar for I thought I had epilepsy all of these years. Then I asked God to decide and I cried for about five minutes and said, "I'll have it through my brain. You can cut my brain but I don't want all my hair cut off so what can we do?" There I was with my prideful self. They told me I could have the "Hollywood cut" which is where they cut through the middle and opened it up in a flap formation. As a result I had my hair cut off half way from the middle of my head and kept that style for years even when l I had dreadlocks later on. My hair grew to the middle of my back from the top of my head. This was a style I kept right up until my chemotherapy years later.

They prepared me for two weeks and my Aunt kept me busy with all sorts of tours so between going to the hospital everyday for steroids and treatment for an infection I picked up while in the Bermuda hospital I was pooped out. Every evening I would get back to our hotel room and listen to all of my messages and write. I figured my column had to go on for my readers so I aired it all out. It was like a soap opera in print and then came the day before the actual surgery. I told my readers if I didn't make it well this is what I wanted them to know. I thanked all sorts of people from family to friends, to pastors to my creative family to lawyers to politicians. And at this time I wish to publicly thank my Uncle Kenny Gamble who wanted me to have a second opinion with a surgeon friend of his Ben Carson. You have always been in the wings for me, you and your lovely wife Fatimah. Also all of my Bermuda Chances 97 music family and Alison Swan (Aunt Jackie who motivated me to move to a conventional doctor) for your sincere interest and inspiring conversations that helped to build up my spirit. Once my diagnosis was out there my friend Wendell went and researched it in the library. That meant so much to know that he cared enough to go beyond his comfort zone and inquire.

Some of my American based family such as my uncle Donald, cousin Nessie, Evie and Karen came to visit me. In fact my cousin Karen had a date scheduled and drove all the way from New Jersey to see me before my operation and then said she had to leave to get back to her date. I thought that was so special. Alison took the time out of her stay in the Hampton's with her then boyfriend Bobby Teitel to keep check on me. Just to think years later they would become some of Hollywood's most successful producers. In fact we both married around the same time and I told her what people were saying and she said, "Who cares about people they either love you for you or not."

The actual day before the operation my friends Cathy and Sharon caught the train from Philly to come and stay with us which has resulted in a lifetime friendship. One of them is afraid to fly so they traveled all those hours because they thought I was worth that much. I'm so grateful to the Showell family; Cathy, Sharon, Donna, Shawn I love you for life. Before they took me in for my operation everyone appeared strong and treated me as normal but I caught a glimpse of my Aunt Estlyn crying and then reality set in. As I laid on that hospital stretcher preparing for my 50/50 I remembered that profound statement. I said, "Lord you know me and you know my heart and I trust you no matter what" and I began reciting the 23rd Psalms which to this day honestly I can't recite the entire thing because my brain gets fuzzy. So who allowed me to know it? My partner, Mr. Holy Spirit. At that point I felt so peaceful and through all my near death experiences I feel extra peaceful because what else could I do but leave my fate to my Creator. That's why I laugh at myself when I get bent out of shape over the routine disappointments in life like being let down, not having enough money for bills etc. If I can face death a few times and look at it in the face than I need to apply the same trust and ask for Godly wisdom.

When I came to from a surgery that lasted for fours there were all of these nurses and doctors surrounding me. They were excited because I opened my eyes; you would have thought I was a baby that said its first word. They were all "gaga" over me and asked me what day it was. Well my brain went all the way back to when I entered the hospital in Bermuda. It was like a reset button and I responded October 24th and they said no it's actually such and such. They were just happy I could speak! When I was waiting for surgery in that freezing hallway I remembered talking with a man who was a Yugoslavian soccer star and some lady was ranting how she told everyone she had cancer. The guy had prostate and the other lady I'm not sure but I do know for sure that the guy wanted to live. The other lady in my opinion sounded like an attention starved lunatic! So when they took me to my room I asked for the man and he didn't make it but that motor mouth lady was told she didn't have cancer and she complained saying, "What will I tell my friends. I thought for sure I had cancer maybe they need to check again." I could not believe her so I replied, "Are you for real? Tell them the truth and you should be happy you're alive!" Then she asked about me and I told her I didn't know but deep inside I felt I did and it was okay with it because I knew somehow I was going to make it.

Later I was in a room by myself and I couldn't walk or just about move so I started having deep conversations with God. I asked some serious questions and He showed me some serious answers in that hospital room some of which I'm being told not to mention at this time for many skeptics and are not ready for my truth, the truth that was shown to me. A truth that goes beyond our human understanding, beyond religion but one of superseded spiritual realms. Let's just say in addition to several other "awakenings" I experienced the realm between spirit and body. A realm where human bodies pass through you and as I'm told this is when your spirit and body are not in total alignment. Some of you know what I'm talking about.

Unfortunately the doctors told me that I was a case that didn't have to be for quote on quote "Any doctor who took pathology 101 would have known the symptoms and what to check for." Now I choose not to be angry or bitter but because my tumor sat for all those years and certain tests were never done my tumor became like a piece of bad meat and lodged itself in my left lobes which affects my speech and balance. It was so lodged that they kept apologizing saying, "We are so sorry we really tried but we were only able to extract 80% and the 20% remainder is inoperable but we will test to see if it's benign or contains cancer cells." Well the result was yes it is cancer, no matter how I disguise it or pretend that it doesn't exist. **The "C" is in my pocket and I carry it, it does not define me.**

At the National Brain Tumor Society's "Race for Hope" walk 2012 in Philadelphia I was encouraged to see so many survivors and listen to a sports celebrity's testimony of her admitting that yes she has brain tumor but her life goes on and she strives for the children that are affected. I was able to interact with others who haven't been checked in years but go on with their lives. There are others who haven't been as fortunate and have survived with their limbs, sight, speech and motor skills being affected. I thank God for my slight off balance, twitching, and speech impaired mishaps. I'm so grateful for being down from 3500mg a day to 3000mg. I'm grateful for my family and friends who traveled specifically to Philadelphia and seriously went out of their way to support me after the devastating east coast storm Sandy. I'm proud of my Hubby for walking with us. I don't take any of this for granted because God didn't have to save me you feel me? I'm here in your face for a reason and part of my purpose is for Him to receive the glory and say, 'Look I'm real here's another one of my miracles!"

THERE'S SO MUCH MORE

It took a minute for me to write about my friend Michael who passed. We were so close and to this day he is the only one who left me anything . . . just saying . . . I met him through my friend Nate who also is laid to rest. As a matter of fact Nate drove all the way to New York to pick me up and bring me and a friend to spend time with him in Philly. He knew but I didn't have a clue that he was dying. Months later I called to ask if Nate was going to the parade and they told me that he had just passed. I had felt his spirit so I called as I normally would. You can imagine my shock. He was my best friend and introduced me to so many people and I still maintain some of those relationships today including my pug.

Michael and I bonded immediately and we would do everything together from shopping to watching movies, to clubbing, to feeding our faces or just chilling. When I joined the church I even had him coming there and he gave his life to Christ. I remember one night we were dancing so much that Mike fell off the stage and was bleeding but did that stop us, of course not. Along with another friend we were the joyful trio trust that! As I'm writing I now know why I'm a loner and that is because so many beings that have been close to me have vanished off this planet including my girl Ms Renee.

I would visit Mike in that hospital everyday and my ex would complain because she couldn't understand why I had to be there so much. I was only there a few hours a day but I would have to argue with her every evening but I still pressed on. I watched him dwindle away and after about two weeks I called my church to sing and pray at his bedside. This seemed to lift him up but then one afternoon I didn't feel up to going directly there to see him. The hospital was only blocks away since I resided downtown back then but I felt strange and just started walking toward Market Street. I went to the gallery and there was a youth choir singing and God knew I needed that to replenish my soul. Now check the order of God.

Because I didn't go directly to the hospital I was late by an hour and as a result his sister had just stepped out of his room leaving her friend there. We were watching the news or something and then all of a sudden he started making these strange breathing sounds and the lady looked at him and started screaming and like my Aunt she started scaling the wall. I haven't figured out what that is all about yet! (Smile) Anyhoo I put my arms around him and held him, stroking his head and told him everything would be okay. The doctors and nurses rushed in and we had to leave the room and at that moment his only sibling, his sister got off the elevator. She started screaming and the doctors came out of the room and said they had done everything they could for him. I went back in the room with his sister and the scaling lady and I just massaged his hands because he was still warm. I kissed his forehead and softly said, "Goodbye my Michael."

I left the hospital and it was a Friday evening, I called my former life partner and told her what had happened and she said she was sorry but we still had plans to go and hang out in Jersey so I better hurry home. No remorse, no compassion and now looking back God was surely holding me in His arms and that was my first lesson in not relying upon a human for compassion. I went to the club but I wasn't myself and she told me to perk up but how could I when I had just lost my other best friend. Even writing about that makes me angry and I do not need to go there!

Days later I was scheduled to travel to Bermuda and was taking a DVD player and some other stuff for her family that I had to check in but because I was late I couldn't make the plane. This male airline steward told me that all the flights were booked for the next five days and I cried my head off. He said there were a lot of worse things in life and that I was acting like I just lost my best friend and I replied, "I did." It was the first time I cried and the tears wouldn't stop flowing and then I felt Michael's presence so I called his sister. I knew the funeral would have been in a few days but I had told him I was going home while he was alive and after he passed I reminded her. She told me that she was sorry I missed my flight but she already had me down to read about his life on the printed program. I mean seriously, all I could say in my head was, "alright Mikey Mike you have me." I ceased crying and the day of the funeral which was in their hometown Coatesville outside of Philly, my former ex dropped me off at the trolley station to link up with some strangers for a ride and kept it moving. I felt alone for I had been to several funerals with her but I guess this wasn't one of her people. I felt like I didn't matter, I felt abandoned.

I was so nervous as I stood before a packed house, I felt like I was going to pass out but all of a sudden I felt these large hands rest upon my shoulders and there was an immediate sense of peace. I don't even remember what I said because it wasn't me talking but I can tell you this people were laughing hysterically. They were saying, "Yes yes that was Michael, oh my God you are killing us with the jokes." At the repast people from all over were coming up to me thanking me for uplifting their spirits and reminding them of how funny Mike was. All I could say was that he had that planned out I was just a vessel. To this day I've never felt invisible hands of such peace upon me. Can someone explain that entire scenario to me? If that doesn't spell out spiritual than I don't know what does! Email your thoughts to **hismultimedia@yahoo.com**

WHAT'S REALLY REAL?

Here I am a week later and the pain in my body is subsiding but I guess my spirit is used to being healed miraculously. Anyhoo my sister made a statement that stuck with me but it was realistic about me getting older. Well with time come age, wear and tear and yes I have to take better care of my body and take less for granted because this is real. At first I took the statement as a negative and my spirit became weighed down. But yesterday morning my Bishop talked about how we talk to ourselves 98%

of the time and often we are bombarded with negatives. How we interpret these messages I strongly believe is also important. When I took my sisters comment as a negative I felt kind of down but then my partner, Mr. Holy Spirit reminded me that while I needed to pay attention to my health I also needed to pay attention to my spiritual and emotional well being as well.

Last night a relative started telling me about various people that I knew who had died or those who had passed on as I like to refer to it. At the end of the conversation they mentioned about a gentleman who had been granted yet another miracle from God. Now at first I was like oh here we go death, death, death but this morning my partner reminded me that most of them have Christ in their lives. I had to transform my mind and make life, and miracles, the focal point or synopsis of the conversation. This reminded me of one of my favorite scriptures that was uttered in service yesterday morning Psalms 118:17 "I will live and not die and proclaim the works of the Lord."

Yesterday when I walked to place the offering my legs buckled and I shouted out Jesus and it was like in midair an Angel caught me! I was shaken and then I ran into the arms of another member and just wept! She once told me I was her inspiration but actually as I'm writing this I realize that she is mine. For it is she and the Holy Spirit that fights brain cancer, liver, breast the whole works so when she gives me pointers I listen.

Therefore when I came home I stood in that kitchen with my faithful dog on the floor and pleaded with God one on one. I repeated scriptures about fighting the enemy and removing ALL negative energy NOW! My God is my protector and over and over I recited "I will live and not die and proclaim your works. Lord you promised me that you will not leave me nor forsake me. Lord you will not leave me for I have work to do" and as I'm writing to you I'm crying because my friends Jesus is the most real thing we will ever encounter! I said, "Lord take away this pain for I want to be able to kneel again when the Spirit tells me to pray. Oh Lord I love you!" The tears just ran down my face as they are right now and as I'm sharing my testimony I'm listening to Wes Morgan's song "I Choose to Worship." He sings about his healing and I'm going to worship my Lord now . . .

I had to take a minute and just lift my hands and worship. I cried out at that kitchen counter with my coat still on and purse intact and those of you who know me, also know that I always have my purse or bag. On a lighter tip they used to call me bag lady at one time. I've been carrying a bag since age two. Well I called on Jesus oh yeah, and started saying my favorite phrase "Thank You Jesus, thank you Jesus" and between thanking Him praising and pleading I laid my hands on those areas that I felt pain and said, "Lord you are not a man that you should lie and you said that we can lay hands on ourselves and Lord in the name of Jesus I'm raising my hands and believing in a healing." Well within minutes I started walking around in circles and for the first time in a while I was able to get on my knees and pray. I said to my dog and my husband if I wasn't here I wouldn't believe this wonder!

Earlier before I started to pray over myself I said "here we go it's going to be another chemo time" but when your back is against the wall you cry out. I believe this is going to be a decade of crying out and believing that the result will be signs and wonders. I am able to move better still a bit sore but NOTHING like the pain I was in. Why? Because God provides for us everything that we need to live, to heal ourselves. The price was already paid for us, we were bought with a cost and that is the blood of Jesus. I was even able to pray for an estranged friend in the industry who had lost everyone around him. I could feel the spirit of depression so I asked for a film about suicide and how God moves in real life situations. I believe the point I'm trying to make this morning is that in the midst of my storm God allowed me to minister to this man. I prayed and we got disconnected but as was prophesized this is the year of reconnections. I was able to call back and say, "What you hung upon me in the midst of our prayer?" And then he responded and I knew that the Holy Spirit had me proclaiming His works . . . . Oh yeah it's on . . .

Later last night when I felt that spirit of loneliness creep upon me I started flicking through the TV stations and my partner said try this station and there it was, a show I produced over a year ago and it spoke about God and purpose. A station with two million viewers and it was almost as if God was saying and confirming that Les you still have work to do! Shortly after a cousin told me about her friend committing suicide I was able to share the story about the show on television as well as the film about suicide that I had asked an associate to mail me. And you know what this house that God gave me is a house of worship and praise and I will show the film here at some point. The house story is another miracle.

I would get on my knees and claim this empty house that sat here for two years. The lady next door prayed for a Christian neighbor. She later told me how one Sunday while she was in the balcony at my church she looked down and there I was. Ms. Renee said God not only gave her a Christian neighbor but also a member of the same church. Tell me God doesn't answer prayer. What's really real in your life?

I know what's real in mine for I went beyond myself the other day and reached out to tell my loved ones who had hurt me severely just how much I love them. So real to me is going outside of your feelings, your hurts, your pains and trusting in someone Higher to catch you if you fall when you are standing on the ledge of your life and you can say, "Okay Lord I'm extending myself again but I trust you to catch me." You see the difference for me this time is that I'm seeking His face, His grace and His mercy in the midst of my extension. I believe we make wrong choices when we insult Him and fail to ask He who created us for directions in our life journey. I often find myself saying, "Lord can I handle this or where should I walk, what angle should I take?" It's the 'should I' conversations with God not the 'what if s' that display our authentic trust in Him.

BEATING THE ENEMY'S HIDDEN DRUG WORLD

You know most mornings early the Holy Spirit wakes me up with a song and this morning the song is "Oh Give Thanks Unto the Lord for He is Good for He is Good . . . Oh Give Thanks unto the Lord for He is good for He is good!"

Here lately I feel that I'm missing my mark missing my purpose by allowing all sorts of distractions and confusion within my life. The music thing seems to be spinning in circles one minute it is mad clear; then I don't hear from people and the next I'm in contact. Those I've helped spit in my face like the success is on their own and I'm feeling tired and drained. Yep I'm drained at my core because each day my wheels are spinning to nowhere. Now I get things accomplished but everyday well most days if I'm not with my church buddies I feel USELESS yeah that's the word I'm looking for. Well this morning after my morning prayer with my boo I decided to give there Holy Spirit free reign over my morning and my purpose for this time is to focus on writing and executing this long awaited book.

You see the book is not about me or you but like the song says is about JESUS. Yesterday when I was with my music buddy we drove across an area and I told him how I used to snort my nose off right there in the projects. In fact I was so high one time I couldn't even get on the plane to go to my own grandfather's funeral. I was a functional

addict and oh the stories and adventures that came with that are a book in itself. Only God you hear me saved me, only the power of Christ delivered me! You see a functional addict sometimes is worse because they can mask their addiction for years because they have learned how to manage, how to a point control things but deep within their spirit they know they are helpless. After the entire drug has control of them!

I was telling my mate how I had a slight heart attack and felt the numbness in my arm but I stayed and contemplated on snorting more cocaine before the scavengers got it. In fact I told them what was happening and they just looked at me and went on getting high. That was the first time I asked God to save me in my spirit because I saw the spirit of death. Another time the night before I was to fly I freebased with some people I had just met and the smoke was so powerful that it knocked my head against the radiator and all I could see were some type of monkeys. The same people left me laying there slightly bleeding and stole the drugs and money. When I came to I looked for the monkeys but they had gone. I now know that I was seeing in the spirit and those monkeys were demons that I had entertained and was getting high with. On another occasion I was having sex with a female and when I looked down between my thighs I saw the head of a lion like creature. It was during that time that my mother and one of my Mother and my Aunt J started praying simultaneously for me and they both turned to the scripture about "coming like a roaring lion" now take note that I was "getting my flesh on" so I couldn't tell neither one of them until much later.

And actually later went like this:

I was sort of punk rocking it with half of my hair shaved and always wearing black. And I used to wear this jacket that looked like something from the matrix all the time even thinking about it makes me smile. It was a sharp long trench like unique black jacket.

I would party at this club that was held in an old church and all sorts of people would be there and they would be doing drugs, having sex etc especially in the bathroom. Well this one night they asked me to attend an after house party which I often did and it was there that my back was against a solid wall in the kitchen. There I was talking to some people sporting a red sweatshirt under my fierce black jacket. Mind you I had left my girlfriend at home. So get the scene right in your heads, standing in the kitchen leaning against an empty solid wall smoking a joint with these new found "friends" and then the unthinkable happened. I looked across the room and out of nowhere this black cat came across and our eyes met. When that happened I swear to God I saw my girlfriend. Then in my mind I said I must really be spacing out and then my back felt extremely hot and then someone yelled that they saw flames and my back was on fire so I did the stop drop and roll thing and these "high" friends beat the flames out off my back. Now it freaked people out so much that I'm sure that memory will remain etched into their brains.

When I got up my favorite jacket had a huge cinched hole in it and my sweat top which should have been flammable was untouched. I was a classic case of human combustion so I held onto the jacket to show my mother which she took and felt it was a demonic act. When I told my girlfriend she proceeded to want to indulge in sexual activity which would have normally not thrown me off course but I was traumatized so this was not helping! Again I looked down and bam there was that lion face with the same cat eyes of the black cat from the night before. And I was not high! My mother, aunt and uncle were in town attending a big service that they had invited me to. So when I saw this again I was freaked out so I stopped her cleaned myself up and ran to that service! This was when my mom and aunt told me about them having the simultaneous prayer. Later my mom told me how one time when my girlfriend called the phone it became super hot like it was on fire. Now when she told me this I hadn't even told her about my back catching on fire and all the "sexual awakenings" we will call it. In fact it's only as my partner, the Holy Spirit is leading me to write this that I am connecting the dots. Like one my aunts said demons followed me and still do don't get it twisted!

My whole life has been a chase of cat and mouse always running and dodging. I would go from one relationship to another and get caught in snares and would find myself praying my way out. I remember calling my grandmother and telling her that I was afraid of this girlfriend and how I woke up to my long lock of hair in the back of my head known as a tail was literally cut off! Snap, bam, gone you hear me! Man I just remembered that my long tail in back of my head was the bomb so I thought so you can imagine my face when I woke up next to this girl touching the back of my head. Going to twist it around my finger and play with it like I usually did every morning and nothing, I was horrified! I maybe laughing now but trust and believe back then it was no laughing matter. Now she claims she doesn't know what happened but really it was only me and her and there was no sign ever of my hair. We always say in the islands 'don't let them get hold of your hair or they will control you.' Well that girl had me wrapped around her finger from changing her grades and risking my job to having her relocate to be with me, to leaving my car that I purchased to having her trade it. Now think about it she would take all of my prized material possessions but never my soul because of my praying family! Thank you mom, dad, my aunts and now late grandmother, I put you guys through it but you always supported me. You may not have liked it and spoke your piece but you forever stood beside me. Lord I love you all for that unconditional love!

One time I went to go on a vacation with my immediate family and I left the car with my girlfriend and when I returned she said someone stole my car. Well I went for months looking for my car and every time I would see one like it, I would be breaking my neck, I loved that car it was my first and only car. Well eventually it came out and she confessed that she gave the car to these dealers for an eight ball of cocaine so that she and another girlfriend could smoke it up. Now you talk about violation of trust! I must say that writing these experiences brings back pain and just negatives in my life but I thank God for saving me. My partner, the Holy Spirit has brought to my memory that God never left me and his angels were always with me. I was the freaky girl who would have the Bible open and would read Psalms 23 when I was getting high. People would be like what the heck but hey it wouldn't stop them, after all it was free drugs so it didn't matter that much. Now it feels as though the whole set up was so religious.

I remember walking for miles with people to get drugs or being at a house where there was a newborn baby and the house burned down and the people ran back into the house just to get their drug equipment. Not their personal possessions or a blanket for the baby but a crack pipe. Let's call it what it was . . . so deep inside I hated crack and what it made people become. In fact I hated the whole cocaine demon thing. And it's not by chance or coincidence that the Lord allowed me to move back into the building that me my former girlfriend used to live at as well as getting high. Hey I even got raped and saw certain things happening prior. I could have avoided the whole situation but I allowed the drug to lure me in. I remember being at a basketball game and the game was exciting and going into overtime when all of a sudden a flash of my girlfriend and some older man came before me and they were getting high. I had never seen this man before in my life and I dashed to our apartment and she had on the inside chain lock so I couldn't just use my key. There they were just like I had seen in my head at the basketball game.

THE RAPE AT GUN POINT WAS SO SURREAL

Another time my friends and I were at a Whitney Houston concert and one of my friends had gotten assaulted by this guy and it upset us all, I mean right there at the concert. So when we were leaving I felt strange as if what happened to my friend was going to happen to me. I knew that feeling of violation since I had been sexually molested a few times when I was young so that demonic spirit was familiar to me. When I arrived at the driveway my former girlfriend was pulling up in a white BMW and they asked me to get in the car and this strange foreign man presented me with a bouquet of red roses saying that he had heard so much about me. Now let's look at this picture in the supernatural. How did they know when I was coming home and why would I have feelings of being violated!

Long story short we left and I was raped at gunpoint and my insides were tore up. That was the one and only time that I speed balled (heroin with cocaine) and I cried out for my girlfriend only to find her later in another room at the motel with a guy getting high. She apologized and I forgave her but at that time she told others in the "life" that the rape and suitcase were lies but we have proof.

My Mother flew in immediately to be with me and we had to go to the rape center at the hospital and get all kinds of tests including pregnancy. The man had given me a curable sexual disease and months later I watched on the local Philadelphia news the same pair of men being arrested and one was shot during the police bust. Sounds unreal but my life was a continuous movie reel! My family lived through it and had to forgive my former girlfriend and look past all that she did. This included setting me up with a suitcase full of drugs. I'm telling you right here, right now that there has always been spiritual warfare in my life.

THE POWER OF THE LIGHT

Later in my life I realized through therapy that I allowed myself to take on a lot of negative qualities in order to protect myself. As I'm writing this, my partner the Holy Spirit is clearly showing me that I took on that spiritual layer of clothing. But you see I always had people praying for me because I knew from growing up that God was never far away. I knew to call long distance in that college dorm to my Grandmother!

There was a time when a friend and I were traveling from New York trying to get back home. We had partied all weekend and the guy put us on the wrong train. As a result we didn't have enough money and at each stop I pretended to be sleeping so that I would miss the former stop and get closer to my destination. Well it was so cold that I had to put my packed already worn underwear from my bag onto my feet, it was freezing. Eventually the conductor came and stated that this was the last stop so we had to get off. Here we were in Forrest Hills somewhere with no money to get back home. Well my friend said she would pawn her chains so we jumped in a taxi and had them drive us to the nearest pawn shop but we were in such an exclusive area that there was none. So we ended up driving to a place where the taxi driver was sure they would take the jewelry. After driving for quite some time my friend changed her mind right there in midstream, like a rock she was not turning back. So now we had two problems; one we couldn't pay the driver our fare and two we still didn't have enough money to return to Philadelphia which was about two hours away. Once the taxi driver found this out he was furious and called us to his dispatcher and threatened to call the police. Talk about dodging another bullet I prayed like a child for her lost puppy. God obviously heard as usual and the taxi driver basically kicked us out of his car with a very strong warning.

So here we were in the middle of nowhere and as we walked to a nearby train station I got down on my knees in the snow and started praying and calling my deceased Grandma Nevida Joell's name. Once we were inside we found a payphone for there were no cells those days. We called the police and almost immediately a man came over and said he recognized our strong accents and that he was from the same country. The gentleman said he overheard our dilemma and gave us enough money to catch the train and a taxi back home. I went to thank him but he had disappeared. When I returned home I was telling the latest escapade to my friends and one of them swore down that I had described a man who had dated her sister and suddenly disappeared. My Mom and I feel that he was an Angel.

As you read this book you will discover that this is just one of many examples of miracles in my path. I choose to serve Jesus above all others because He has never left me no matter how many times I may have left him. Miracles such as the lame man walking, raising of the dead, water into wine maybe miracles of the past in story book form of the Word but they are still happening centuries later all in the name of Jesus. He is still moving mountains, casting out demons, and healing the sick in the here and now . . . I'm proof! Jesus is my comforter, my best friend and I have 200% confidence in Him. I look at the power of prayer just in my family.

I have a cousin who was shot in the head and the prayers that went up OMG! The doctors gave him one in a million chances and he is that one. My Uncle who fought Parkinson' disease and the doctors had given up saying, "This is it." But Jesus said, "Oh no I have the final word and it is not time to quit!" This is yet another example for Him to show up and show out. My nephew got in a motorcycle accident and split his head, he cursed out the doctors all around him but my Mother and Aunt Q pleaded the blood of Jesus openly. He got in the accident on that Friday and the next Friday the doctors said he didn't need surgery and sent him home. This is whom I'm proud to serve. The Way Maker!

In my own life I started having these severe seizures. I hit my head against the radiator and the persons I was getting high with looked like monkeys. Well about a couple of years thereafter I was driving with a friend one night when suddenly I saw these monkey figures and out of nowhere I felt my spirit slipping from my body and I tried to get out of the car. I was trying to bite the pin up on the car lock on the door in order to get out. My eyes were in my head my teeth felt like they were being forced out of my mouth and then Jesus stepped in and it was over. You see my mother puts anointed oil in all of our shoes and when she feels something extra she anoints our shoes with a little extra oil and that very night she placed a little extra anointing in my shoes!

Another time I was at my Grandmother's house and we were all sitting in her bedroom when suddenly I was attacked and pushed on the floor and this time I felt my body giving in because the force was so strong and I didn't feel like fighting so as my spirit started traveling in a dark whirlwind tube . . . . All I could hear was my Mother saying "Lord please don't take my child" and suddenly I was bounced back. There was the bank scene where I was upstairs smoking my cigarette with my smoking colleagues when out of nowhere I saw this huge black crow like bird flying straight for my neck and it knocked me out of my chair and they say that my head hit the concrete floor so hard that they could hear it two floor stories beneath. My body started violently convulsing and all I could do was hope God would help me. Well I ended up going in the ambulance in the middle of the city and they injected me with dilantin. I didn't know God like I know him now and back then I didn't believe that no weapon formed against me would prosper. I loved the Lord but hadn't accepted Christ as my personal savior. I was going to battle unprepared. I know for sure that if it wasn't for my praying family where would I be? Up until today those that were sitting with me my when I suddenly fell out of my chair where it looked like an invisible someone pushed me are still stunned! Many see me as a walking living testimony ten times over and my hope is that for every witness of these events that they see Jesus, the light in all of this. That they recognize that God is ruler of the light that overshadows the invisible ever moving darkness.

It's All in the Knowing!

By now you may have figured out that quite often I have these visions and dreams and not to mention supernatural experiences. When I was younger some people thought I was psychic or a white witch and I played with it. However now that Jesus is my Lord and Savior I know my identity. My Aunt and Mom used to say that I was always surrounded by witches and warlocks but that is because they know the calling that God has over my life so their assignment is to block me. I now know this and I'm comfortable in the knowing. You see it's in the unknowing that is scary and we tend to seek out all kinds of answers.

I remember years ago while in college I was at this party and I used to dress quite gothic back then, which was my thing. One night I was partying at this church that was transformed to a club and we used to snort our noses off in there. Often after the party we would go to actual after hour parties at various places, the speak easy, clubs and homes. This one night I was at this house and I saw this black cat pass me and our eyes connected and I felt the presence of my girlfriend at that time. So I went on talking and I was standing in a kitchen with my back against the wall and suddenly my back became real hot. The next thing I know I was doing the drop and roll thing with my back in flames. People were screaming and trying to beat out the flames. Even then God held me for I was calm and knew to drop and roll without ever being told that, well not consciously anyway. I was wearing my favorite matrix black jacket that night and in the back of it there was a huge scorched hole. However the red turtleneck I had worn underneath was untouched as were my black pants. I was in awe and gave the jacket to my Mother which she kept for years. Now the joke is, those same gothic associates that I was with who acted like nothing scared them were so shaken that they said I blew their highs and questioned who I really was. Deep huh? Looking back I really put my family through it no wonder they are still sane! Thanks family you all know who you are.

On another occasion we would drink to pass out and we would get so drunk that one time I ended up in some couples bathtub with them bringing me back to myself. I know for sure someone drugged my drink at a hangout bar that I frequented at that time. We would have these drinking contests between the Bermudians versus Americans and Bermudians are known to handle their drinking. This one time me a fellow college mate from my country and I drank so much and were proud that we were winning and then it hit us. I was on the dance floor and suddenly dropped. Then they were looking for him and found him passed out in a bathroom stall. As a visual it was funny I'm sure but then to add salt to injury I had to get back home and I went in this car. As we were driving all plastered the people realized that I was the wrong passenger and made me get out on the side of the highway and then I hitched a ride home with someone only to realize that this time I actually knew the people. There was God rescuing me again! I mean He rescued me so much that He should have gotten tired but He didn't give up on me thank God! And you know even though I was not walking with Him as I should He was with me. I wasn't a true friend to Him like He was to me and for that I'm truly sorry, please forgive me Lord!

I can recall driving with my cousin and our Greek roommate and the brakes failed on the car on this winding road in the rain and I prayed and we were able to maneuver the car to a safe grassy spot. Even back than I was known for my faith despite my wayward self. I was the one who would drop to my knees and pray in public and those around me would see the manifestation of prayer. One time I was on my knees at the post office pleading for God's help and the next thing I know I was receiving a package. Another incident was when I fell to my knees in New Jersey and asked for my deceased Grandmother's help and then God sent these two Angels who helped us and then disappeared. It's all in the knowing!

Look at the time when I was dancing on the floor and this guy who hadn't seen me since my drinking days was telling the bartender that he wanted whatever I was drinking because I appeared plastered and happy because I kept grinning and couldn't talk. What he didn't know was that I had long stopped drinking and I was actually having a partial seizure on the dance floor. When he came back with some drink I looked at him and all I could say was "Thank You Jesus" repeatedly. Can you imagine the look on his face, it was funny. I was too embarrassed to let anyone know I was having a seizure but look how God took over and used me. I was that donkey that the Bible speaks of for the Lord spoke through me to that man and I know he will never forget that "Jesus moment!" When you know that you know that you know who God is and the power of Jesus name you will never be ashamed of your identity again.

ALL BRAND NEW

Publishers have been contacting me and one of the things I make clear is my relationship with Christ but I am quite clear that we DO NOT want this to be another traditional Christian book for this isn't about religion, no this is about a way of life no judging! I mean let's face it I've been there done that and He still chose me and is using me. Like a good friend of mine said God saved your life, now you have to ask him what is it He wants you to do for Him; after all He saved you for a reason. Now that particular friend may not be a traditional Christian as we put it for she still smokes her cigarettes with her glass of wine but hey wisdom! Out of our entire time together those words were the most epic. She loves the Lord, fears him with all her heart and hey I don't know if she has accepted Jesus Christ as her personal savior so let me call and ask her . . . . Ok let me get my cell phone and call her . . . . its ringing . . ." Ok G let me ask you a question . . . have you accepted Jesus Christ as your personal savior?" Her response . . ." Yes I have." My response "Thanks that's all I called you for, the words you said to me yesterday were so poignant as to God saving my life and how I have to ask Him what is it that I can do for Him . . . . thanks sweetie . . . talk to you later."

Well there you have it, it is about your personal relationship? Wow just read a little of this to my Aunt who is facing her health challenges and she agrees it is personal. Now I told her it's your turn Auntie this is going to be your testimony. Unfortunately at times like these we see who our real friends are and she told me through this she didn't realize how many friends she had or how many churches back home were praying for her. She said something profound and that is she doesn't feel like talking to any negative spirits. And I agree we have to pray to ward them off either out loud or in our minds and hearts.

LESSON IN THE REJECTION

This morning I was in the bathroom asking my partner what should I choose and then I realized while sending a friend of mine a documentary that had been rejected over and over that the lesson is in the rejection. And ironically one of the film workshop choices I have to make is about documentary rejection. Now I don't know if that is confirmation but my partner will reveal it to me later. Anyhoo it was brought to my attention that every time I was rejected I learned something new. The more I was given reasons as to why I was being rejected and told to tweak this and that I learned more. I guess what I'm trying to say is that although we may get down emotionally and feel like giving up we can ask God to show us the lesson learned. For example my first Christian song came as a result of being asked by some parents to write for their daughter. I interviewed the girl and developed a sense of what she liked and composed a customized song to fit her personality from lyrics to instruments. It took time money and stepping out of my lyrical box. Before this I wrote relationship songs not realizing that the foundation was being laid inside of me to write the ultimate relationship songs, the Grammy songs for God's ears.

Getting back to the point, the girl's parents all of a sudden became unreachable and one day at a conference I saw them and asked what happened and they said they were no longer interested and the result was a completed song with no one to sing it. I mean I did the demo voice and later casually presented it to a label that was interested and offered me a deal based on the song but I wasn't ready. That song's title I began to see everywhere and as I walked closer with the Lord I began to see supernaturally what was happening. That song is "Sing Praises" and it is will be on our first released worship compilation.

Another song God gave me that I thought was for my cousin but when I went into the studio to sing it I had seven seizures during the laying down of the track. This occurred so much to the point that the engineer would look at me and say "Thank you Jesus" because even He knew that was the cue for what made me get through. Now after all of this the song I thought I had recorded for my cousin was never about her or for her. Her management wouldn't let her sing the song or any other song that I had written. Now check the scene it was my team that got her there and negotiated the contract for her while missing trains with these new managers. I literally took her package and marketed her to them without the coins. Why?

Because I believed in her and still do and she now is doing some national things with major recording artists. I hardly hear from her but my dream is still to see her walk across the Grammy stage. My Bermudian writing partner and I wrote and produced her songs. Then we had her compose her first song ever about the death of her friend which played on the radio but you know what? It hurts but it wasn't meant to be.

Later on an associate of mine sang the original version of that song that God gave me walking down Samson Street. We felt that because of all the attacks during the laying down of the track, the song was worth more and shelved it for years. Time went by but I wanted to hear His voice not mine so my partner, Mr. Holy Spirit told me to transform it into this great song for the Lord, now look at that chess move. Another time it was the documentaries and each time I learned and at the same time He was rebuilding my catalog, who knew? God knew . . . . So let's stop allowing our human emotional roller coaster to go off track and start pulling out all of our pitfalls and start restoring and using them as empowering blocks to build journeys of success.

This brings me to a scripture that changed my outlook and that is Psalms 118:25 "Oh Lord Save us and grant us Success" and He will. You weren't meant to get that job or have your song sung but that person or film placed or whatever the situation. Whenever you face rejection know that it's not always the enemy sometimes it is God blocking or diverting us back onto the path that he has charted for our lives.

I'M AWAKENED

My partner alerted me to the fact that the reason as to why I'm going through all sorts of persecution is because yes I'm being redefined and changing and people don't like change. Also the Bible is being fulfilled and it states that in the end times Christians will be persecuted so after this revelation I feel better. Over the past few months all sorts of strange things are happening and it's always those closest to me. I mean I have to write about this because this is a part of my journey, as the pages turn in our lives we write on those pages and some things we can go back and edit but while the pages are turning we can't go back. So let me just brief you on a few things. I have been disappointed over and over my mate is always going somewhere but with me nowhere.

Nine out of ten times something happens and we never get to our destination, concert after concert. It's funny because we used to enjoy going but there's a spirit of confusion so we have to work on injecting life back into our marriage. We live separate lives to the

point of no social contact other than eating meals. Now this loneliness took me to a place and brink of feeling depressed but I have cancerous cells in the remaining part of a brain tumor as well as systemic lupus so I have to seek God in this marriage that He ordained. My partner Mr. Holy Spirit said this man was going to be my husband before I knew and I fell in love with the spiritual side without ever knowing the flesh. We didn't have sexual relations until after we were married which is unheard of in this modern time even amongst Christians. But what I fell in love with is what I'm trying to change. so that we could become more intimate. Here is what I recorded in a moment of despair.

Sometimes in life you could still be lonely and be with someone. This is the worst feeling of rejection and abandonment when you are actually with someone who doesn't talk or interact with you. One moment they are warm and the next they are cold as ice and this makes me feel like giving up. Sometimes I want to give in to the odds that the doctors say I beat. My heart is so sad and the only thing that keeps me from suicide is my partner, Mr. Holy Spirit. It's hard to fight lets keep it real but I know my God has His eyes on me. For if his eyes are on the sparrow than I know He's not going to leave me nor forsake me. As I go through this brief victim mode of not being able to drive in over a decade or being approached, Lord I need you as I breathe you.

REMAIN STANDING

I may not have a car but I have a transporter and supporter. My Lord will never leave me nor forsake me. He is not a man that He should lie! He promised me that He'll never leave my side and my Lord and Savior has proven Himself time and time again. You know I remember on one of our pod casts my sister and co hosts saying that if God were not to do another thing for her He has already done enough. Well my friends that has stuck with me and like I was telling my Aunt last night there are those in your life's journey who are there cheering you on and wrapping your injuries for their benefit not yours. When you no longer are of use to them they disappear just like the wind. The more in tune we are with the Holy Spirit we can feel them coming and going but thank you Jesus, for the Lord I serve is unchanging. He chose me before I chose him just like the worship song my partner, the Holy Spirit gave me. And I'm strongly being directed right now to write that.

Unfortunately we look to one another for that perfect support, that unchanging mentality and the ONLY assurance we have is that when we accept Jesus Christ as our Lord and Savior we do become new creatures, new beings! Like anything in life it takes practice, sacrifice and commitment going against your flesh for it is hard because we are so used to the natural shell. But with Christ it is true ALL things are new and yes we can change. Although we may slip and fall with Christ in our hearts we can get back up, recharge and do better until we are renewed. As long as we are breathing there is hope. There is the hope that we can change, there is internal joy, an internal peace that resonates on the inside and manifests itself on the outside. So when someone asks me the question of how I'm doing, I used to say that I'm hanging in there but the power of life and death are in the tongue. Words are powerful so I'm learning to change my response to I'm blessed and still standing. God willing I will have mastered that response by the time this first book is published so it will become natural for me to simply say, "I'm still standing!"

Is it Possible?

Last night my fiancé and I went to visit my estranged uncle who I hadn't seen in three years. He had watched me get my butt beat by my HIV infected transgender tenants who owed me money. I had to talk to God for a while after begging my uncle for the money he promised to pay me back. It never registered that the Holy Spirit was having me make a mental list of the positives and negative attributes this man had in my life. There were more positives and as a result I made the choice to forgive. Forgiveness is a deep release and one of the harder things I had to learn and it takes repeated practice. Don't get it twisted it is not all peaches and cream.

Let me get back to the story because you all know by now that I can go all around the mulberry bush to make my point. And I must say that the fact that the Holy Spirit and I are writing this book makes me realize that it is a method of covering all bases so your heart and intellects are triggered to another awareness level and senses that you may have never thought about! Wow I guess that answer illustrates the possibility of there being a reason for going around the long way. Thanks Holy Spirit because I could not have humanly thought of that. Coming home on the train after having an enjoyable evening with my uncle whom he had just physically met one of the things we talked about was mysterious possibilities? I told him there are so many things that I have personally experienced that I know it is possible but that doesn't minimize my relationship with Christ instead these experiences have strengthened my relationship with my Father and I feel blessed to peak into the unknown. Now what I'm about to talk about many traditional followers won't understand and may see it as the devils work but what if? Is it possible?

Years ago I was getting high on some strong marijuana and a bunch of us had some serious past life experiences. I remember being this man on a horse who had raped and killed all of these people as well as my mother being my sister. When I became sober I could still see these images and noticed how my relationship with my mother was more of a sisterly nature. Then I looked at how maybe this was the reason I was in an alternative relationship and when intimate felt male domination. Well that's all I'm going to say on that for now don't want to be too explicit for it is my first book and we don't want to be banned. But let's remember the whole purpose is to put our experiences out there in the hope of saving others! Now that past life experience was like I said when I was high but I could not get those visuals out of my mind even while talking in my head and as I'm writing at this very second I can see the man who I remembered but now I have another visual which I'll share. A few years ago I wanted to know more about what I experienced even though the church frowned against those things that are unknown.

So I signed up for this class where this lady had been on some international shows and was known for dealing with regressions in order to help you deal with your now issues. You know the reasons as to why you feel certain emotions but can't explain it. I was always trying to save someone and then when they pooped on me I felt abandoned. I mean this trend continued no matter how many times I attended church, my relationships with people were a vicious cycle. Anyhoo I attended this class one evening and we had to move from the church hall to the actual church and lay on the pews. I forgot to bring a blanket as they suggested and I was among the few people of color there but once we got started no one noticed for we were nothing more than an array of human beings with curiosity and the desire to learn about ourselves. I put religion aside and said, "God here we go please show me what I need to see just as what I need to write at this very moment. The one thing that I'm known for is my integrity even by my enemies so I assure you that what you are reading are my truths, my experiences and my journey. All I'm doing is sharing to inspire others so they can see how my personal acceptance of Jesus Christ as my Lord and Savior has made situations while living in this earth more bearable.

Just like when they told me I had this brain tumor I read that book about life being lessons repeated until learned and that gave me a more meaningful perspective.

That evening as we laid on those cold church pews the instructor turned off all the lights so that it was near pitch black and all you could see was the light from the flashlight that she held under her chin as she spoke to us. She told us how she hoped that we could experience one of our deaths in order to understand some of the underlying issues we now face. For me that was right on time. As she was talking I said to myself how can she expect us to experience anything with all of that babbling?

Then all of a sudden I saw myself on a cobbled stoned street that I thought was England. I was standing there as a white woman with a grayish dirty tinge on my face dressed in a bonnet and holding a little blonde dirt faced girl's hand. She was my daughter and she held onto this homemade cloth doll with blonde strands and drawn eyes and a mouth. We were standing on a corner and then all of a sudden this old carriage like car hit us and I could see it now the cloth doll flying in the air and my hand stretched out and all I could see is the face of the little girl looking blankly. It seemed so real and I could feel the sense of lost but in my mind I said yeah this isn't real because the church doesn't believe in this so prove it Holy Spirit that this is happening and is a part of my journey. And even now I'm discussing with Him as to what to say for I don't want to scare or offend anyone. I just turned to the Bible to Acts 12: 9-11 and for the first time I'm reading about what happened to Peter and hey Holy Spirit these relate to me. Gee thanks partner!

Okay where was I? Yeah after I said prove that this is real I saw my great grandparents talking to one another in a field of red flowers and my great-grandfather was standing. The lights came on and I was back. Um time travel, I must look into that with God. Anyhoo standing I had only known him to be in a wheelchair and man that was it for me. She asked us to sit up and write quickly words that described the feeling we just experienced and mine were Saving and Abandonment. Some people were upset because they didn't experience anything. Later I asked family members was there ever a field of red flowers and the answer was an astonishing yes, a garden filled with wild poppy flowers. Now how could I have possibly known that?

Weeks later I was at me favorite Kmart just doing my routine browsing and as I was riding the escalator I noticed for the first time these pictures and I had to call my Mother because these were the same streets where I had the accident in that session and all of a sudden all the feelings came rushing back with the visuals. I could see it so clearly and my heart and fingers are racing as I share this with you. Now there is an area in the city that I've always felt drawn to even from college days. There is a restaurant which to date I'm yet to eat at and it is called the Tavern where everything about it is in the 1800s and I know now that is the area I had the accident at, right at that corner and I'm sure I lived in that area. For a time I couldn't figure out if I was the mother or the daughter but as time has gone on I can feel in my spirit that I'm the mother and I feel that I abandoned my child and as I'm writing I could see my hand stretched out and I know that I was trying desperately to save her. I may have saved her physically but I'm left with the mental scars of abandonment. So you tell me why are my issues today forms of saving and abandonment. Is any of this possible? God did mention about unrevealed mysteries!

ALLOW GOD TO MOVE FREELY IN YOUR LIFE

You know it's funny because I was thinking and saying out loud that it had been some time since I had the cramping that I first got from my lupus. I mean my body would cramp up so bad that one time I was in the pool and they had to carry me out. Another time I was in bed and I had to have my partner rub me down. I remember this one time she told me how she was feeling sick and couldn't go to church and that was the night after my intense cramping and I said, "I have to go to church to give God some praise for all that He has gotten me through." Now that I think about it I was very involved with my other "gay friendly" church. We used to travel, I was part of the choir and loving it and I miss that church. In fact one time when it looked like I was dying overseas it was that church's footage that I had taped of the MCCP choir and other churches singing in Baltimore that got me through for the Holy Spirit was so present. I would lay there and look over and over at my choir's delivery of the song "I lift mine eyes to the hills, whence cometh my help" well I think that's how it goes but the point is I could feel the Holy Spirit and that is what got me through.

Writing these chronicles reminds me of so much that I couldn't possibly write it all!

I was in the hospital in Bermuda and I knew I was dying and called for a certain American Minister. I have tons of Ministers in my family could have asked for anyone of them but I specifically requested him. I felt hey if I'm dying why not listen to that small still voice after all what did I have to lose no matter how crazy it seemed to me. Anyhoo the Minister came and I asked him if he had ever met a "gay Christian" and he said, "No!" I told him, "You have now and I have a message from God to give to you." I had a Holy union with my former life partner who I was emotionally tied to at the time and was living in the life. So I went on to tell him how it was going to take him to wake up the people and help make a change in that particular society that was afraid and worshiping a Bishop of the cloth who had gotten way out of control and into the power range. Yep unfortunately it happens to many Christians who get the power bug. Those readers in Bermuda remember the outcome I'm sure. Many humans period can't handle power and become dictators; and that is why it is so important to seek His face and pray for humility.

Well months later this same Minister got fired by the Power Bishop ranger and this created a spit in the church and the result was another church being birthed out of that. Then the power ranger became real sick to the point he couldn't speak for cancer took over and within the course of two years he died. I guess what I'm trying to say is that even then and there in my near death state God used me to speak to that Minister who got fired and had to return to America. None of this surprised me because I delivered the message God told me. I was obedient and because of that and other numerous experiences I do not question anyone's heart relationship with the Lord. I didn't know it then but the Holy Spirit was my partner since way back even if I wasn't truly His. It wasn't until I completely surrendered my journey to Him that I began walking hand in hand. Now I know there are those out there that disagree but you can't disagree with God's love and the healing power of Jesus.

Years later I saw that same Minister at a funeral and we both happened to be back in Bermuda, the same place at the same time and he remembered the warning that God had given. Listen up, if God can use a donkey or a burning bush to get his message across then why not you. I look now back at the sequence of events or God's order and I can say as my deceased friend JoJo Sharon would say, "Yea God."

The order had to go as it did for me. To become sick again overseas, to go through a cheating breakup that nearly took over my essence and my being to the point that I aggravated my lupus and cancerous brain tumor. I had no other choice but to go on chemo and I had no other choice but to cry out "YES LORD, IT'S YOU and Me!" He will break you down boo and in that midnight hour you will feel His power but whether we obey or not is a choice as well. I recall when they couldn't get any blood out of my veins so they had to go via my private parts and I said, "Jesus I trust you to carry my pain" and you know He did. Another time they tried feverishly to get my blood and because I now had blue veins due to the systemic lupus and all the vein poking from the MRIs, Cat Scans, clinical trials, heart problems etc they were in one word "shut."

One time in the presence of my only niece these Indian nurses were so tired of watching the main nurses poking me with needles desperately trying to get blood so they began crying out loudly, "Jesus please help" and all of a sudden the blood stated flowing. So just as people are moved in and out of your life, don't get too discouraged I've learned that when you make Jesus your number one friend you will realize that His blood will cover you and guess what you will start forgiving, loving, laughing and believe it or not trusting again for after all our God always has a plan we just have to be still and listen!

WORSHIP IS OUR ULTIMATE DESTINATION!

Well I'm finally returning home to my Hubby and doggie after traveling for a day. What started out peacefully ended up shifting. Yesterday morning I was so at peace after a wonderful prayer summit; one man termed it as simply a date with God. Destination Summit covered all generations from age 82 to 22. They treated us like the princes and princesses that God designed us to be. However as we know after a good feasting with God the enemy gets angry and tries to throw all sorts of bricks at you. As a result when I was traveling between destinations my plane got cancelled and out of habit I was going to catch a train home. In fact when I found out that there was a three hour layover I originally told the organizer that I would catch a train home but my bag ended up being too heavy so I had to put it on the plane rather than a have it as a carry on.

When I arrived in Newark I found out the plane was delayed even further by another five hours. I thought about getting my stuff and going for the quickest route and catching the train. My independent self was going to be like Nike and "Just Do It" and even glanced at the air trains passing the window. Gather this thought with a visual. My partner, my guide, my light and my best friend said, "Stop and call your husband" so I obeyed. My initial intention was to board the train and call him from there and go straight to the house and have him drive to the airport later and get my other bag. Notice the rush! But now I'm grasping the concept of marriage and obedience.

When I called my boo he told me how he had these dreams of train accidents and in one of the dreams he saw the train turn on its side and this spooked him. I told him what my intentions were and he said, "Oh no, whatever you do no trains on this trip!" I told him that somewhere there probably was an accident and to pray for the people so that the results wouldn't be too bad. I'll want to make mention that after that I googled train accidents on April 16th and 17th and well you can see the shocking results for yourself. Let's just say we serve a mysterious but compassionate God!

Long story short the plane ended up being cancelled altogether and customer service suggested that I take the train but I told the representative about my Husband's dreams and said you know about these things because you are from Africa. I called the organizer of the summit who told me to ask for a night up and that is what he did for me with a food voucher just like she said.

I went to this beautiful hotel, had a great meal at no cost. Notice the word "no cost." Later I told my Hubby that I would catch the train home the next day because I didn't wish to upset his passenger's lives who he takes to work with him in the morning. He agreed but insisted on taking them which is an hour away from where we live and then he said he would come and get me from the airport because again he didn't want me catching a train on this trip. And check this my Mom kept telling me not to put my other meds in the bag that I was sending through but I told her I had enough with me and that was just the overflow. I traveled early the next morning and when I landed I walked into a Minister who I had on our television show and asked him if he had seen himself on TV and he was so excited that he said, "Did I see it I had my son tape it!" I told my Husband and he said, "What that same edited portion" and I was said, "Yep." I felt good knowing I assisted in making someone's life brighter.

Naturally in the chain of events my bag didn't make the airline switch like they said it would. I went home and when five hours went by from the latest time they had given me that the bag would be delivered, my partner prompted me to visit this worship song we had composed but I didn't have all the lyrics just the title and lead hook. It is simply titled "He's Calling Me" and when I started worshipping with the song and singing "Greater is He that is in me than he that is in the world, He's calling me, I worship you Lord, I honor you, I glorify your name because you are calling me, so put aside All distractions and take position, can't you hear Him calling you, just listen!" And then there was a knock on the door and my Husband yelled," Babe are you expecting somebody?" And I responded, "Yes my bag!" And there it was being delivered late but right on time in the midst of worship. I posted on face book how the lesson was patience and peace beyond understanding. I couldn't understand why I was at peace because in the natural I should be livid. That was my lesson and for all those around me.

The ultimate message is that when you worship you come to that destination where you are with the Great I Am and no one can touch that! For in true worship there is delivery and deliverance. "I expect that right now Lord as my Mother is in surgery we expect nothing less than Greater." I reached home one day before my Mom's surgery and next week is my two Aunts. Thus **the peace beyond understanding lesson** is for them as well.

IN THE MIDST OF PAIN

It took me literally hours to get up and start writing this morning. So much has occurred over the past week I have to ask where do I begin. When my partner first awakened me I listened to a timely message on the Talley about how there is about to be a movement of the Holy Spirit that will sweep across nations and how America needed to get back in alignment. This quickened me to start texting people who were on my heart that God wanted me to drop a word to. A word of hope; one of fulfillment and empowerment. Sometimes we all need that grain of promise in our lives. So even in the midst of pain and that I am physically, I have everything to gain because I can feel His presence and that revives me and keeps me striving!

I was just thinking for those that saw me line dancing a few days ago at my cousin's retirement party from Air force One they would be shocked to see me now but hey that's how it goes with these challenges. If it's not the systemic lupus or the brain cancer acting up it's an attack on our finances, marriage, family members or church. "Lord right now in the name of Jesus I rebuke all of these afflictions against my body. Lord take away the pain in my hips, my back, my knee and the jerking in my hands. We've been on this journey for over a decade and I know we still have work to do." Like the scripture says Psalms 118:17 "I will live and not die and proclaim the works of the Lord." Psalms 118:25, Jeremiah 1:8 and Jeremiah 1:19 and the list go on. At this very moment I dress myself with the full amour of God.

My dog is up just staring at me and I'm saying to him do you see it and then I'm pleading the blood of Jesus over this room and this house. You know animals and young children can see what we can't see, that being the invisible. This morning when my husband and I prayed before he left for work, we prayed for protection against the seen and the unseen devices of the enemy. This stuff is real believe me. The other day while I was taking an afternoon nap I was having my back massaged in my sleep and I was fine with that but then suddenly I felt this coldness about to caress my nibble and I bit it and literally awoke with my mouth chopping down. From the view of an onlooker they would have seen me wake up to a biting motion. Now I literally saw in the spirit this huge grayish blue green like snakes body, octopus thing slivering away and I could feel its coldness. I can't really describe it but it was just as real as me sitting her typing and talking to you. I frantically called my pastor's wife. So when I was reading about clothing ourselves with full armor that is preparation for all that is to come. I told my husband and I was not afraid but just glad that I have a Lord and

Savior that watches over me and I now know who I am and that is a solid warrior in the Army of the Lord!

WHEN YOU ASK GOD WHY?

When I was raised I was always told not to ask God why? But when so many incidents are occurring one after another I had to ask God why. I kept feeling that I was the common denominator and mass hysteria was twirling around like I was Dorothy in the tornado. Well I went to sleep and my partner woke me up and I opened the Bible to Job and my eyes fell on the intro and how God doesn't want us to feel guilty. My partner reminded me that I have to learn to call on God in the midst of the storm but I was calling on man such as my friends and family and relying on my own feelings instead of the greatest source in my life, my Creator, my master, my friend, my all in all. In my head all I could hear was this hymn "There's a sweet, sweet Spirit in this place and I know that it's the Spirit of the Lord, there are sweet expressions on each face and I know that it's the Spirit of the Lord. Sweet Holy Spirit, sweet heavenly dove stay right here with us, filling us with your love. And for these blessings we lift our hearts in praise without a doubt you know that we have been revived when we shall leave this place." All I could do is cry and worship him. In my head all I could do is say I love you Lord and I hear your voice.

It's funny because He reveals so much but I have to learn to get in the habit of when He shows me things to ask for direction right on the spot. The other morning I woke up to a song I don't even know and that was "Lest I forget Gethsemane" and the rest I can't remember. So I asked someone where was Gethsemane and they told me that is where Jesus went to pray before he died and he cried. Well yesterday the incident that happened to me I became the outsider as I watched a family member go with a bunch of authorities and just look down at me literally. My partner brought it to my attention that moments like these will continue for we reside in an unstable world but God never changes and His arms are stretched wide so that He can love and hold us tightly when the fiery darts come.

They usually come from those closest to us but we have the shield of faith which is confidence in God to overcome. We have the victory and we must remain suited for the enemy is forever chipping away at our weaknesses. There are no days off with the enemy and his posse so why should we become so comfortable in our own skin and think that we as believers won't be attacked. Think about that scripture "He comes like a thief in the night" seriously and we must always be prepared with our swords for our battle is not against flesh and blood.

BARREN ALL OVER AGAIN

When I was growing up I would experience painful and heavy period cycles. Sometimes it was so bad that I had to wear two tampons and two giant sanitary napkins along with three pairs of underpants and a pair of stockings that we cut and my sister termed them "stocking underpants!" Didn't dream I would have endometrial cancer.

I know God has a plan but it's the painful hurts that we have to deal with that push us into our destiny. Mine comes at the expense of being barren in so many ways and losing those kids is like the doctor telling me all over again that you can never have children. Years later I tried to adopt and they said because of my condition, the lupus and brain cancer I could not. The loss of losing what you naturally are designed for is so deep that it cuts like a knife.

Your Health is God's Wealth

You know I've always felt somewhat inferior when it came to what I amassed materially. Many of my family had the latest gadgets and I was still somewhat in the dark ages. I remember going shopping with one family member and she scoffed at me loudly and embarrassed me because I didn't know what the latest gadget was or even how to use a kindle. Well once this book gets published it will be on Kindle! Another had accomplished some things and that is all some family members could talk about and I realized when I woke up this morning that subconsciously I was chasing after their approval. I had produced many shows, songs etc. but that wasn't where they were at. Even writing this book didn't make that much of an impact but I realize that the more I write what is in my head that it is for my own personal therapy and health.

Last evening we were discussing one of the times I had been severely ill and having a good laugh over it, well at least now we can laugh. Years ago while it was happening it wasn't nobody's joke. Let me take you back a bit to just one of the many health sagas and I'll show you how God is first and how humor prevails.

I was going through an intense break up with legal issues and I knew that my doctors had hinted at chemo for a while but I refused. However after my Holy union was legally ended I returned to my original country to die. It was there that the illnesses decided to go buck wild! I have an apartment back home and it was vacant so my Mom was praying that God place the right tenant. At my former job this lady I'm friends with knew we were looking and felt that a new employee moving to Bermuda might be a perfect fit. Now on the other side in a another land in Barbados the lady told her friends that she was taking this job in a foreign country but still had not found a place to reside. Her friends and family thought she was insane but she felt that if God was guiding her to this job then He would also lead her to her new home. On the other side thousands of miles across the oceans my Mom

was praying that God place the right tenant and her faith was super strong so when the lady connected the two it was ONLY A GOD MOVE! Check this:

I came back home moved into the side apartment and met the new tenants and felt her warmth. She had no idea about my brain cancer or systemic lupus, titanium chip in left breast or osteoporosis. I was battling seizures and grieving over how cold my relationship ended. It was like the title to one of me and my Bermudian writing partner Wendell's songs, "Cut like a knife" and trust and believe it cut me into pieces. At the final meeting in a large board room I took the Bible and opened it to Psalms 91 just as my Mother told me and placed it in the middle of the table. Therefore when they had to hand me something they had to go across this powerful Psalms. My ex had asked for more money and assets after listening to her new friend, a powerful lawyer. They requested another property if I didn't take care of certain papers in a short six months knowing full well that the doctors had now ordered me to take chemotherapy. I guess you could say they left me right before my treatment. Yes I had my faults but this was inhumane. Their new friend who was also a friend of mine wanted to leave me with nothing and capitalize on the fact that I was physically ill and actually told me to go and take care of my health. Can you believe that and they were right! So I presented a long recap letter from my side as to why no more money should be given and I was guided by my partner, Mr. Holy Spirit, and my two cousins the entire night prior to settlement day. That day we signed the papers with the divorce lawyer I left immediately for New York. We speak about "same sex" marriages not being legal but I lived it right down to the legal divorce.

After I left the building I traveled via bus to Chinatown in Manhattan and I never let them see me cry but I wept as I walked all the way from Chinatown to Times Square and for those who know NYC that is a walk. I cried and talked to God the entire time. When I reached the Marriott my family had rented the Presidents suite and when I saw them we hugged and cried and then my Aunt Estlyn treated us to Oprah's Broadway show "the Color Purple." I cherish that moment for I went from devastation to elevation! It was also there where I realized the category that certain friends and family fell in and about how people are placed in your life for seasons and reasons. An Uncle who I hadn't seen in years was the one who sat with me through that legal process because my lawyer couldn't show up. The Holy Spirit instructed the letter writing and the finding of documents to support facts within the letter and chose my two cousins to be my assistants. God never leaves nor forsakes if you just believe and ask Him to guide you. My legal separation was the beginning of the rest of my life!

As I'm writing this I'm taking the time out to say thank you Lord for leading and guiding the development of this book. And I know it's my part one book due to the visions. As I type my hands have spasms and like a fish out of water they often just flop amongst the keyboard. But I know my Father has that worked out as well, I just know which is the title to another song. It's funny my husband who often says due to my chosen song titles, "You remind me of that man in a movie, you want to hear it I wrote a song about it!" I've never seen the movie he's referring me to but I can relate to 'Hey, you want to hear it? I wrote a song about it!" Yep certainly can and I just know that God will bring me through for every trial and tribulation is my testimony for others. It's not about me and never has. We need to get that concept; it's not about us people. God uses and allows circumstances so that He can show off!

God placed that new tenant who was a staunch prayer warrior. One morning as she passed the apartment where I was staying she felt the spirit of death but proceeded to go to work. She didn't know us like that but deep within knew that God had placed her on assignment. When she passed I was inside fighting supernatural forces. All I could hear in my head was that former friend who was now with my ex saying "It's not about you Lesley Ann, concentrate on your health" in a deep off beat British monotone voice." I started having these seizures and every time I tried to speak I couldn't. I then remembered that the tumor was located in my left lobe, and my speech area.

A specialist had said once that he found it amazing that my speech wasn't effected and tell you the truth it is and now when words get mixed up or I can't pronounce something I blame it on the tumor but that doesn't stop the fact that I'm learning another language. Even writing and editing this book is a challenge because there is so much content and I just want to be aligned with the messages my partner, Mr. Holy Spirit wants me to release at this time.

Imagine I'm having problems with my given language but yet seeking to learn another. I equate that to my relationship with Christ and how despite the fact that I have some difficulty reading the Bible it doesn't stop me from being taught by my partner, Mr. Holy Spirit daily about the Word in other ways. We can't let our limitations limit us! We must strive beyond and yes that is the title of one of my appointed television shows. Go ahead and smile thinking about my Hubby's comment.

WE OVERCAME THE ENEMY ON MY BIRTHDAY

Well today maybe my birthday and I'm in my room praising God because I just grabbed a pit bull at the throat and shouted out loudly "In the name of Jesus you will not have my dog!" I had no fear while cars stopped and the strength and boldness of God in me was wrestling these animals which had demonic presence. I was on my cell phone when I had a foresight. I could hear something in the atmosphere that wasn't rite. There was a guy across the street with two medium sized pit bulls and one was unleashed so I put my phone on the sidewalk while the person was still talking I asked us to be covered by the blood of Jesus as one of them came to attack my baby and I shielded him. The guy came running and the other one was trying to come. The dog was actually dragging him across the street and I shouted, "So you see there is power in Jesus name" and he was out of breathe saying, "Yes mamma I can see it!"

And the result is seen as Well the person on the phone was like what the heck was that and all I could say was that I'm going to get my praise on at some service. These are attacks and it's confirmed that I know what I know and who is my personal Lord and Savior. But I'm asking you to unite with me and rebuke the spiritual warfare on us, our families, our friends, animals and all the passageways that Satan feels he can get a foot in . . . **"We denounce you demons in the name of Jesus for He is Real!"**

Well everyone had asked me what I wanted to do for my birthday prior to the dog incident; as a matter of fact my Husband had given me some money and told me to do whatever I wanted to do with it. I just told everyone that I wanted to do something peaceful. So that's all I kept putting into the atmosphere was the word "peace" and they say name it and claim, that is what the good Word says. And guess what that's what I got. I went and told my Husband that I was going to go to one of two churches since it was a Saturday evening. Then I got a call from one of my girlfriends saying she had sent me a text but strangely I hadn't received it. It was inviting me to go to one of the two churches I felt led to attend. This was the first time in my life that I wanted to attend a praise service, I felt compelled to worship and give thanks in a corporate setting. Attending watch night was nice but this was different for people are expected to attend a church before the New Year rolls in but this wasn't expectancy or a tradition this was my birthday. The day that God decided to release me into the atmosphere and onto this planet called earth.

I was actually the first baby born that year. My Mother called me in the morning and said, "You better do something on your birthday and not lay just around. Remember I was stuck in that hospital over the holidays since you were due on Christmas but decided not to come out until January." She said she spent all of her holiday seasons; Christmas, Boxing Day and on New Years Day she was in labor all day in pain and I said, "But guess what Mom it was worth it because I'm here and I promise to do something today that will bring me peace." Before the close of my birthday my girlfriends treated me to beauty treatments with a facial, a massage, line dancing singing and praising God. I had a blast and it goes down as one of my most memorable birthdays or as I like to refer to it born days! Thanks G and K!

THE REASON WHY

Every time I hear the word "why "I automatically think about how one of my artists sings it in a song. Anyhoo you have to just hear it and it'll stick with you the way he says "why?" and the other artist says, "Because she loves me so much." Well the only reason I'm here communicating with you is because He loves me so much. Part of my purpose is delivering the great commission by media, to convince you of Christ unconditional unfailing never denying love. It's a love like no other that will bring you through when humans and possessions fail you God does not. He doesn't write anyone off even the serial killer has a soul and that is why He sent his only son Jesus to die for you and me. He paid the price already and all we have to do is make Him Lord and Savior over our lives. He has given us power through the Holy Spirit that lies within us. Awaken that force within you and let me introduce my partner who directs my path because I made the choice to accept and follow Jesus. Yep it is not all glitz and glam believe you me. You may be persecuted but you have this assurance and undeniable peace that is within once you accept Him as Lord and Savior over your life.

Yesterday I went to get a special gift for my cousin who was retiring from Air force One. She was the first woman of color to ever work on that plane and has gone down in history as the first. But let me tell you my girl is a die heart Jesus follower and her first love is Christ not position. I guess what I'm trying to say is that all of the five Presidents from Bush Sr. to Obama had a secret spiritual weapon on board that protected them and that was a representative of Jesus. That's all I'm saying. When they were the only plane flying in the entire sky during 911 they had Jesus on board do you realize what impact that has?

I was in a section of town recently that reminded me of some of my former friends from my former lifestyle and I was prompted to call one of them. Now I have passed this store and street countless times but today was different. A thought of a memory made me physically stop to make a call. A call I hadn't made in over three years. I couldn't get through so I said okay it probably wasn't meant for me to call her. I started having funny memories of this certain area that definitely was a part of my journey and I missed the people. I had turned off my phone but when I got up this morning and turned my phone on there were texts that one of my hang out buddies who I had thought about at that very spot I stopped at had passed in her sleep. Now I wasn't even in contact with them but had the urge that prompted me to call and that was nobody but my partner who is within me, the one I personally refer to as Mr. Holy Spirit, partner, the Spirit etc. I don't know I feel death nor should I say peoples' spirits in general. Just like my cousin's wife when I found out she was sick I had a vision of her passing and I was like Lord what about the children. Then she had to go on life support. As you read on you'll find out about my Michael Jackson experience and that really brought things to light.

Back in the day I couldn't understand it but now I embrace my gifts that God has given me and I encourage you to do the same.

Yesterday when I was traveling back and forth I started reading this book entitled "The Rules of Engagement" "the art of Strategic prayer and Spiritual Warfare" by fellow Bermudian Dr. N. Cindy Trimm. I had on my list to write about Ephesians 6 but I was waiting for my partner to tell me the right time. So I read about the armor that God gives us and last night I felt an attack on my body and the Spirit got me up to bring up all of this green stuff. You see doctors diagnosed me with systemic lupus and 20% remaining brain cancer, osteoporosis etc but the God that I serve takes care and has his angels watching out for me.

Yesterday morning in my meditation I read about angels watching over us and after my blizzard and disappearing men experience I know this first hand. So to sum up this portion, this morning it was Ephesians 6 that got me through the night for people have passed for less reasons then my medical conditions. Therefore fluid in my lung was not an option for I have work to complete and one of them is delivering this book of experiences into your hands. For those that don't know Ephesians 6, it contains 6 sections of armor that God has given us to fight the spirit realm because it's real so don't kid yourself the battle is quite valid and becoming worse as the time gets closer. Satan is bringing out his weapons and there are no stops, the gloves are off. Here is our armor from top to bottom to encase the human spiritual being. You must wear it and always be aware not paranoid just aware!

1. Helmet of Salvation to protect our minds

2. Breastplate of Righteousness to protect our hearts where our emotions are housed.

3. Shield of Faith to fight off the attacks from the enemy's camp.

4. Sword of the Spirit which is the only offensive weapon God provides us with and that is His WORD. (Memorize scriptures)

5. Belt of truth is used to keep us girded and grounded so we won't wander.

6. Footgear of readiness and motivation to spread the news, the gospel, the testimonies, proclaim God's works.

Now I try not to be as my loving hubby calls it "thumpish" but a keep it real Christian. So there I'm done for today unless my partner tells me otherwise. And you see obedience is better than sacrifice just thought I would throw that one out there as a bonus. Thank you Lord!

REORGANIZING SPIRIT WITH MIND

Well it's been a while so I put pen to paper or in this modern age finger to computer keys, either way it feels like it's been far too long. I just thank God for allowing me to communicate daily with Him through my prayers and general internal talk. I can't imagine what it would be like if I stepped away like I do when I step away from my pages. I may not write due to a bunch of distractions, life circumstances or I just don't feel prompted to journal and that could be because of me or I'm not obedient to my partner, Mr. Holy Spirit. Now quite frankly I talk constantly with my Lord and Savior and quite often I say to myself wow I should put this in my book or that in my book or I will say to friends, "now that is one for the books." But you know what it's all in my book of life, no escaping it whether we write about it or not it all gets recorded. The other day someone sent me a video about the big bang theory and all the galaxies and how religion came about and that it is so naïve, which is the term we'll use here not the explicit as they used.

They went on to say that we are naïve for believing that God created all of this. I shared the post on my face book page along with a note that although there may be a million galaxies I still believe and will not be shaken from my knowing that there is an extraordinary God. I mentioned that I have had encounters; I believe that there are other life forms and I still know that my God created this universe! As I write this I'm being ministered to. In fact I know that there is a God who controls all of this and that is why I do not get caught up in second guessing the Spirit inside of me. He is the strength that gets me out of bed each day or the very breath that I take. I ask for answers to my circumstances or even more so guidance to the right door but as humans we second guess it. I know just as God is removing the clutter out of my life whether it is people, material things or character flaws; He is also reorganizing my mind, my time and I just have to learn to be more attentive.

The other day I had put on some boiling water for my soup and I came up to the office and my dog was acting strange so I thought it was because of the heat. Suddenly I felt prompted to look for my medication and after a short time of searching upstairs I was led downstairs to the kitchen to the pot on the stove where all of the water had drained out and it was just about to burn and get nasty and my partner casually had me turn off the pot. I posted on face book the occurrence along with whether this is science or something much greater, such as God. You know we always hear that saying in church "let me decrease so that you Lord may increase" but how many of us really take into account what that actually means. Science says we become one energy with the universe and yes I can agree with that but how about taking it a step further and believing that we become one with the Spirit of God that resides in each of us. What about becoming one with the presence that you know is there, greatness, something that is so full of light, that knowing that remains outside of our emotions, our feelings such as pride, or fear.

When we speak words into the atmosphere whether it be by mouth or print we have to take responsibility for that. You ever hear that saying we are that what we eat well how about we are that which we speak and rightly so since it comes from the heart. Whether we are trying to influence, manipulate or hurt what we deliver is powerful. The Holy Spirit inspired me to write the song "It's Time, time to change our hearts, time to renew our minds." At the end of the day it's time to transform our lives from the clutter and chaotic ways of thinking to leaning on Him, not our friends, pastors, or mentors. Give Him a try first and ask for guidance and direction and trust and believe once you step aside from you, you allow the gateway for manifestation of greatness. I am going through a situation right now, one of those 'oh God I need you and only you can fix it' circumstances. Instead of running to drugs, or friends I gave permission to my partner, the Holy Spirit to guide me, direct me, lead me and between my emotional bursts of trying to call a friend, a prophetess, and getting busy signals or just the ringing God allowed me to connect with the right persons who have my back not my neck. I ended speaking to two persons and each of them resulted in prayer. I didn't ask for money, a plumber or an answer I asked for one accord and had them touch and agree with me.

You see when your earthly partner doesn't want to pray with you go to wherever it is that you need to go whether it's inside of yourself or outside of yourself whatever it takes to open up and cry out to the heavens, that God will align you with His will. And let me tell you I just kept seeing and hearing the words hold your tongue and I obeyed and in less then twenty four hours my earthly partner aligned with me in prayer and asked for miracles. It is all about being on one accord in every circumstance, being one in spirit, mind and soul and the result is you will be whole. You will be able to carry out your purpose beyond adversities because you are in alignment. You can't honestly tell me that you haven't figured out by now that we are fighting constantly against spiritual warfare. That's what it's always been about the fight against minds, bodies and souls. So let's reorganize our way of thinking, let go, let God transform us bit by bit and watch our world change. You may go through tests but the way you handle them will be different and as a result their impact will differ.

Look the reality is that only God truly knows the corners of our lives and we can only see down the streets of our journey so why not give it to the navigator, the number one GPS of our lives. Just punch in this is the situation and this is what I would like to see happen and if it's your will then let go. He knows all and is all there is, ever was and all there will ever be so therefore what we wish to see may not be all that He wants for us. He may see the lessons, the healings, the reorganizing in the comfortable patterns of our old ways of thinking, and figuring so we must just open ourselves and trust in He that is greater because He is the ultimate creator. The ultimate fix, the solution maker and most of all what I constantly need to be reminded of, He is my matchmaker.

AS I LOOK BACK OVER MY LIFE

This is an actual written account of what occurred prior to me coming to the church where I eventually met my husband. These were friends so I thought, ones that I had toured with and housed. Here is part of what was sent to the Police Commissioner at that time.

I will point out that this in no way applies to every transgender individual for I understand now that my fight was against demonic beings. If I hadn't lived it and had the proof with witnesses and hospital bills I would have thought it was some twisted attempt of a horror movie. Written one year after the horrific incident.

December 10th, 2007

To Whom It May Concern;

It has been nearly One Year since the unthinkable occurred on the afternoon of December 23rd, 2006. And as I write this letter it truly is for To Whom It May Concern, for those whose human souls have compassionate and emphatic hearts. Hopefully these documentations will make a positive impact in our lives. As we are a city that faces extreme occurrences of violent acts we must look at the core of our problems and not just the inhumane results. Those that are HIV positive we should assist and be threatened by their status. A positive HIV status should not be used as a loaded machine gun! The reason why it has taken me almost twelve months to write this cover letter is due to the fact that I had to revisit my hellish nightmare. However it was a nightmare that would lead me closer to God, and my Lord and Savior Jesus Christ where as a result the Holy Spirit led me to my church home the next day on Christmas Eve, December 24th, 2007.

I had rented my house to two transgender individuals and was told that since I was a Christian I should not discriminate and rent the house on 2xyz Latona Street to them because NO ONE had given them an opportunity in life. I heard the foster home stories, the job and school discrimination stories as well as the entire "outcast stories." Needless to say I rented the house to them and when I went away three months later they abruptly ceased paying the rent. When I went to visit the place with my uncle there were several people just camping out there along with animals? Again I gave them the chance to defend themselves and they stated that since they were HIV positive status they could apply for disability and social security and therefore would be able to pay my rent. I noted that they would receive a notice to vacate if they didn't pay by an agreed upon date.

Well months went by and on our agreed upon date I personally served them a notice to vacate and this time when I went to my house there were young boys sleeping on my living room/dining area. The animals were unkempt and the dog was attached to a cable cord. The stench was unbelievable! The tenants were not home. I was told by the young boys that they paid the tenants $200 to stay at the house for a month. I now understood that my house was a haven for young runaway gay boys. They referred to my tenant J.M. as "Mother" and my former original tenant M.L. as their 'Grandmother."

I understood the lingo but when I went upstairs they were fearful and screamed "Oh mother is not going to like that." When I went upstairs they had the largest flat screen TV I had ever seen, as well as computers, wigs, costumes, handcuffs, nets and chains hanging from my ceiling as well as scattered ID's of various ethnic men who appeared to have been taxi drivers . . . .

I rushed downstairs and the neighbors were gathering outside. I remember when the dog was a mere puppy and he remembered me so I took him off the cable cord and walked him on the sidewalk just to get some air and to pray but as I was walking the dog back to the house I was approached by J and M. One of the young boys who had a visible attached colon bag had telephoned their" Mother" and "Grandmother." I handed them the notice and M said you aren't a Christian all up in my face and I shouted, "I plead the blood of Jesus" as he stood in my face. He placed his hand around my neck and pushed me off the sidewalk in front of the house and into the street where I landed on the back of my head. J and M knew that I have a brain tumor for they had been hired and performed for CARF in Bermuda. This was a cancer charity I had founded before I knew I had cancer to research the illness and assist its victims.

As I lay in the middle of the street a circle of neighbors surrounded me including my uncle who was afraid to get involved because of the attackers HIV status. All I could do is look up and it was like a scene from a movie and I just remembered feeling helpless on my back and speechless as my future fleshed before me. If only I had listened to others, if only I had not been so kind to these people, if only I had never let any of them move in, if only I had done things differently! Then I realized this was my destiny and I must literally exercise the Jesus step of turning the other cheek and in this case if I didn't I would give them a reason to scratch me and I know HIV is transferable by the mixing of blood. All of these thoughts ran quickly through my mind and then I remained calm because I literally felt the presence of Jesus! Then my legal tenant J who wore a weave pulled my dreadlocks and twisted them stating "Ah you thought

I was the nice one but I was the one who was going to FU up, you dizzy bitch!" As I looked into his eyes I saw nothing but demons. And I secretly in my heart made a vow to Jesus that if I got out of this I would turn my life over fully to serve HIM 100%. The neighbors had called the cops who were situated close by at the 17th District and three police cars arrived on the scene. One white who appeared to be the leader and two black who acted in a rookie capacity! Of course everyone scattered and the attackers all rushed in the house. I went to enter as well since I was the landlord and owner and M was no longer residing there but purposely squashed my fingers in the door, he was pushing so hard that one of the young boys behind the door was screaming for him to stop. The police had me wait in my uncle's car while they went into my house with my uncle and closed the door.

The white cop stated loudly, "If you don't stay in the car I'll have you locked up!" So the message here was simply we are on the attackers side. I understand that they did not wish to be caught in any cross fire but why loudly state that in front of others. They could have pulled me aside and told me in a respectable matter since my assault was the reason as to why they were there. Needless to say my uncle who had nothing to do with the house struck a deal with all of them. Now here I was the landlord, embarrassed by my tenants, the young boys, the neighbors, the police, hurt physically with my head and hand as well as emotionally because my uncle looked on as I was attacked and never tried to help me. This was the essence of the lesson in self preservation!

Well after a while the three policemen emerged from the house and the white cop just looked at me with a look that I'll never forget but maybe he was frightened by them. The two black cops were more compassionate and told me where to go to file for an official eviction and also if I experienced severe physical pain to go to the hospital. Later that night I experienced pains in the back of my head and my hand was hurting were they had crushed my fingers. However I had made a pact with God the next morning and I found myself on Christmas Eve at my now church home. But later on that Sunday I had someone drive me to the hospital where I had to talk to more police and have a CAT scan due to my pre-existing brain tumor and they did not wish to take any chances. I was between insurances so I was slapped with a near $5000 medical bill and I remember months later during the sheriff and official eviction two young cops stating, "Oh you could just pay the minimum on the bill." Forget the fact that what happened to me was wrong. This was a visible display of city violence. And Audora (J) and her/he followers stated boldly in front of these young cops, **"You could not have been that hurt cause you would have went straight to the hospital and not waited 24 hours and the event was not that dramatic, Miss Drama queen since you cops never arrested us. In fact we took care of you in front of them so you know I must be fierce!"**

And they are right the original incident on December 23rd, 2006 that afternoon was NEVER reported. I had to have it reported twice. (DC#0617067244 and then DC#063982655)

I spoke with Commissioner X Y Z (name withheld to protect privacy but it was stated in the actual letter) when he visited my church one Sunday and told me to contact his office directly but I needed time to heal so here is my cover letter and package. I am giving copies to Captain B as well in hopes that a precedent will be set for respect. That being NO LANDLORD should be attacked by their tenants. And police should not be threatened when it comes to them doing their job; they are in control and therefore by

No means should be viewed as less than such. When we have police being viewed as less than we will continue to have violence!

Thank you for addressing this situation in some way. WE DO NOT NEED tenants terrorizing other neighborhoods because they flash a positive HIV badge.

Sincerely Yours,

Leslie Ann Virgil
(Attached are eviction, med reports etc)

WHEN YOU ACCEPT THE 'WHAT IS' IN YOUR LIFE

I was listening to Donny McClurkin's Caribbean Melody and I just started jamming in my bedroom for it is a natural thing because it's my roots. But what I really wanted to discuss was how I was looking at the footage I had of the children worshipping God in Guyana. It was so intense and real without inhibitions or limitations and I just started weeping. My God they just were really getting in deep and I asked God to please let me get back there and to other countries and just continue to minister and do His work. I was crying when I first got there because I just couldn't believe how God allowed me the privilege to stay alive to do missionary work in South America. It has really been something for when you have the medical doctors telling you one thing and the doctor that lives within you tells you something else, it is a spiritual awakening! I was watching a TV show with my hubby and in it a young girl died as the result of clinical trials and this struck a chord in me. You see when you truly go through life changing events than everything becomes personal. You begin to relate to life on a different awareness level.

Just knowing that I took medication at the beginning stages of my condition and knew something wasn't right when a hot rash overtook my body and my breathing wasn't normal. So I called one of my doctor's and they said to just keep on taking it. Now even though I wasn't walking with the Spirit like I am today my partner always prompted me to do something, to take some form of action. I called my doctor in the United States and I was instructed to stop taking it immediately because it was poisoning me. I say this because my ultimate physician is the Great I AM. Due to insurance purposes I'm living off faith. Again I'm past a decade with brain cancer and almost a decade with systemic lupus and the breast chip. God had me survive the endometrial cancer and I couldn't have come this far without God first and my support team. So the "what, who and how" in my life is my partner Mr. Holy Spirit, the fun team, the spirituals, my medical both conventional and holistic, the adventure team, my Reiki, the music buffs and the film heads. But above all of these is my Lord and Savior Jesus Christ, the only name that these lips could utter to break through the dark walls of this thing, that relentless blocker we refer to as cancer!

It's All About the Call

You know this journey of life may seem meaningless, tedious, and just out of whack if we have no call to answer. Imagine just wandering around aimlessly waiting and getting restless and out of shape because we are waiting on a call. We don't know which phone is going to ring or whether it will be via a text, email, or skpe but we just know deep within our core that someone, something greater is calling us. Now that call is our purpose. The reason for our entry into this realm is all about the Call. Often we go through life seeking, always trying to fulfill a need that we don't even know for sure what it is. We fill it with religion, family, music, material possessions, drugs, sex, clubbing or whatever we can find to fill that space. And like my transcended friend Ron says we try to fill that space and what we need to fill it with, is God! When you fill it with God you'll learn how to converse with the Holy Spirit that is beyond this realm. You'll learn how to ask questions, receive answers, be guided, submit and the next thing you know you become totally dependent on Him. Now I don't get caught up in the gender he or she thing I just refer to my partner as a He but it is an invisible person. Either way I don't care because this is my true stable, unfailing friend, my confident like no other. Getting back to the original message when you begin to know where to look and how to receive it is only then that you will be able to 'Answer the Call.' Now be prepared He may call you to do some things that are totally outside of yourself and comfort zone but if you just trust Him and put your hand in His God won't leave you believe me.

Answering His Call is the best thing I could have ever done. It's better than sex, drugs clubbing or even my music. There I said it my music. God spoke directly to me about my first music assignment. I had two small record labels, and publishing for a hot minute and then I asked Him while I was under an IRS deadline "what should I call it Lord?" He said, "Hismultimedia International." You know the first name came from a record executive asking me after a recorded successful three day music show, to go home and think of a name for a side label. In the middle of my sleep I was awoken to "Hisrecords" and I said that's a stupid name. Then I went to my alternative lifestyle church and the Pastor talked about His records and the Spirit within me let me know that was confirmation. I came back from a life or death brain surgery and entered a famous music executive's office and he signed off on it.

I would often ask the Lord why does the world embrace me more? Why do I face so much spiritual abuse? The only church that embraced and recognized God's calling on my life from young is the church I was raised in, the Salvation Army. From young I had my first Christian play there, "Danny Learns the Hard Way," a modern look at the story of the prodigal son. Then we had the singing groups, "the Young Inspirations." They were some of the best times of my life. The sleep over's, the picnics, the vacation Bible school and the Junior soldiers class effected me so much that I dreamed of becoming a Senior Soldier and eventually a Salvation Army Officer who would travel the world spreading the Gospel and helping others. All I ever really wanted to do was spread hope Lord.

Tears are falling down my cheeks because before I leave this earth I want to make an impact, be a life changer for you Lord. I want to be a representative of your glory, your grace, I want to tell your story and share with the world just how amazing you are. You saved me over and over from myself and for that I will hold your hand because you have been so good to me. Like a friend of mine said in our pod cast, Lord if you never did another thing you've already done enough. So I will fight for every gift you have placed in me to share with the world. Lord I will stand up against the blockers because you gave your life for me so that I may live. You sacrificed your all; you gave yourself away for me so that I could be free. So the least I could do is to be your true friend!

The Ultimate Survivor Cocktail

I was looking at a TV show last night about the various cocktails of prescription drugs that they put people on for life threatening illnesses. I was like wow and then my partner, Mr. Holy Spirit reminded me about myself and going through clinical trials for several years with a variety of cocktails and now in the past few years we've got it right with a dosage of nearly 3000mg a day of a variety of drugs. As I listen to Mary Mary's and Kiera Sherd's "It's the God in Me" I am also reminded that the reason why I've lasted this long with my life threatening illnesses of brain cancer and systemic lupus is because I am on the ultimate cocktail and that is the Trinity. Yep I don't deny that the Father, Son and Holy Spirit live in me and are constantly with me so it's the God in me that keeps me from making wrong choices! You really have to trust in the Spirit!

Recently I had an illness break through with some serious seizures that took my speech since that is the area where the brain tumor resides. I had been taking this aloe plant mixed with my distilled water almost daily for seven months and I guess I overdid it. Most people take it for a few weeks but no one told me the severity of what could happen. My prolonged usage wiped all the medication out of my system. All I heard were the positives and I relied on that man's word and the healing of cancer. People can tell you things that they come across and are well intentioned but until you live it and know it my new motto is "Never Assume." It's like the Word people can assume and read it, recite it but do they really know it and live it?

For if you really are a Jesus believer wouldn't you start showing it. But who am I to judge I'm not here to judge anyone so I'm just saying. God wants us to test Him, try Him, and wear Him and know without a doubt that He is real. So as I'm preparing my cocktail drugs for the day I was thinking that my ultimate documentary would be the story of my life depicting what I go through but in reality I'm blessed. You just do what you have to and be aware and don't just assume.

I balance my conventional therapy with holistic and of course my spiritual. I do this because I have to, it's not like I have a choice. I may get a little down on occasions because I start having silent pity parties of not being successful but my partner, Mr. Holy Spirit reminds me that hey you are still beating the odds so you are being successful by still living and striving each day to do God's work. Now don't get it twisted there is a lot of work to surviving! The list goes on like the chip in my breast and here lately I've been dealing with a lot of fluid around my heart so it gets pretty painful. But I now know what it is and years ago I didn't with all of the mucous collecting in my left lung. It seems like I'm just a lefty, left side of brain, left breast, left knee cap, left leg. Yup a lefty all right, just a bit of dry humor up in here! I used to say to my doctor well is it just a little bit of cancer, how are we doing? Notice I say we because I've got to include my partner for without His direction where would I be. My doctor would look at me like I'm crazy when I used to ask is it still there? "Really do you think it's still there?" Her response is always "**it never left!**"

Ok let me ask this question. How would you deal with a stranger in your house my readers? You would try to evict them right but after awhile when they keep returning for longer stays you may give up. Or start embracing and letting them know and shout, "Hey I'm in control, this is my house and if you want to reside here than you have to play by my rules!" That is how I look at my illnesses who are strangers in my house. Now the people who ask about your situation and you tell them the truth with "Oh the cancer is still there" and they respond with "Oh we all have cancer cells blah blah" and it becomes about them, then they are not the ones you need to be sharing with. Listen up be aware some don't really care so zip it! And if you really want to share and not deal with the drama talk to God. Ask for guidance in your footsteps for your partner will direct you, just tap in. My relationship with the Trinity since I've gotten ill is TIGHTTTTTT! They are my all seeing eye the God in me like the song says. As a songwriter you know when you pen lyrics and the message that you are displaying. Therefore when I say my Lord and Savior I mean just that. I use the word "My" because its personal and "No One" can question that and "Savior" because that is just what He did Saved Me. Just to think I could be a functional addict on street drugs like I was while I was in clinical trials. Now if that is not a suicide mission! But you know He never forced me to make a choice to fight for my life but the more I tapped into the Holy Spirit the source, and made Him my partner only then was I able to access the power that I needed to fight those demons and make the right decisions. You see even though all the balls are thrown at my left my Lord still reminds me that there is a right side to balance it all out.

Yesterday someone from my church admitted that they relapsed and I held them and told them my story and the only way out is to tap in to a Higher Power and for me it's the Trinity, for me it's calling on the name of Jesus Christ. For living this Christian life is sometimes more emotional because of expectations and that's were it becomes hypocritical. I keep it real and I don't proclaim to be anything I'm not. I keep it simple and follow Jesus. I let the light shine within me for I take it seriously that I maybe the only Jesus that others may see.

IT WASN'T UNTIL

Here lately I keep saying this phrase out loud and you know what they say the more you put it out into the atmosphere the more real it becomes. The phrase is simple but profound and goes like this "it wasn't until I knew I was dying that I began to live." And guess what it wasn't until I awoke to another phrase this morning that I realized the true meaning of the first phrase. Okay I don't mean to sound scattered because I'm actually more in tune today then I was a year ago or even yesterday. You see this morning I awoke to feeling calm, peaceful and joyful. I heard this "It's Time to Recognize the Power of The Holy Spirit That Lies within you!" I mean I knew I had a restful night listening to the silky soul XM station . . . I was jamming in my sleep to Melanie Fiona, Ledisi, Anthony Hamilton and Janet Jackson. I love music and was created to deliver messages through it so I don't get too caught up in the debate between the secular and the inspirational because I think it is quite obvious in the lyrics and the way the song makes you feel. For example right now I'm listening to Atlantic Starr's "Secret Lovers" and at the time this song came out I was full swing into a hidden relationship.

Songs mark a time and place in the space of our lives. It's stories unleashed from within and can make you feel relaxed, pumped up, feed your anger, make you feel sexy, and inspired and for some they just remember being wired if we want to keep it real on this journey! So much so that Mariah Carey's song "Always Be My Baby" invokes the first television show that we did that made an impact on our society and helped to develop the lives of our cast.

My partner just had me connect the dots as to why I have the confidence in doing a reality show because I've already done one. I was so motivated by what the Lord awakened me to that I'm pumped. I asked my partner while in the bathroom who should I share this message with? What format should I use? And then I recalled the message from my mentor Dr. Mike Murdock on the keys to wisdom when he said that we have to stop investing energy into that which does not change and I said that to someone yesterday and instantly felt empowered. You see we can't keep feeding the roaring beast the same food and expect it to calm down. We can't keep feeding it that which fuels its temper; we need to start feeding it that which soothes. I once wrote lyrics to my cousin's music and called it "Music Soothes the Soul." In this life we need to be soothed and awakened for all the right reasons.

Not just in and out of season. So awaken that which lies within you that you were destined to utilize to bring forth positive change! Unleash the partner that lies inside of all of us. Walk into it, walk with it and embrace its power and release its authority. After all it is time for us to break the chains and walk into our calling!

Don't Let the Demons Knock U Down

My partner just threw my attention to the fact that there are some chapters that use the same exact lingo "it's funny because" and you know for the past week I've been dealing with the fact that there are demons living in my house and that isn't so funny at all. I tried to avoid this chapter from making it into this book but this is my life's journey with my partner, the Holy Spirit. Therefore how could I avoid sharing with my readers something that is so profound in my life! It would be like inviting you to dinner without the utensils. Ah, now I know for sure that just came directly from my partner because I've been so worn out by one demon in particular that I was about to call it quits but my Lord and Savior wouldn't let me.

I understand why Jesus is referred to as our personal Savior because that is exactly who He is. It's like what the group Destiny's Childs singer Michele Williams sings "Rescue Me" and "Have You Ever." Have you ever been in love like this before with someone who is so steadfast, always there, so intense that you know that you know? Well that my friend is the love of Jesus. Some call him a powerful prophet but to me He is the Son of God who saved my life and continues to save me hence the title, personal Savior! My partner gave me the boldness and calmness to confront face to face literally this demon who comes to visit and tries to take over but with every beat down I've learned to throw down. It's like being in a boxing ring and each time your opponent swings you have to master their moves. Now I can say the phrase "it's funny because . . . ."

Last night was the last straw where I was able to combat the demon and tell him in his face that you met the right one, the right family, a praying family so if you want to fight we will fight in the spirit. I spoke in tongues to it and looked directly in its eyes calmly. I told it that in the past I would scream, cuss and sometimes react with violence but God has me in a place where it will no longer have power over me or my emotions. I told it that I loved my mate and I know God placed us together for a reason to minister together and he was worth fighting for. You see I asked God to show me directly what is this disorder that I see my baby fighting with and he showed me dead on. Over the years this demon has followed me from relationship to relationship and I've wrestled with demons that once resided in me until I was delivered. I could feel this energy shift and heaviness. I recognized the dark zombie like look and shift in behavior. You know the saying how the enemy comes in the same format but just with different faces, different places but always the same style.

It didn't matter which person or gender it was for I confronted it with three people and as I'm writing this I 'm just experiencing a breakthrough. I remember the first time I encountered it and that was when I was molested when I was young by someone I loved and trusted and that was the first time I saw the dead eyes, that cold spirit. Thanks Holy Spirit you are right on. Now I'm here jamming to Kirk Franklin's tune "This is It" from his CD "The Fight of My Life" how timely is that? Just as he sings "I've made up my mind for I've been there before" and my partner just reminded me that everything must change. If we want different results we must change, allow our Heavenly Father to change and transform our minds so that we can take our rightful positions. God did not give us a spirit of fear but one of sound mind. So last night legion must have been shocked as I looked at him straight in the eye because I knew my baby was there and the Lord placed us together as one not for me to run. Now being human of course you get tired and upset but you have to trust in the Lord with all your heart and lean not on our own understanding and that is not just a scripture to recite it is living truth.

Many of us go through life trying to get back that which we lost, that which was stolen from us as children. Whether it is our security, our innocence, our trust, or our family unit. The fact remains that we all enter into this world the same way no matter where we are placed; we all speak the same language. It's not by coincidence that every baby on this planet speaks the same language and can relate to each other. No it is because as human beings we are meant to be on one accord and it's the stuff that separates us from our initial truth. We all have the same alien look inside our mother's dark wombs where we reside in water for nine months supported by a feeding tube. Like seriously have you ever really thought about that or looked at a fetus? There are no mistakes when it comes to God. We are His creation, His design so imagine how He feels when the adversary tries to steal us. You know how we feel when someone steals our ideas or breaks up our relationships so just imagine how our Creator feels.

WAKE UP AND GET YOUR PRAISE ON

God is just too much that's my boo for real. You know Bermuda once had hundreds of people dancing and singing with floats to "The Presence of the Lord Is Here" by Byron Cage and it was just so moving because you had everybody grooving on the sidelines including the children. I videotaped it and wanted to use it in my last documentary WE R 1 but I had some technical difficulties but now I know why it wasn't included at that time, it was because it was to be included in a time such as this. God operates in our lives in seasons and he knows what to release at what time and at what exact location. You see at that time Bermuda wasn't in the eye of the storm that it is currently in. I went home for ten days and within that time there were three fatal shootings. And it hasn't been a month since I returned and there have been two more; so much so that outside law agencies had to be bought in to simmer the pot. But the pot will continuously overflow because we fight not against flesh and blood but against spiritual warfare. Therefore what we need right is a Spiritual Awakening.

That's kind of deep since that was one of the first songs I recorded and released years ago . . . . one of the lines went like this. "What we need now is a spiritual awakening. Like Bob said we can't give up the fight until all of Africa has been united . . . you don't have to be in a church, you could be in a club it makes no difference where you are we need a spiritual awakening and only then will all of Africa be set free." The Holy Spirit is telling me this morning that the song was prophetic and when I talked about Africa I was really talking about God's kingdom and this planet earth for we need a Spiritual Awakening. In order for the pressure pot to stop overflowing we need to turn it off and start over from the foundation. Okay Holy Spirit let's flow with this; you ready readers here we go.

In order for many of our lives to get back in order we need to place ourselves under authority and we are not talking about just under fleshly law but Spiritual authority for we are spiritual beings housed in temporary flesh and therefore we really operate in the spirit and get deceived by our flesh. What we face are the spirits we struggle with, our inner demons and all of us need deliverance in and out of the church which is only corporate. Today we encounter flying saucers that are coming at us left and right and if we can't see them than we can't grab hold of them to stop the negative flow that is circling this planet we are out of orbit! For it is not only Bermuda but the world that is spiraling out of control! We need the Holy Spirit to step in each of our lives in order to put things into proper perspective and in order to do this we need a spiritual awakening for again we fight not against flesh and blood but against principalities. How many read it and don't understand it. How many repeat it but don't grasp it. How many of us love to recite but truly don't believe in the power of words that once released into the atmosphere take on a life of their own. That is why the Bible says the power of life and death lies within the tongue. This is real talk my friends we just need to know how to do battle.

Once you know what you are fighting than you know how to fight. After all you can't battle successfully against an enemy that you don't truly know how powerful they are or better yet where their weaknesses are located and once we learn this we learn how to defeat them. You have to war and fighting just in the flesh doesn't swing it when they are coming against our minds.

It is time to get back to our foundations and do some serious warfare in the Spirit. Let the Holy Spirit take over and unite and I do not care what denomination you are join forces and unite! We have to strengthen ourselves and stay armored memorizing Ephesians 6: 10-18. It's about truly putting on the armor of God and covering ourselves from the crowns of our heads to the very souls of our feet with the blood of Jesus. Our heads wear the helmet of salvation. Our bodies wear the breastplate of righteousness. We hold it together with our belts of truth. We wear footwear that is the footgear of Christ just ready to spread the word. Like the other meeting I was at just running for Christ, people everywhere just running for the Lord and we were clapping as if at a marathon. We carry the shield of faith 360 degrees and check this out that is all of our protective gear but our ONLY weapon is the Word of God and that my friend is our sword. Um now that I'm thinking the other day that was my movement in the spirit, the cutting motions of the sword. Child we were on fire for the Lord.

This entire Christmas season has just been amazing I love it so much that I'm steadily just seeking His face, His grace, His mercy that endures forever. The Bible is a living book. Whatever church, meeting, television or radio the messages all flow as if they are speaking directly to me. I used to say to myself jokingly that all the Ministers must get together and say, "Hey this is what we are going to speak on" but I know it's the Holy Spirit. And I just love it! I tell people the high that I encounter in Christ is greater and more fulfilling than any of Satan's earthy drugs. There is no hangover or guilt or shame or the loss of jobs, family or friends. Getting drunk in the Holy Spirit is so exhilarating that you can't help but want more. I'm telling you this movement of release is real and the adversary is angry because humans are waking up and getting hold of the secret to this war and it is all in the praise and worship my friends. It's only one name that demons flee to and you know I know and that name is Jesus!

Just the other day I had to go to the hospital to see one of my specialists pertaining to the lupus and I'm learning from the older saints about not claiming diseases because than we take ownership of them and they begin to control our bodies. Remember words are powerful. A deepie huh? So I texted people and asked others to pray for my results and then I was there for a couple of hours and my results amazed them. My one doctor that didn't believe in God now knows for sure that there is somebody out there bigger than you and I because he says I'm a medical miracle and I'm going to speak to medical students next month pertaining to my medical testimony regarding my journey of brain cancer, lupus, osteoporosis, titanium chip in breast, and the removal of female reproductive organs due to endometrial cancer. So I decided to have it recorded. However I'm asking the Holy Spirit to lay out the presentation. I will keep you posted since it isn't until next month. Well no time to be nervous just have to ask my partner, Mr. Holy Spirit to protect me for I've been preparing for this my entire life.

You know what I'm saying. This is the opportunity to show off His work and like I told my doctors that we can not forget about God in this!

It's All Inside of You

I'm here listening to me and my partner, Mr. Holy Spirit's songs. The lyrics are on time for me this morning. You know God is "A True Friend" and it talks about being just that. Those attributes that make us a true friend and the reverse. We always hear about how Jesus is our friend but how can we be a friend to someone who gave His life, gave His all. It talks about committing our ways, submitting our pride, stop being selfish and start trusting totally by putting our hands in His. This song is a modification of Psalms 37:5 and I always envision that picture with the hand reaching over the wall and the hand reaching up. This brings me to that dream I had of jumping into the vast blackness and being asked about my faith and when I did, I saw written in red about belonging to Jesus. It said "You are now a servant of Christ."

There is a personal situation in my life where I jumped and followed God's voice and the visions and signs He gave me. So far it's been like a roller coaster but when I look back I know my assignment. In the natural I would have NEVER chosen it but God puts us through tests to see how far and how willing we will go to be that True Friend. We say it, read it in scriptures and even sing about it but are we really willing? It's like the song "I Give Myself away, so you can Use Me." We all cry, feel it, get all emotional because deep inside we know it rings true. We were created not for ourselves but for God's enjoyment. We were created for the plans that He created us for, not our own. It's not about us but our Creator.

I've experienced several situations where I know I have to trust in His plan for I would have lost my mind because of all the deceit and hurt. You know when you create something and then someone plays it out not the way you intended or when someone listens to you, meets with you looks at your draft, your blueprints and then says we can't do this or that at this time due to the great line . . . budgetary constraints (we don't have the money) and the next thing you know there they are executing what you laid out with a slightly different twist, maybe 1% different but you know it was yours. For those that may have experienced this, remember the hurt you feel? How disconnected we feel from those we trusted? And I talking about creative deception or what I like refer to it as 'creative thievery.' So how do you think God, our Creator feels when we do the same thing to Him? It's no different. That is why we get all fuzzy and emotional to certain songs or sermons because we know the message rings true to our hearts.

We all fall short because we are human but how many of us are willing to first accept that we are wrong. Secondly that we must take the painful steps of dying to our flesh and coming out of our comfort zone to do what is not natural to us. How do we trust in something that is not seen or tangibly felt but yet we are so willing to trust gravity or the air? We get so caught up, me included in 'us.' Like my neighbor asked me the other day who is us? I don't want to start getting my preach on but this is serious we need to do some self examination. This is the first step and after that it's like a baby walking until it becomes natural. However we have to start first and continue. Every habit began as having a bit, a bit of something, a bit of dominance over our spirits. You have to commit to make it a habit and then it becomes a part of who you are. Learning to say no to your natural and yes to the supernatural takes practice but if you don't start you'll never know how the other side of the coin of your life can be. What wonders and joys lay waiting for you. So just trust in Him and submit yourself starting today and don't be too proud to ask for His help. It's not easy but with practice we will meet the mark.

KEEP HOPE ALIVE IS MORE THAN A MOTTO!

Have you ever had a situation where you felt you were walking amongst them. It's almost like sleepwalking but you are awake. The enemy is continuously throwing darts at you and it comes to a point where you get tired of ducking. All you can do is stand. People that you think are in your life for the right reasons maybe the wrong reasons. Those you see as anointed maybe self appointed. Those you praise turn around and cause you shame. Dark clouds go in and out and the ONLY thing you can hold onto that is never changing is our Lord and Savior, Jesus Christ. No matter what He answers the call. It may not be when we want it but as He stated in the Living Word He will not leave us nor forsake us. You know God is a God of order and preparation. He will allow His children to go through but will do so for their good. This is a concept that caused my husband to give up but check it out not give in. You see once the seeds are planted they are there to take root. Tenants that gave us a hard time God removed and the one that my husband thought was the golden one stabbed us not only in our backs but in our necks.

I sort of glimpsed at this snake when I saw him trying to befriend my husband at a wedding reception. He never could look directly at me and from day one when he got the apartment he treated me as less but he and his girl were always up in my hubby's face. I would tell him how they made me feel and he always made excuses for them but the way I see it they were my husband's lesson. It was prophesized a while back how we would have a business and how my husband would want to just give things away and that he should listen to his wife and that was the beginning of that prophecy coming true. If this would not have happened to us it wouldn't have allowed my husband to see me physically cry out to the Lord and submit and fall on my face before the Lord. The Holy Spirit got me up this morning to take me back through Jeremiah 1 where God constantly states that He will rescue, that's the key word. That word I woke up to, and then there on television it showed two situations where people thought they had gotten away with murder for decades but in both cases the murderers were convicted.

This same tenant who suffered from a physical disability secretly moved and abandoned us and then lied on his offer and caused us hundreds of dollars. The last words I said to him before he hung up the phone on me was that I needed to see what the Holy Spirit wanted me to do and then I called my husband and laid down on the concrete outside my church. Now there is another situation but before I write on that let's see what God is going to do. My partner has told me to hold up and let it unfold so I have to submit to my partners will not my own. I'm telling you I have to smile because my partner, the Holy Spirit is my baby and is ALWAYS right. He is my comforter, friend, my all seeing eye and I'm telling you I don't know what I would do without Him. I'm listening to Darius Brooke's song "I Will" and that corresponds with what I'm saying

God's will works for me. Hey we have to keep hope alive for His word tells us so. Like the song says "Hold on (Change is Coming)." God doesn't make mistakes so don't give up; keep the faith those are the lyrics. And that's what the message was last night how big is your faith, for that is what sizes our God. In the midst of writing this my husband just called to tell me thank you for holding on and keeping the faith and those were his exact words.

Look I'm not saying that there won't be trials and tribulations but I do know this that God is not a man that He should lie. No matter the pain, our spirits determine our will, our flesh, and our emotions. When you're going through pray, when things are secure pray and when you see no way out pray. We have to pray without ceasing and sometimes I smile and say, "Lord here I come again I know I sound like a broken record." But on the other hand my partner has me just thanking Him and constantly asking for protection and bleeding the blood of Jesus. I guess I have become like my Grandmothers "Nevida and Annie," just like my family jokes about. My stepson said yesterday morning when I anointed him and his cousin with oil that I anointed him twice already and I said "Well that's double anointing." We went from him asking me "What's that, what are you doing, oh I get Holy water at my school" to now "Hey you did me twice." I even anoint our dog everyday and my hubby's shoes just like my mother who passed this faith practice down from her Prophetess Mother and from my Prophetess Grandmother.

I come from a family where praying is as natural as eating or drinking. Now my husband doesn't come from that background. So my partner, Mr. Holy Spirit had me look at Ezra the dramatic prophet. He not only knew God's word, he believed and obeyed it. I was led to turn to Chapter 10:1 and it talked about how this prophet threw himself down and openly confessed and repented and his weeping brought others to sorrow. My partner told me to get out of bed and prostrate before the Lord and pray. My songs came on and I started to talk to God about how many times He has bought my family through from accidents, shootings, death, and murder and how we all know how to cry out and praise the Lord.

I feel so blessed to have such a wonderful family and fortunate to have been raised with such faith in God . . . Alleluia it was my Husband seeing my reaction to the Lord and my weeping beyond the church walls that continue to make the difference. And that's what Ezra did, it was his humility that made the difference and my partner is teaching me how to be that example in the midst of the storm.

ABUSE STANDS FOR WHAT?

I'm sitting here talking with a friend after crying my eyeballs out. I allowed myself to be spiritually abused by members of my church again. I was in a meeting one time and heard a young girl state how something so tragic caused her to turn from God. This bothered me so much and I had a vision in my sleep and in reality I connected with a gentleman who was showing Christian and Inspirational films at his church with free popcorn, drinks and soda. Make a long story short I went back and forth with members in charge at my church for almost seven months to show a family movie that was about saving lives for Christ and suicide due to bullying. My snow boy who lived a few houses down committed suicide at age 21years and I know that demonic suicide spirit first hand. As the Lord would have it the movie was shown a year later and I had the opportunity to speak with that beautiful child and we hugged. After a few more disappointments I literally asked the Lord to show me what He wanted me to see. I opened the Word and there before me was the translation "Don't waste your energy on those that continue to oppose you." It's where Jesus says to shake the dust off your feet.

One of the things I'm sure about is that God will never leave us or forsake us. Sometimes along our life's journey we get locked into modes, behaviors and patterns. They may change slightly but we have to totally give it our all and then and only then with a renewed mindset can we change. Quite often we need a heart transplant. I know that falling in love with Jesus can certainly do that. I constantly hear the phrase that the only person blocking you from fulfilling your dreams is you. This is painful but true for when I look back over my life in all of my abusive relationships I am the common denominator. I am afraid of rejection and abandonment so unconsciously I get involved with people that will do exactly what my inner most fear is. You know the saying that in a hundred persons nine times out of ten you will gravitate to that same individual. Different face different place but same setting.

I look at Satan as that, he knows our innermost fears and always provides a different face with a mask in a different place so that you feel it's new but then the masks come off and you realize that you are being hurt over and over again so you have to ask yourself the question what you can do. You and I must change and do things differently. When I was recovering from brain surgery it was one of my most peaceful moments just before and after the surgery. I read a book by Dr. Carter-Scott entitled "If Life was a game, than these are the rules."

The book talked about life being lessons repeated until learned. I realize that I have to learn the lessons and because I haven't I'm repeating them in various areas of my life. In my spiritual life I keep presenting proposals and then I watch my ideas tweaked and put into action without me before my very eyes. I react to my personal life by being defensive after being hurt over and over and as a result I shy away. Just writing this makes me realize that I must revisit these books and take the bull by the horns for if I want things to change in my life than I need to trust my God and ask for direction from my partner as to how to walk new because the season that I'm about to enter will require that. I need to rise above the emotional games and seek even more of His face as I go from glory to glory. "Lord I humble myself right now and ask you to show me how to love those who have hurt me. Show me how to love myself more so as to avoid these circumstances and most of all is to be aware of all forms of abuse in all relationships."

HERE WE GO AGAIN

Yesterday morning I felt so out of sorts because I couldn't sleep the night before. So many people were tugging at me to do this and that and my peace was shifted. It's amazing how we can literally allow people and things to disturb our space. To blow smoke into our blue skies and therefore allowing them to become grey! What I'm learning is that when you feel the negative energy shifts ask the Holy Spirit to cover you with the blood of Jesus. We have to remain covered and protected. Read those Psalms and practice those positive change tools daily. Keep yourself safe, your mind, body and soul. AFTER ALL THAT IS WHO WE ARE MIND, BODY AND SOUL.

I know I felt weary but nothing could have prepared me for what I was about to face; more severe attacks. Thank you Jesus that I recited scriptures before I left home and meditated with my partner, Mr. Holy Spirit on Isaiah and calmness. I was even inspired by Him to change a lyric from Holy charm to Holy calm. Deep huh and I was wondering what on earth Holy calm meant. Well that's just it; it is not of this earth is it? It's supernatural, unexplainable but can be experienced! I tell you this journey is something there is never a dull moment. Let me tell you briefly what happened:

I was going back and forth with industry agents and some were demanding deposits without showing us anything concrete. That to me was strange and I just didn't get a good feeling. Then I had some paperwork that had to be done and I felt in my gut that it wasn't going to happen even though I wanted to believe in this individual. Well they didn't surprise me because the Spirit told me what they would do; there was the pattern of disappointment. Then I get home and my cousin, sister and several friends informed me that my email had been hacked. I panicked and asked my partner to lead me literally as to what to do. Look I don't know about you but my personal relationship with my Lord and Savior is candid and truthful. I've learned to be like David and just talk direct. I respect but I'm real and He answers, teaches and disciplines me over and over until I get it. I embrace my partner; Mr. Holy Spirit so when the trials come and the so called friends have gone it is my Lord and Savior who has wrapped me in His arms where I remain safe and calm. That sounds like one of my God inspired songs but it is true.

Songs for me come from Him and my experiences. Therefore when I received the news of my deletion I released that. I'm on the road to God's completion for the plan He has for my life! Now I need to update my face book status to let my peeps know that I no longer feel violated but exonerated because in deletion there is completion in the road to freedom. Hey He knew I was going to take forever to delete and rearrange my contacts so He presented a way in which I would be pushed to shred the weeds in my life so that I could move forward! We have to make room for new seeds to be planted.

WHEREVER YOU GO THERE I AM

This is an appropriate title because when you think about it there is No place you can run to and hide that God doesn't know about. It could be in that crack house, snort house, holding arms so they could inject themselves, being raped at gun point, orgies, hanging from a roof but wherever it is God is and has been there with you all the while. Now the twist is we haven't always been willing to let Him into our hearts and become our Savior. Once we let Him in that's it, that's where the work begins but I tell you this that is when everything begins to make sense and if you stick with Him He'll guide you through.

Yesterday I read on face book about an event that triggered some things for me. Now the night prior they had a clinical social worker at my church talking about forgiveness and the root. For me I explained how I had superficially forgiven my ex and then months latter I had to call her, that's right her and ask her for forgiveness and immediately I felt this thing, this spirit lift off me. That was the first time I felt true freedom in forgiveness. I shared my testimony and the next day I saw this post on face book. Well I had talked to my partner, Mr. Holy Spirit before I responded. You see throughout my life I've always had ideas stolen that I discussed with others, spent money and assisted in others dreams of recording, publicity, interconnecting them with people etc and the result most of the time is the same. Or should I say was the same, thanks for correcting me partner. When they feel that they have arrived they forget how they got there. It's almost as if they got there solely by themselves!

My vision was so clouded that I could not see how God had orchestrated and connected the dots. I mean as recent as last night this guy I had worked with told me that this girl who was on my label had gone back to the same recording studio I had financially backed. She released her CD and signed with another label stating that she was never signed and once confronted said, "Oh well we only released a few songs!" This same chick had called me years ago because she had no place to sleep but I couldn't help her because I had to set boundaries for I had been taken advantage of from so many freeloaders. Now I'm not saying that she was one but she was my test and didn't even know it. Like for numerous people I was nothing more than an ends to a means but that's cool Jesus has me. I used to fight behind the scenes for peoples stories to be told, CDs played, music made etc. God has finally brought me to the place of recognizing that for every person or situation that has rejected me or used me it was Him orchestrating my life.

I now know that learning from my bad choices and forgiveness are tied in one lesson. Even at church I've had problems getting articles printed, choirs being featured, inspirational movies being shown and the list goes on. I always tell people Satan comes in the same format, he doesn't change his game plan. Think about it. He's always presenting the same game but different faces, different places, adjusted situations but the same game even in the church.

Now that I can see through my spiritual eyes I thank God for the lessons and praise Him in advance for the ones He'll bring me through because I know my identity in Christ. Now I can say to all those who crossed my path, I say thank you for kicking me as my Bishop would say into my destiny!

I was just saying to my partner that I could write a whole book on the Healing in the Rejection. You just wouldn't believe how many times this has happened to me and I'm still learning and I sometimes say God you must get tired of me coming to you and He probably says, "there she goes again the rescuer but that is my child and as long as she holds my hand I've got her."

I remember getting high and when we smoked weed I would have my tape recorder interviewing people on various subjects. My hubby and I laugh about how we all used to think things were deep, like super deep until we got high on Jesus. Check it, he would say, "well if up is down then down must be up, and that's deep man." Please child, what's deep is getting so high that you get trapped outside of your body. Your spirit watches everyone doing everything at the same time and then as usual you casually float back. Then you experience the one time that you can't get back in and you end up pleading with God to let you back into your fleshly temporal shell. After God let my spirit back into my body I made the promise to never touch coke or crack again and guess what I never have.

Yeah my drug life is a movie in itself from the angels that were appointed to be beside me to me being seen as a freak because I would have my Bible open and then after I took a bump or hit I would grab the Bible and start reading it. Especially Psalms because I would see the demons jumping off the wall or hear them through people saying stuff like "oh we got her and she isn't having none of our stuff, after she helped us use up hers, we are doing all of this here" and laugh. I used to say I can hear you and they acted like what? How did she know that's what we were thinking? Now what I didn't know was that I was hearing their thoughts sometimes.

Yeah like the song says when I look back over my life and see all that you have done for me, Lord you have been so faithful! You could have given up on me but you didn't because you knew your plan for my life. All I could see was the earthly which reminds one time I was getting high on weed and I was talking extra spiritual. This guy who I was with ran this line, "okay we've talked enough spiritually can we now get earthly?" I will always remember that for it was and is such a profound statement. For those who can't figure it out he meant can we now get busy.

The cocaine just had me clinging to the Bible for my life and people would say I don't want to get high in here with the Bible or can she leave but they had no problems getting high on my supply. Then others would ask me what I was reading, so even in the midst of the white clouds God was ministering. And when I got clean through Him I went back to some of those places and some of the people would say pray for me. I remember seeing this girl who was the girlfriend of one of the dealers and she would always look at us with her nose turned up flaunting all her gold as if we were cockroaches. But to my amazement this same chick was there begging for rocks and the lady of the house who had suffered from a stroke told me to get out because she said you have moved on and you don't want to be caught up with this. Those demons have whips and that is why you could be clean forever and out of nowhere have the urge and the only way to fight it is with my partner and yours, Mr. Holy Spirit!

Some of you reading this know what I'm talking about. Just anoint yourself daily and cover yourself with the blood. If trigger situations occur plead the blood of Jesus against it and remember your shield and sword. "For there is No Weapon formed that can harm you." "He arms you with strength and makes your path safe." "Although he stumbles he will not fall for the Lord upholds him with His hand." These are just a few scriptures that have covered me over the years.

TRYING TO BE A REAL TRUE FRIEND

God inspired me to write a song with that same title and for you songwriters out there you know that when you write it means something. Words jump off the page into the sea of music and once matched together they become alive. They have to partner in order to make sense, become meaningful whether negative or positive. We send forth vibrations into the atmosphere with our songs. I posted this in my status one morning on face book. I'm going deeper but this is how I feel about the gifts that God gives to us. We have a choice and can match them to come alive and make sense, thereby making a difference in this world and its atmosphere. Or we can sit on them and selfishly keep them without matching them into the great sea to make them come alive and become fruitful. He doesn't give us anything to hold within our palms for He supplies us with everything to give away and to pass on to bless others. Isn't that what true Christianity is about, passing it on.

I always remember a song my cousin Quiletta sang in girl guides, "It Only Takes a Spark." She and her group performed that at our former Salvation Army church, "Newlands" and my Mom's singing group there was the Newlanders. It is funny how there is power in words, break it down NEW LANDS. That is what God wants us to conquer, new lands, and new territory. Jesus traveled to new territory, He moved around He didn't stay put. So the songs He gives us in our hearts are not for us it is for others just as the lessons He gives us, are to teach others and how? By becoming living examples even when we stumble we must dust ourselves off, get back up and walk in our new suit that He has fitted us with. We are no longer that past creature but a new creature in Christ. Now check that term "creature" not human being. Pay attention people He's always talking to us even if we don't want to listen or pay attention to details. It makes no sense to just be "churchin" when Christianity is a lifestyle; we have to work this thing!

This brings me back to being a true friend. We sing songs like "I am a friend of God" by Israel Houghton but are we? Don't get it twisted He is our friend but are we His? Think of friendship in the natural form. Would you want to be that friend who's always reaching out, always giving, always spending, always listening and always there as the shoulder to cry on? Just always giving away you. When God gives you something it is not meant for you to be selfish with it. He wants you to share it. He wants you to be a true friend back and return that compassion. I ask myself why is it that every time I offer the ideas, events and whatever God has given me to the Church I get shot down. Now when I offer them to the world they embrace it. Does the world embrace me more? You know the only church that has embraced and recognized God's calling on my life from young is the church I was raised in, the Salvation Army.

From young I had my first Christian play there, "Danny Learns the Hard Way," a modern look at the story of the prodigal son. Then we had the singing groups, "the Young Inspirations." They were some of the best times of my life. The sleep over's, the picnics, the vacation Bible school and the Junior Soldiers class effected me so much that I dreamed of becoming a Senior Soldier and eventually a Salvation Army Officer who would travel the world spreading the Gospel and helping others. All I ever really wanted to do was spread hope Lord. See the alignment.

Tears are falling down my cheeks because before I leave this earth I want to make an impact, be a life changer for you Lord. I want to be a representative of your glory, your grace, I want to tell your story and share with the world just how amazing you are. You saved me over and over from myself and for that I will hold your hand because you have just been so good to me. Like a friend of mine said in our' Keepin it Real 4 Christ' pod cast "Lord if you never did another thing you've already done enough." Therefore I will fight for every gift you have placed in me to share with the world. Lord I will stand up against the blockers because you gave your life for me so that I may live. You sacrificed your all; you gave yourself away for me so that I could be free. So the least I could do is to be your true friend!

WHAT'S IN A SONG?

Let me tell you when God speaks and breaks you it is quite real. It goes beyond confession in public or breaking and weeping amongst a believer setting. When God speaks and asks you a question you answer not with your words but with your heart. You know God gave me the gift to write songs and for decades that was my identity but the closer I get to God I realize that I have a new identity and that is in serving Christ. My identity is a Christian, a servant of Jesus Christ. When you take on a title you begin to live that title. Well for years I wrote lyrics and melodies, arranged and eventually produced. God gave me Chances 97 which was the gathering of various unsigned artists before a panel of music executives who critiqued them and had production or possible record offers on the table. This was successful and led to a host of other events such as Gospofest, Night of Bermuda Stars, Revelation of a Star, Rockin it Clean Live and Praisefest. Even though at the beginning of some of these events I wasn't walking with God yet He was always walking with me. I remember working for this company and my contract was about to run out and one night I had this dream about a host from BET and the gathering of all these people and the next morning it was so much in my heart that I set out to find this host.

Well it just so happened that one of the girl's I worked with was close to him but I didn't want to go that route because of various things it would entail. So I prayed and even though my prayers may not have been as deep and sincere as they are today I still asked God to lead me? Check this, my cousin who's a film camera woman and video director called me and guess who her roommate was, the same host! I therefore resigned and left the company and on faith set out to start this new adventure. I had a tight staff of three and that included myself. The result of the music conferences and showcases was the downloading of information, correction and protection. That was when God instilled the concept of self discipline with regards to working a project and here we are over a decade later! That was a springboard for many things to come. I've always worked for myself other than the one job God positioned me for when I had the realtor battle and was new at the beginning stages of dealing with the brain cancer. He ordered that as well for He knew I would need insurance for the surgery. God is God and He does go before us but that is another testimony.

We know our steps are truly ordered and yesterday God literally had me spring forth the well within. I gave my testimony of gratefulness and I publicly repented for any sin that I may have committed knowingly and unknowingly on my knees. Hey at this point the Holy Spirit is making it apart of who I am and being funny I guess next he'll have me bring a mat so that I may literally lay before him. I was excited because I was asked to do some music for my church and I was honored since in the past my churches weren't that interested in my gifts. Anyhoo these leaders would say that I should manage their kids or at least mentor them.

So check this, that night I went home and the Holy Spirit my partner directed me as to how to musically compose a song on this program. Well I called it Always there but He had me change the title to "Abba Father." I presented it to the pastor and his kids and the lead son said it was too melodic. Well when the Holy Spirit instructed me to write it I listened for each band member's parts and the instruments they each played. Later the son said they couldn't do anything with it because they needed lyrics so I waited until the Holy Spirit gave me words and in it He even had me write the name of Jesus who we refer to in Hebrew, "Yehsua." It talked about living fountains and breathing Christ and stuff that made no direct sense to me at the time but I've now learned that this is truly worship for those lyrics become so intimate between you and God. Thank You Jesus! I even had been instructed to write talking parts. It became so intense that God would wake me from my sleep to write. I presented this to the lead son who told me they couldn't play by ear and therefore I needed to present them with chords and progressions. In addition to all of this he had the nerve to ask me if I wrote something would I put his name on it. Of course my answer was yes, I don't care about that stuff I just wanted what the Lord has given me to get out! All sorts of music were given to them and there were the same excuses. One day I invited an associate of mine who sings to the church and she sang her song and fell in love with their worship band. When she asked them if they could play music to her song you know their answer was yes! "Sure" their father said. And I said, "I thought you couldn't play by ear!"

Now keep in mind when I was doing secular music I had no problem finding artist. As a matter of fact they found their way to me. The irony was that the name of the label was "Hisrecords." A name that God gave me in my sleep that I just couldn't shake. I was asked by a major record executive to come up with a name of a subsidiary label for all the artists they had seen with potential in the Bermuda showcase. I said it was a stupid name but then there was so much confirmation that I knew it had come from God! Well that bothered me so much that my husband said he would sing it but God allows situations and people to kick you into your future and I'm so glad they and others pushed me into mine. I was at the door of my destiny hollering and screaming and clenching onto that door knob but fear had me paralyzed me from walking through that doorway of countless Divine opportunities.

WHEN HE SPEAKS DIRECTLY TO YOUR HEART YOU KNOW

Well here we are another morning and for the first time my partner has prompted me to continue where I left off. Usually when I write I just jump to another subject but today I'm continuing and this is a new level in consistency. So here we go like I said my husband jumped in like the shining knight and I allowed a man to save me and took my eyes of what God wanted and it became all about what I wanted. I mean I prayed for anointed persons but it still was who I felt could contribute to this God project. Anyhoo I gave him the lyrics, full song and instrumental and after weeks went by I approached him. In my first year I'm learning that to question him is not the answer trust and believe. He told me he couldn't get with the way the guy was singing the song. Now at first when I gave him the words and sang it he could relate. Then after time went on when I asked him after hearing nothing he told me he didn't have time because he worked so I said, "What about when you drive back and forth to work can't you learn and listen to it then?" He got angry and I told him to give me back the CD. Now what I really wanted was him to say ok babe I'll learn it but he gave me the CD so I guess that was my selfish desire. We later attended service at this men's shelter that I had been trying to get him to attend for two years. I personally felt that we had accomplished something. Being that he is the Pastors Armor Bearer he came and that didn't bother me for I was just excited that he came. While we were waiting in the other room he started to sing this song and our Pastor said, "Why don't you sing this song today at afternoon service?" And he said, "Yeah if the band could back me." the Pastor said yes they could. Now remember this is the same band that couldn't play by ear. Now my husband said he didn't know all the words so one of the girls hooked him up. Remember he was willing to learn them in a flash.

The service at this city shelter was powerful, they may have been small in number but mighty in Spirit and just thinking about it makes me what to shout out a hallelujah! Later when we were driving home and dropping off the Pastor the Lord started speaking to my heart. Child when he speaks directly to your heart you listen. All of a sudden tears started streaming down my face and I was trying to hide them in front of the Pastor and my Husband and then right after the Pastor got out of the car and we drove around the corner I started boohooing just like a baby; I'm talking crying my head off. You would have thought I lost a baby and that's what happened check it. The Lord asked me would I give up my music for Him and I said, "But that's what has gotten me through my illnesses all of these years. I mean yes you first but my music is my life." He replied ever so clearly and forthright. "First of all it was Me and Me alone that brought you through all these years. It is Me for I created you and the music within you. Will you give up the music for Me?" After going back and forth and weeping I finally said "Yes Lord I will give up my music for you!" In an instant I experienced a relief and immediately stopped crying. The rest is history for He started having me redo my previously written songs and compose new ones with savvy beats and tracks. Let's remember I may have arranged and written songs but never in my life had I ever composed music from scratch. I had purchased this music program and downloaded it on my computer and God literally used me as the instrument to make His music. I became the pen that He used to write new lyrics and even this book. The Trinity is real; don't ever underestimate the first team, Father, Son and Holy Spirit. They guide me and direct me and it is one joyous journey no matter what the enemy throws it builds character, faith and trust in the ALL knowing!

HEARTBROKEN BUT BLESSED

I literally have been up ALL night reading the Bible listening to all kinds of music, praying, anointing my living room with anointed oil and just trusting God for peace and stability. Last night while we were in our weekly Bible study I felt this chill and I mean I started shivering and after that there was the breakdown and distraction. I'm learning to recognize those demons more and more but this is the first time I felt the open coldness like that. Yesterday a former get high mate of mine called to let me know her husband passed and all I could ask was his soul okay. She had joined the church and said that they had both stopped getting high cold turkey five years ago but from seeing him sneak in the past my spirit felt that since he wasn't going to church his spirit wasn't as strong as hers. Well that's how the day started and then I proceeded to get my paperwork in order for the apartments. I washed, cooked, cleaned a little and then rested my back and got a quick snooze. Now I reminded by hubby to pray for future tenants that God would place, and I had my mother pray the night before and my cousin the morning before so all I had to do was trust in God for I had been going over my finances so I just threw my hands up and said, "God you got this just direct me which way to walk."

While getting the papers together and fussing with my printer a cousin of mine told me one of our cousins had died and I sort of expected her death because she had been ill for quite some time and her daughter passed after a short bout with cancer a couple of months prior. I had seen her the last time I was home and she wasn't even diagnosed and when I found out she was sick I tried to get in contact with her from out here and sent messages but then she passed. I just wanted to share the good news with her about Jesus peace and all that He has done for me. Her mother was Seventh Day Adventist and had her personal relationship but her daughter I feel made her peace at the end

Last night I found out my girl who was recently diagnosed with lung cancer that had rapidly traveled and just like that she passed. I had just sent her daughter some positive information about a man who had been diagnosed with cancer and 30 years later is still living. Gosh I needed to be reminded of that because that is ministering to me for I often feel as though I'm running out of time.

This particular lady is my cousin's wife and he was the one dealing with colon cancer for years. I just wanted to let her know some of my positive stories just like she had asked me to tell her husband over a year ago about chemo. And who would have thought, she was the picture of health when we were shopping over a year ago and gone just like that in a finger snap!

My heart goes out to her children and her sister in law who is remaining. I guess my lesson is to try harder to contact those who I know have cancer and as a matter of fact I'll be calling this lady I know out here who I just spoke with and told her I would call her back. She's fighting in the hospital and told me that I was encouraging to her. You see I have been diagnosed with brain cancer eleven years ago and I've got the systemic lupus going on as well as a reduced mass in my left breast and osteoporosis. Lord I'm blessed and like I told the lady yesterday about that scripture Psalms 118:17 "I will live and not die and proclaim the works of the Lord!" And you know what, I make this covenant with God today as I'm writing, that I will proclaim His mighty works in my music, my films, shows, and writings whether they be articles or this book. My purpose is to provide hope, encouragement. Even though sometimes I get lonely and feel down because I need that same encouragement from another human. But we'll keep those pity parties very brief!

Wow I love music, I'm here listening to Joss Stone singing L-O-V-E and isn't that what it is all about? God our Creator is love and I love making people happy or providing hope and I'll be doing this until it's time for me to cross over but in the meantime I have a lot of work to do. So partner please keep me grounded and focused not on man but on the Master plan that has been laid out for my life. "Lord I promise to make you proud and maybe if I say it out loud it I can have it marinate within my spirit. Lord thank you for the gifts, thank you for the trials for without them I wouldn't be having this conversation with you right now. Lord I thank you for my health, my family and my faith. Lord I LOVE you and I'm in love with you. Thank you for the memories and all that is to come. Thank you for making me be still so that I can listen to your voice, thank you for taking people out and placing others in. It's like what my friend Nyeah stated on our pod cast. "If you didn't do another thing I would still thank you because you have already done enough!" And guess what my heart feels mended. YESSSSSSSSSSSSSSS Lord you did it again . . . I tell everyone Jesus is my boo and I'm not being disrespectful He is my everything!

BEYOND DESCRIPTION

I told my hubby this morning that the stage I'm going through in my life right now is confronting all of my fears. My fears of losing my integrity, fears of rejection and fears of abandonment. However it's like my Bishop preaches and teaches which side of the comma do we want to live in? The side of just living or have it more abundantly. I choose more abundantly and with that choice comes the challenges against self. One of the things that I prided myself on was integrity and everyone could depend on my word. Now I see integrity as one of the gifts God gave me and I love to provide people with hope, being that bridge from here to there. So when factors are beyond my control to make things happen I get fearful but in reality if I trust my Lord and Savior as much as I say I do I would do what I can and let God be in control. This is the lesson that I'm constantly learning.

One of my sponsors has been promising me some more funding for my music project and as a result I put my trust in him and told others that the project is on. Behind the scenes I feel as though I'm begging for the sponsor's commitment and as I'm writing this I realize that I'm giving this sponsor way too much power. Therefore "Lord I come to you humbly and ask you to help me want to be in your will! Thank You Jesus." Okay that's one lesson and the others have to do with the outreach film project. "Lord I give it back to you, I recommit this project that you gave me in the first place and I realize that the resistance only builds my perseverance. Lord I promise to lean not on my own understanding of resistance but to trust that you are God and God alone and you obviously know what you are doing. I'm not being sarcastic but real with you Lord for the only one I fear is you for at any given moment you can pull the plug. Lord my friend that's in the hospital, please save his life so that we can record and proclaim your works!"

In the midst of writing this I just had a church associate pray with me. She prayed for finishing and removal of hindrances. You see at the end of the day it's not about you or me but what our purpose is and once you know that you begin to see how all the dots are connected and the roles you play in this game called life. I live strongly by various scriptures and they are my affirmations like my repeat "I will live and not die and proclaim the works of the Lord." Psalms 118:17 Someone said to me the other day that I should say affirmations at the beginning of the day and when I think about it I do. I affirm every morning with whatever my partner desires for me. I know sometimes I feel that with all my challenges I need to get things done and remove the clutter out of my life. Thank you my readers for you have helped me to distinguish what is needed and as a result my partner is removing the clutter starting with my mind. This journey is beyond description that's how smooth and real this ride is.

IT'S NOT JUST A CLICHÉ

Every morning I wake up with nausea and can feel that demonic presence. I'm on day eleven and yesterday there was no barricading of the door. I called out to Jesus loud and clear and trust and believe the entire block knows His name from my mouth. I understand spiritual warfare quite well and know for sure that I'm on the right path. Now don't get me wrong I fall short and am tempted but God does make that way of escape. For what I'm going through now I've been through before and in the past I may have talked to God but I didn't let Him provide me with a way of escape. I took matters into my own hands and quite often my way was not the best. The other morning I walked across a neighborhood that had changed drastically, not so much in the outer as it was in atmospheric presence.

So many times we dress up on the outside but we carry a smell, an odor of the demonic. Many think that demons, witches and warlocks are fairytales but they are quite real. If you are in tune with your inner self you can feel the energy shifting and you will always be given a clue when you listen to that still inner voice, that gut feeling isn't called that for no reason. It's not a cliché when they say listen to yourself or there is power in the name of Jesus or prayer works. No these are not clichés these are real happenings and we need to be more aware of what really is going on. We can't get so caught up in the fact that we are supreme beings because we are created in the image of God so everything we do, say and are on our own is in stone. Oh no boo don't get it twisted while we maybe supreme beings and are created in His image but we aren't the only beings you feel me? There is more in the invisible than the visible. The time we live in and on this planet isn't dress up time it is dress down time. It's time to get to the naked truth, the basics. For me that statement about taking care of home and cleaning your home is not a cliché but my life's battle that will end victoriously! We can't close our eyes to what is . . . . and that my friends is more than a cliché so in Jesus name go forth and fight those entities that are taking up space in your closet. I guess that's where the term space invaders comes from.

It Matters

When people say making memories doesn't matter well they do. Yesterday I received news of a vision I had seen some time ago and I'm telling you some things you wish you hadn't seen or felt but God places you in times and seasons so that you can see and feel and most of all plan ahead of time. I'm so shaken right now I have to step away from writing this. Oh Lord please help me . . .

Okay it's been twenty four hours and I've had time to process. Yesterday I had to stop writing because the tears were falling all over my computer and then my partner led me to call my prayer partners and we ended up going for prayer early in the morning. My family is going through it with afflictions one after another and all within a short time span of a few weeks. My Dad got his results and that was the straw that broke this camel's back. I pray for peace for all of us. And today my other Aunt is going in for surgery. I listened to them when they came to visit and they were all on canes talking about scheduling their doctor's appointments and I was like "wow." We went from conversations of maintaining health to all of this within five years! Now I can see why they always ask you to make a five year plan because we don't know what will happen from day to day. I mean just look at me who would have thought but it's all about the fight, the right to take back the authority that God has given each of us. He has given us the authority to say, "Mountain move!" So to all the mountains in our lives we just need to have faith the size of a mustard seed and it can be done. Yes the Lord has the final say but until then He didn't instill in us the DNA to give up or give in. We have work to do; we have to fulfill our purpose that He has given us.

You know I was just talking to this young artist that I've had for four years and we groomed him to become developed for his dream of rapping and singing. Now he wants to quit because he isn't signed and it has only been a month since we released his CD. I'm asking the Lord to give him patience and guidance. All he wants now is to be able to make money and become wealthy because that is all they see hear and are constantly bombarded with the invisible stringed dollar bills. That's right my partner, Mr. Holy Spirit just gave me the insight that every dollar bill comes attached with a string and it is up to us to develop the "no strings attached mentality." Like I told him, we must be careful what we put out there, what energy, what words. For words are sometimes more powerful than actions. We have to constantly speak to ourselves, pray over ourselves and realize that at the end of the day when the lights are off and the audience has left the building, we are left standing center stage answering to the audience of one. Therefore everything we do every word we say, we must remember that at the end of this life's play it does matter. For it has never been about us it has always been about the one who created us.

SITUATIONS CAN CHANGE

Let me just illustrate the effects of the last forty eight hours and the results of the unpleasant news. I spoke to my estranged uncle for the first time since he gave me and my Hubby directions in the snow storm last Christmas, well I did call to say thank you but anyhow I spoke with him at 3:30 in the morning and told him the family situation and he agreed that prayer does change things. Or in his words that prayer seems to change things. So I said, "Well can we pray right now and we prayed." That was a miracle okay. Then my sister dedicated her life a few weeks ago and didn't tell the family but my big mouth dad approached her and she said yes but she wasn't going to be a fanatic. That was a miracle.

My Aunt asked to be kept in prayer and that was unheard of. My other Aunt once given her earthly death sentence started to attend church regularly. My Aunt Es cuddled me in her arms when I was going through with my countless seizures and the Holy Spirit directed her to tell me to say in my head, "Cover me with the blood of Jesus." Then she told me to say, "Thank you Jesus" in my head and out loud every time I felt a brain attack and that saved my life. I want to take this time to say thank you Aunt Es for being obedient to the voice of the Lord.

I have a Jewish friend who never believed in prayer or religion but just was proud to be Jewish. He remembered I had prayed with him for his Mother and he called me saying the prayer actually worked and now he believes a little bit. So this morning I was able to confidently ask him to pray for my family and my Dad and he agreed.

Oh how could I forget with all the turmoil I had a bad dream last night or let's just call it a nightmare which I hardly ever have? I was being followed and chased and then I was running in a wooded area and I tripped and fell into this pit. I tried to pull myself out and when I was climbing out this dark blue force with a hat kept pushing me back and we wrestled and finally I bit it and again I woke up to a mouth opened biting motion! Then I was out of breath and looked at the clock and it was 3:29 a.m. and my partner told me to open the Bible. I turned to Psalms 108 and it talked about how there is victory in God's strength and with God's help we can do more than we humanly think. I felt calm and went to go back to sleep but my partner had me get the Bible again and turn to Psalms 110 and only He had me turn to that page because I sure no I didn't on my own. Now in 110 it talked about the credentials of the Messiah and that Jesus is the Messiah and the translation said that we can't straddle the fence and say that He was just a great human teacher or a great prophet but that He is the Son of God and came to save us and we must proclaim Him as Lord. And you know what? Even Oprah gave Him credit at her last show as being her source and the song we mixed last night talked about proclaiming Him unashamed. Well I know He is my Lord and my Savior and in adversity we all can be transformed so **it does matter** don't kid yourself!

THE NAME
THAT BRINGS CHANGE

You know the sayings from scriptures such as "the prayers of the righteous availed much" is so true; after much crying, praying and just saying God take it. It is after that when you begin to walk in peace and learn more and more what it means to have a personal relationship with God. To really know what it means to call on the name Jesus and know that you know that you know that name is super powerful and that it is why it is the name above all names? It causes continued change, it brings about results, an unexplainable peace when walking through the storm, riding the waves, starving in the valley, climbing the mountains and just worshipping Him in the midnight hour.

Every time I think of the name Jesus being powerful I smile because I remember this couple who were in my life for a minute. I had rented an apartment to them and they worshipped a whole bunch of things, including a smoking Indian with an alter of money, waving incense and plenty of weed. I remember talking about Jesus and the wife saying, "Yeah they say that name is powerful, it's one of the more powerful mantras." Yep they still owe me money right up to this day but I look at it as they were in my life for the season and a lesson. I met them at a drum circle meeting and they were saying how they had fixed up this house and the cousin owed them thousands and then he kicked them out. It was Christmas time and I had an empty apartment so after trying to find confirmation in a mutual friend who blatantly told me, "Now I don't know them like that." But I took them in anyway despite what I felt in my gut, my fleshly emotions felt sorry for them. They were good for the first few months and I hired them to work on another house. And if that wasn't enough I invited them over for Christmas with some others who had no one to share it with and told each person to buy something from the dollar store. That was our gift exchange.

We enjoyed a phenomenal Christmas with the acoustic guitar and congas. They all served a moment in time and Lord knows I've dragged my Aunt and Mother through some characters in my life's journey and that in itself should be a book! I could see God changing my relationships, teaching me discernment but my relationship with Him is only becoming more intimate. For that I love you Lord and my family more and more and in the great words of my co-host, "if He never did another thing He has already done enough!" It's tough to watch people come and go through your life like a swinging door. Being a landlady you learn to not get personally involved. You learn the meaning of reasons, seasons and lifetime relationships.

Yesterday I was with a friend and watched them go through torment as their Mother's life hung in the balance and all the family could care about is the money, the extra millions like they needed it. My friend has a heart of Christ but the church wouldn't call him a Christian. I told him last night that I wanted to go by and pray with his Mother but that didn't happen. He and his family felt that she was just laying there and didn't know anything. I had the opportunity to tell him that just because a person is lying there and doesn't look like they can hear, they can and I know this because I've been there.

I was able to share my testimony of when I couldn't speak and was being dressed and people were saying, "Well she wouldn't know what we are putting on her" and in my head I was like these idiots don't they know that I can hear I just can't respond. So I told my

friend to tell his Mother that he loved her and that it is alright to go towards the light. Being released is another book on its own. Just letting someone know that you genuinely love them is what really matters! My own Father's birthday was yesterday and all I could do was feel my Mother's pain a thousand miles across the ocean. He goes to the hospital this morning and I am praying that He realizes just what it means to be loved. Lord I'm praying as usual for another miracle of softening his heart and the realization of the words he always said to me when I was dying to live, that God has it and I just want to be there for him. I love my father, my mother, my aunts, my husband, my son, my dog, my cousins and of course the list goes on. I try not to think too hard about my niece and nephews or siblings because of the severe hurt, but the love is still there otherwise I wouldn't feel the pain. After all you can only hurt from the pain that you feel from that which is real. So this morning I'm looking at my baby sleeping on the floor all pushed up behind his bed and I say to myself what really matters?

Money is fleeting so is fame but real love, real caring relationships are the most important. God has shown me so much within the past few years that I feel like I'm in the school of acceleration for getting my heart, my thoughts, my actions and my mouth in alignment with my purpose which is His will. I'm being prepared for what really matters and that is professing and displaying genuine love through every bit of my being. Now that is what really matters don't you think? Lord I just pray that you will give me that personal human affection that I long for. Please don't leave me hanging in my fairytale of what love should feel like. We need to get to a place where we can get over human imperfections.

TEARS OF LONGING

You know when the doctors said that I would never conceive it took a lot out of me.

I was in a same sex relationship at the time and one of my family members response to my sad news of not being able to conceive was . . . "Well it's not like you planned to have children anyway." Are you kidding me? I guess because I was living a gay lifestyle I wasn't human. My spirit was crushed by this statement. What about the choice, the option as a natural woman to want to bear a child. And what does a mother mean to me my partner asks? It means adding value to this life. Bringing change, making a difference, displaying unconditional love with affection, direction and ultimate satisfaction. Being loved and giving love that is untrammeled!

Well I can't have natural children but I have sown into the lives of many children both near and far. I find that children overseas in countries that aren't so modern have a deep appreciation for what you do and more importantly for who you are and represent. I guess one of my greatest gifts to this world is children and the elderly. When I receive letters and phone calls from my past students abroad it fills my heart with so much joy. Now maybe something is wrong with me because I can't figure out why my past students from my county don't even remember me teaching them yet those in South America do. Clue me in maybe it's the Jesus in me but seriously I can't say that about all of my Bermudian students. I had one girl say to me while I was in line at the movies at home that she is who she is as a result of me. What a statement, what an honor.

The other day I received a letter from an overseas student who I was thinking about and she shared with me how she was getting married and detailed info. Another called to say she was kicked out of the house and living on the streets. I experienced a young boy just clinging to me and told his mother in front of me that he wanted me to be his mother. Wherever I travel it is always about the children. My missionary work is about sharing my faith not just in word but in my actions. I was just crying and talking to God about how I yearn to see my kids again in South America. I filmed each one asking them what they wanted to become and it grieves my heart when I know that the majority of them can't because of their economic situations. You know we take for granted our opportunities.

I shed tears because I know their hearts and I pray to God for their protection. I was given the class with some special children and my heart loves them so. I would take pictures of those that weren't in my class and talk with them about their dreams. Look I just know that one of my deepest desires is to bless them, make a difference in their lives. As I'm writing this I'm weeping again to God because I just want to be blessed to bless others. I think about all the money I wasted on cocaine and the wrong people. "Lord I just want to bless others in your name. I just want to plant seeds of hope. I want to plant seeds of your love and be a listening ear. I long for the day when I will see the families in the villages; I pray that the grandmothers will be alive when I visit." I'm taking my tears and declaring in the name of Jesus that I will visit next year and make that reconnect. I tell others the story of the little girl that was too poor to attend dance classes but we discussed her options and possibilities and the next year I went to visit they gave me the news that she was chosen by the country to participate in a major event. I tell of the village that was building stone houses and we discussed working together and how they used to construct in unity in my country. Can you envision how many houses were built with neighbors and friends over a drink or a meal?

My play Granny, Mrs. Myrtle Edness would tell us stories of when the women would be cooking while the men laid stone and mortar.

Then once they finished a house they went on to do the next persons and the trend successfully continued until we became more modern and the togetherness went south once the dollar strings became attached. Now in South America they are keeping those basic trends in the villages and the next year I visited they had finished a few more houses. I feel so connected with those less fortunate. And maybe it's because I'm a rescuer so that's where I feel most needed and appreciated.

Um that makes sense because in my everyday life all I was doing was getting in relationships were I was the rescuer and then I felt used. Thanks for pointing out the correlation partner, now I know why I'm so connected with missionary work and have a handle on whom to bless and not to bless! My partner just reminded me that I do it here in America. For example there was the guy that begs at the bus depot and in return opens and closes the door for people at this particular restaurant. When I saw him last night I was excited and said, "What's up Snoop ?" and he said, "You are the only one that calls me that everyone else just calls me doorman." I named him that from the first time we talked because I couldn't believe how much he looks like an older version of the artist "Snoop Dogg." We had a chance to share stories and I had the opportunity to drop the seeds of Christ. Thanks partner for bringing t hat to my memory I feel better. I now know why they say writing is healing!

RISE UP AND WALK

You know for the past ten days God has allowed me to go through and get through. Last Friday before last I walked all over the city and even visited some former places and ran into a few people but kept it moving. On my way home after literally walking for what equated to be a few miles I caught the train and at the transportation depot I saw the man I named Snoop and he had a big smile on his face. While we talked I observed decent looking people coming up near us to the drug dealers asking for fat ones which is a term for fat drug bags or crack rocks. I could feel that familiar evil presence but I dare not say anything.

I was hungry for Chinese food and mentioned it to Snoop who said he knew of a good one just down the street. So we crossed the street and he ran between the traffic before me and I shouted, "oh Jesus" because I didn't want him to get hit and then I crossed the busy street and he said, "yeah Jesus is the only one I could turn to" and then he shared his drug story with me. He lost his family and home due to being addicted to crack. He said he almost died and is now on disability living in a building without heat and running water but Jesus let him live. I shared some stories with him about my struggles and let me tell you that restaurant wasn't just down the street it was a few long blocks which meant more walking but it gave us time to talk. We waited for the food and I gave him my change which was about $1.50 and he said I didn't have to do that because he was enjoying our talk but I told him I knew I didn't have to but I wanted to. During that time we shared a few laughs while looking at the loud visibly drunk students and then the unthinkable happened. This bronze skinned guy came in with an extra grill of front teeth that looked false and brown. He looked like he had a Halloween mask on but he didn't. He looked and moved like a zombie trying to fit in asking if there was a park nearby. All of us looked in silence as the guy asked for directions. I mean the drunk got sober, the Chinese storekeepers and all of us jaws dropped! I was the only one who answered him and then everyone else added their two cents. It was a pause in a movie scene for sure. After the "alien" guy left everyone was saying, "Can you believe that?" We all agreed that we had never seen anything like it. He had an alien mouth that you only see on TV, or movies like Star Wars or something. And the thing is the guy acted like he was normal, maybe he was from somewhere else but he definitely didn't appear of the human race right down to his weird bronze skin color. As I'm writing about it, I'm squishing up my face and I can still see him or it!

Shortly after the shocking encounter I saw that my bus was coming and "Snoop" said he would run ahead to stop it. All of a sudden I couldn't run and when I reached the bus I was so out of breath that all I could do was crack a joke and apologize to everyone on the bus for waiting for me as I panted like a dog in heat. I told them what a workout! Now you figured I walked my behind off that night and then when I got off the bus to go home there were these guys in a car similar to ours that had broken down. I went into the house and got my dog to walk back to the guys to see if they were okay. Wow just sharing this night with you is wearing me out but check this. The next morning I went to make a sudden turn and bam my knee pops, my leg twists and collapses. I guess it was saying, "Oh no you don't, enough is enough?"

I literally had to drag myself on the floor with my dog hollering for help and all I could do was cry out to Jesus. I called my mother who told me to get the anointed oil and a friend came over. She watched me crying and dragging myself because I could not stand on it. This entire incident reminded me of after my brain tumor surgery when I couldn't walk or when I realized I had systemic lupus with the dog barking. I didn't need another repeat where I couldn't walk and had to use a wheelchair or a walker. I cried out to God.

You talk about pain it was as if every bone and muscle had splintered. And my husband was moving his things out of the house at the time and left me and all I could do was pray. Remember I said I was walking because I didn't want to go home for that spirit of darkness was having its way trust and believe. But like it says in Romans 8:28 "All things work together for the good of those that love the Lord" and yep that is so true. Without going into too much detail hours and hours later I listened to my partner, Mr. Holy Spirit. Against the advice of my friends I called my husband and told him to come home for his wife needed his assistance. Some more friends came by to offer their assistance and one was a registered nurse and she was on it. Eventually my husband came home and that spirit behind him started to go there and I calmly said," Not now!" I told him I was at peace because I had just released him to my Lord and Savior. I had to concentrate on getting better for me and those that really love and appreciate me, including my South American students who were in contact with me to the point were every time I thought of one of them they would contact me. I started bleeding the blood of Jesus against that spirit and prior to that he said he was going upstairs and I just put my trust in God completely to the point that I was able to rise up, grab those crutches and hop to the kitchen. Then all of a sudden he came back like a lamb saying he wanted to get me something to drink and how I shouldn't be on the leg.

After that moment he was like a different person and nursed me back to health. He carried me on his back and I say this to say that what Satan meant for bad God used for good for it was the first time he had seen me down literally and I believe God used that opportunity to bring out characteristics in both of us. With me it was being able to receive because I was ultra independent and with him it was being compassionate which was something that we always argued over. I told him before getting up to hop to the kitchen that God gives us opportunities and I had made peace with my circumstance because I had released that which I had no control over. I was tired of making him understand what I was going through. Out of nowhere I found myself saying these words "You may have broke your mother's heart but here is your opportunity to make it right!"

After hopping around I was able to show my friends in action how I believed God first and refused to go to a hospital because I wanted to try Jesus, you know the name above all names. The successful remedy for healing my leg were prayer with anointed oil, my eastern treatment and Reiki along with traditional ice packs, rubs, peanut oil, faith and trust in God. I promised them all if I didn't get better I would go to the hospital but my faith in God is super strong. Then last night my dog got attacked three times and I started shouting the name Jesus and my husband started holding him saying, "In the name of Jesus be healed D" and was surprised and happy that it worked. Yeah the attacks come but there is power in the name of Jesus and it's not just a song. Consequently this morning when that spirit of darkness attempted to enter and I could feel it in the pit of my stomach I obeyed the voice that said," Rise Up and Walk" and guess what I walked to the bathroom without the crutches. Now give me a high five!

The bottom line is that there is supernatural power if we believe, receive and take authority. Command it! In the midst of pain my friend heard me repeating the name Jesus and then commanding healing. We can't just say it we must believe it. Hence that scripture "No Weapon formed against you shall prosper" means just that NO WEAPON, financial, health, deception or even death! We must recognize that we are spiritual beings in these lovely fleshly bodies. It's funny because I always say that God sees around the corners of our lives and He definitely knew that I had to get my walk on before being laid up . . . What a sense of humor you have Lord . . . hah hah hee hee. Can you imagine if we knew everything about the lessons that we are to learn? Most of us wouldn't want to go through the fire in fear of being burned and I guess that is why God has us operating on a need to know basis. Gosh I love you . . . you are so awesome Lord. Now I'm worshipping to "Simply Redeemed" by Heather Headley and Smokie Norful. Let's march on and have a great day.

IT'S ALL ABOUT THE APPLICATION

I was telling my cousin that the Holy Spirit showed me that going through this surge overload proved to be the test for the application in my situation. And no matter how many worship services we may attend, or conferences, or read and recite the Bible or participate in a zillion movements at the church; without applying God's word we are sitting ducks or showboats just displaying peacock feathers. What do peacocks do at the zoo just parade around but are they serving a purpose other than looking good? Now don't get me wrong visiting the sick and shut in, performing powerful prayer vigils, exorcising unwanted spirits are all important but what about going out of our comfort zones to assist our fellow beings? What about when no one is watching or keeping score, well other than God.

You know I am thankful for following Christ when I speak to the homeless on a regular or get down on my knees wherever my partner instructs me. Or pray for someone softly at a hotel side kitchen or pick up the phone and let someone know that I am thinking of them. I guess I go into the extreme with I go dancing with my survivor sisters or visit with long-term acquaintances and sit at a bar discussing God. I mean the fact that I don't indulge in alcohol in itself is a testimony to others. I used to care about getting teased when ordering a Shirley temple or club soda but now it doesn't bother me. I know Jesus broke the religious rules to show His loving kindness to all including those whom others detested at that time such as the prostitute or the adulterous woman at the well. When I think about the majority of people that Jesus demonstrated compassion for they were not what the church considered to be the 'in crowd' but rather the 'out of bounds crowd.'

I remember someone I considered to be in my spiritual family telling me that she defended me telling someone that I had prophetic gifts and that I derive from a family of generational prophets and therefore they shouldn't look at how I dress! What is that supposed to be mean when the same spiritual close ones started shutting me out when I needed them most like preparing for my wedding or dealing with my Aunt's life changing diagnosis. Don't get me wrong I would have it no other way for my Aunt Es was there with me every step of the way with my brain cancer. However my spiritual friends abandoned me emotionally and I now realize that was a lesson from God. I had no one to call but there was and is a friend that has never left me and is unfailing and we know that name, my number one . . . JC . . . Ironically my partner and I composed a song the night before I left to be with my Aunt and it is simply entitled "There is no other name."

IT'S ONLY A TEST

I was talking to my Mom and we were all crying about my Aunt's life changing prognosis. I told her that all I want is a hit song to show my family and share the finances with those that have been there and those who are in the world that need it. I was listening to some secular or as I term it regular radio and often I hear people singing songs with the name Jesus and scriptures in the lyrics over what some consider secular music and that is what I want to do. People seem to be afraid to sing about our Lord and Savior over the secular airwaves. Many feel that there should be separation of us and them. But who is them? Would Jesus discriminate? The good book says we are to come out from amongst them but we have to live amongst them and show them for how else will the masses know! Many will never hear His name any other way then being Bible thumped. Most are turned off from those who live for judgment. When I go in stores and hear the singing duo Mary Mary's song "It's the God in Me" and I observe the clerks and shoppers all saying, "Hey that's my song" I smile. It feels great that we are making an impact especially when I hear them singing those lyrics that resonate within their spirits; I know that's about answering the call. When I hear the cars drive pass my home blasting "It's the God in Me" I rejoice because I know that Jesus is alive and we are proclaiming His Holy Name.

IT'S A NEW DAY

Do you ever find that when God gives you a word or a saying you start seeing it everywhere? Well I used to get upset if someone had the same phrase because I was so used to people cold heartedly stealing my ideas but as I study the word more under the guidance of the Holy Spirit I'm learning just how connected we are. When you stop to think about it, how stupid and prideful we are to think that only we can receive. Sometimes in church I love to play with it and get the words out before the speaker just to confirm the works of God. You see many think it's a joke or a mere coincidence that God puts things into alignment and how is that when He created us we didn't create Him. All I'm saying is that the more aware we become the keener our senses are. "The closer we draw to God the closer He draws to us" James 4:8

I'm so proud that I'm actually not just remembering scriptures but burying them in my heart and living them. Now for me that is a new day for it is something that I have long prayed for and I love to learn. In the mornings when I study with Him He answers all the questions in my head. And why not He knows my every thought right? You know the closer I walk with the Spirit the greater the flow, the greater the anointing to have a burning desire to create positive change. When I say I love the Lord I mean just that. He is my number one baby and my love is so deep that as I'm writing the tears just swell up in my eyes. He is my everything and it's as simple as that. In Him I live, I move and have my being. Because of Him I was inspired to record the song "A Better Me."

I understand the whole philosophy about the Word being alive because it is. There are so many examples but the most recent was last night when an associate of mine blasted me for not making money my primary focus. Now yes at this time I'm short and hate living a certain way but I also know that my attitude as my partner had me write in a song needs adjusting. Waiting upon the Lord is no easy task but it builds my strength. If I have to identify with anyone in the Bible it would be my boy David. God even comforted me with the fact that I allowed my associate to make me feel alone. I felt under achieved because I wasn't making money. But my Father has never let me go hungry!

MY COVENANT
"THE PRAYERS OF THE RIGHTEOUS AVAILETH MUCH"

This may sound crazy to some but my pet is like my child and I know he has feelings. When I had my chemo he would know I was sick before I did. He would act all crazy and then I would throw up. I know the enemy has tried to take me out several times whether it being physically, emotionally, spiritually or financially. Thank the Lord for Ms. Renee my neighbor who I pray and share with. We even discuss praise reports and testimonies. Yesterday morning as I was glorifying the Lord my partner, Mr. Holy Spirit who often gives me intense feelings in the pit of my stomach that I would experience every time before there is a shift in the atmosphere. That evening before we praised together I had a dream about this girl who I'm tied to spiritually and due to a third party we have become detached. In my dream I saw her going to these two events with this entity. I felt grieved almost like a death and awoke feeling gloomy and couldn't figure out why after all it was only a dream right? Well the one thing I've learned is that when I dream and there are lingering feelings it's a sign. When I got up and checked my phone this same girl who was in my dream had sent me a text saying she needed to talk to me. I immediately replied with a text and felt wow that's deep. Now that's one of my favorite sayings "That's Deep."

I have been going through personal problems and check it out the night before my dream my hubby made it clear that he was going to wake up when he felt like it and then see his son. I stopped allowing myself to get upset when he didn't want to attend church and now since my neighbor goes to my main church I'll get a ride with her in the morning. I began going out of my way not to ask for anything. This is the wall I began building to protect my emotions. I felt I was doing an empowering thing when in reality I was feeding into one of Satan's tactics.

Just to think that we both dreamed about getting a car and it happened to be the same car from a dealership that one of the church brothers dealt with. We were so in sync that we both picked out the same car without ever consulting one another. Yea God; when we obey you things manifest. Now the bottom line is that every time God blesses my husband he seemed to move further from the Lord. Therefore we have to stay steadfast even when our flesh doesn't want to. Early this morning I received some news of proposals being turned away due to monetary constraints but after my morning study the only scripture that came before me again is James 5:16 "the prayers of the Righteous Availeth much."

To tell you the truth for months I didn't even know where that scripture was found but I found out. You see it is only prayers that have made my husband turn back around and God is teaching me to study and be quiet and again keep my hands off the wheel. Thanks to Rev. Love for leading me in my deliverance.

In church Sunday that same scripture was mentioned after my neighbor and I spoke about it and then I asked this scholar for an interpretation and between the good doctor and my neighbor I now know the answer to my hidden questions. I just know that if I stay fixed on the mark God will reveal even more. For it is not by chance or coincidence that I just happen to be placed at various segments of several successful people's lives who are financially wealthy. I happen to be in the studios with certain groups and then bam they are receiving Grammies or others are on TV and covers of magazines or I'm with my family and their songs come on the radio and I wish secretly in my heart if only I could hear mine. I know God has me positioned to where He wants me in His chess game called 'R Life.' I've just begun to actively pursue MY music or should I say our music.

FLASHBACK OF HIS GUIDANCE

Ten years ago my Aunt accompanied me with my brain surgery and now I'm with her in the same hospital and yesterday just before I went into the room to get her diagnosis from the doctor I received a phone call from my fiancé. He told me that they just laid him off from his job exactly 5 weeks before we were to be married. While trying to comfort him miles away the doctor called for my Aunt and me to come in. I had to rush him off the phone and switch gears for I was about to await my precious Aunt's fate. A chronic illness where most people live for 2 to 4 years. Well after being there for what seemed like eternity I had to change my brain from my wedding and fiancé and ask the Holy Spirit to guide me to ask the doctor the right questions . . . . That was one day that only my partner could have guided me through with every step. I had to be strong for her and went in the bathroom to call various family members and cry. I called my then fiancé back to encourage him some more because I didn't need him returning to the street scene. But most of all I recall walking across the parking lot talking to my sister and having her break down on the phone and it was there that God showed me that He is in control. I had never ever heard my sister weep like that before. Sometimes in our humanity He reveals His truth. Psalms 18:32 "He will arm me with strength and make my way safe." Here we all are years later and God is still maintaining us.

JUST HAD TO SIT THROUGH ADULT STORYTELLING

You haven't experienced anything until you experience what it is like to be relaxing in a hammock at a house overlooking a beautiful lake and then comes the storytelling. When I look over my life at all the good memories that make me say "You've got to be kidding me or you had to be there moments" well this is in my top ten lists. I remember being with some friends and they would house sit. One time a friend of mine who was mesmerized with this lady had the rest of us who were in relaxation heaven come and sit inside to hear her read. Actually my friend ordered us to come inside as this lady insisted on reading this story out loud to us like we were kids! I mean was this Sesame Street or what? We would be nodding and she would holler at us when we would doze off. One friend would start snoring loudly and my other friend would get totally red-faced from embarrassment. Talk about crazy times with some crazy friends that God removed and then reconnected in another season of my life.

My Aunt reminded me when I told her about this experience that I should be able to identify with how the children must feel especially during those stories that are according to my nephews . . . boring . . .

I miss my crazy friends a lot but I'm trusting God in this new season. I was once told by my original discipleship leader that God is funny with His mathematics and doesn't see it as we do. Therefore what we view as subtractions are actually space movements for God. In His infinite wisdom He releases people, places and things from our lives so that space is created for Him to do a work within us. So when people cry to me about friends disappearing from their lives I assure them that sometimes God removes so that He can add wonderful genuine beings to our circle so that our lives can be enhanced and empowered for positive manifestations and more importantly reflect the loveliness of Jesus to win souls. Yeah it hurts because we are human but the pain of their departing gets less and eventually will be filled by others. Another thing I have learned is that this too shall pass and it does. I have had so many friends removed from my life over the past five years that I have had no other choice than to seek His face totally! My partner, Mr. Holy Spirit reminds me to turn and feast on Psalms 42 when I feel confused and lonely by God's mathematics for this is more than a story.

MANY SPIRITS BUT THEIR NAMES ARE NOT HOLY!

Ummmmmmmmm God is good for in that short break the Holy Spirit which I feel compelled to write about in full. Many people are talking about the Spirit this and the Spirit that but the Holy one just told me to ask them what Spirit are they referring to the next time I converse with someone who's talking like that. For there are many spirits just as there are gods but who are they when you call them by name. That's why I always say, for me I've chosen Jesus Christ as my personal Lord and Savior and folks why? Because He saved me from a sea of hell but I always respected Him no matter what I was doing even when I was high.

When I think about that word "high" we as lost souls were seeking back then a way to escape or attain a higher state of being. But there is only one Trinity, one Father, one Son and One Holy Spirit/ Ghost who can take you to the ultimate high and it is wavy! I say wavy the words of another cousin who was senselessly gunned down for talking on his cell phone. Yeah that's right talking to someone else with his earpiece on I'm told and someone thought he was talking to their girl and when he turned around and said no I'm on the phone well the guy still shot after him, his brother and a friend and the result was another close relative dead over a spirit. That's right only a spirit of darkness could have made a man kill over embarrassment in front of witnesses and the girlfriend that he in his mind was defending. Only a spirit and we know that spirit's name was not Holy . . . .

HOPE DEFERRED LEADS TO A SICK HEART BUT DREAMS FULFILLED ARE A TREE OF LIFE
(Proverbs 13:12)

After traveling for hours and taking five trains to get home was no easy feat but after being pounded with conversations that were weary on my soul from my spiritual sisters; I felt down and for the first time in a long time and was about to have a full blown seizure so in my heart I cried out to God and popped some pills.

Any hoo this morning I got up and worshiped and then I started reading my daily Proverbs and thanking my Father for the ones that I was able to memorize in my heart; that being Proverbs 3:5, 6 which jumped off the page while over a friend's house. Later in conversation with my mother she mentioned how this same scripture was one of her favorites and started reciting it. And tell you the truth it isn't until I'm writing this morning that the Holy Spirit is reminding me that my relationship has become tighter with my Mom in the spirit. Oh I can feel my prayer language exploding in my spirit, "Holy, Holy, Holy, that is who you are Lord, I will praise your name forever" and there goes another song thank you Lord . . . Okay let me go and record this I'll be right back . . .

Ok I'm back. You know I was concerned about my Aunt but when I look back over our journey together we have traveled the world, shared so much that it is only fitting that I should be beside her naturally . . . she is my second mother and the term spiritual mom should be given to her not someone I really don't know because they used that titled when they were approached and I went along with it; well that was for a season . . . Titles are deeper than most think and have true meanings just like the title we give to our Lord or the Spirit, we can no longer say them so casually.

As I stated earlier my Mother and I are tighter due to our spiritual connection and now I see that happening between my Aunt and I. We always had a supernatural bond and believed many out of the box things due to our personal experiences but now this is a new season and I'm looking forward to it as a matter of fact I welcome it! I believe this is how we have to look at this journey called life. As confirmation I was getting excited about God placing scriptures in my heart and I just wanted to memorize even more so we, thee and me came upon Proverbs 12:28 which states "The way of the Godly leads to life, that path does not lead to death." I'm going to give that scripture to my Aunt as well.

Then as I was reading the Word and thanking God for getting me to memorize I was watching Bobby Jones musical showcase on BET and there was Israel Houghton and the New Breed singing about the promise of life. Talk about confirmation sometimes God does the ultimate to get our attention . . . I mean let's face it ; it took almost three near death experiences to get me away from the power of cocaine. And that's funny because someone was saying they realize I'm not lying about some of my testimony because I always tell the same story. Like really? Can you believe that; they must be used to people saying stuff for attention. Well this is the truth baby and for those that are reading we keep it real . . . . In the past I would talk to the Lord and ask Him questions and as my Mother had taught me from young I would just open the Bible and wherever my finger landed I would read that as my answer.

Throughout the years I must have talked a lot because my Bibles are all highlighted and falling apart. I would carry my Bible everywhere but I couldn't memorize scripture as others who would. Then when my Aunt was sick one of my uncles who is a Minister called and gave me some scriptures to give to her and one of them I was excited about and you could hear that I caught him off guard. The Holy Spirit had me share scriptures with her for it was almost as if I had kept them in my heart specifically for her! Psalms 18:16-17

Having the Time to Say Goodbye

I'm riding the Amtrak with my Aunt Es and we are going away from the hospital for the holiday weekend before both have to return to the cold reality of the hospital setting. As I flip through pages reading about Michael Jackson all I can hear in my head is his song, "Gone too Soon" and of course I sing all sorts of lyrics in my head to the music and keep coming back to "Gone too Soon." Our lives resemble a train ride passing through towns some familiar and some not so familiar, some we know by name and others we've only heard of or read about but at the end of the day all of us on this train have one sole purpose and that is to get to a destination! Now obviously we do not all share the same entry and departure points but needless to say we are all on this mode of transportation for the same reason, that is to travel, just as we are all in this body loaned to us by our Creator. The train is temporary and even if we tried we could not remain on it forever neither can we remain tucked within our shell that being our human clothing that houses our spirits. Hey you all know the sayings "life is too short or live each day as though it were your last" well all of these aren't clichés but are actually based upon truth.

There's Something about that Name

Let me paint another real life scenario; my Aunt and I left Boston and while she went to be with her other nieces I came back to spend time with my husband on his birthday. We had decided to spend it with some family friends hanging out having a blast at a water park. While we were there we went on this ride and literally all got flown into the water without warning. I for one was gulping in water and the others well let's just say we all were dunked. Anyone looking would have busted their sides from laughing. I mean it wasn't exactly the hottest day but it was one that we were all grateful for because it wasn't raining. At one point we saw the rain clouds and they passed right over us, which in itself was a miracle considering all of the torrential rainstorms we had throughout the entire summer so why would this day be any different? None of us wasn't that overwhelmed about getting into the freezing water other then the youngster who was with us. There was this ride that we didn't have a clue of what we were in for, we each just grabbed a tube and by George we were going to 'wear out' this water park for it was the last day of the year that it would be opened and we were on it. Well that water ride we had no clue about overturned one guy in the tube and it knocked his glasses straight off his face falling to the bottom of the pool. Now earlier his girlfriend and I were looking at his glasses and I noticed that they were chipped and she said how he needed to get them replaced. And here we were a few hours later and thank God we had noticed that defect.

There were two lifeguards, one on the left and one on the right. We spoke with the one on the left and he said to her boyfriend that they would have to get a diver and that he should come back in fifteen minutes. So we all went off and did a few more rides, the majority were fun and others well my body kept getting stuck in the water tube I don't know what that was about? Anyhoo we were having a ball and then we decided to go back to the lifeguard way past the fifteen minutes. I went on an adjoining ride with the youngster and I could see the boyfriend storming off and everyone else just looking sad. So I asked what was going on and they said that the other lifeguard on the right gave the glasses to someone else minutes before we came back. Everyone was saying how stupid that was and how could you just give them away yada yada. The God in me like Mary Mary's song made me go to the other lifeguard who had a smirk on his face and he immediately began defending himself saying what did we want him to do for it wasn't his fault.

The Holy Spirit led me to be calm and ask him did the other party properly describe the glasses and I told him that he had no idea what he had just so casually done for we had drove a long way. I looked at his nonchalant spirit and I said, "I plead the blood of Jesus" boldly and he instantly changed and became more compassionate. Then within minutes of calling that name that non followers say has a lot of positive energy, a diver came up and handed him the glasses. Meanwhile the boyfriend had left to go let off some steam and the rest of us were standing at the other side. I looked immediately at the glasses defect and called for the girlfriend who confirmed that these were the right glasses. I said it's all about Jesus and the guard smiled and we shook hands. You see even in that God was performing a miracle and the result was that we enjoyed the rest of our day and night. Boy how I love the Lord in good times and bad times He'll never leave me nor forsake me and through every trial He is teaching me that it is not about us for truly it's about the bigger picture.

There is No Justified Moment

You know that scripture Proverb 3:6 which is one of my favorites that I live by "Acknowledge Him in all thy ways and he will direct thy path" is a scripture that I've taken to the tenth power I mean I anoint my computers, my dog, my hubby's shoes, stepson everything with anointed oil. When the computers act up I speak "In the name of Jesus not today Satan." The other day my toilet began to rise as I flushed and I said again in the name of Jesus. Like the song and scripture says walk in authority and while people may think I'm insane or weird, it works if you truly believe. Try it!

The morning that I was leaving to go back to Boston to be with my Aunt. I got up and the Holy Spirit directed my hand to the sections of my beloved dog where he had been insanely scratching over the past few months. We couldn't figure it out and we didn't have the money or transportation to take him to the vet so I tried home remedies and would bath him and he remained cool for awhile and then it would start up again. At first we thought it was a game you know chasing his tail but then he took that to the tenth power and would not only chase it but bite himself. Well I prayed, for either he was going crazy or something was wrong but we couldn't find any fleas. Well that morning God had me place my hands amongst the thick fur and go straight to those areas that had the most ticks I have ever seen. There were entire families ranging from big to small. They were buried into his tail and next to his upper ear. I poured my trusted anointed oil and demanded authority and drowned the creepy crawlers.

As a matter of fact I was multitasking when it was brought to my attention that my baby couldn't walk for his legs were giving out so while my boo was holding him I was picking and brushing his coat. It never ceases to amaze me how with God it is all about the timing for if my baby had lost his balance after I had left to return to Boston my boo wouldn't have been able to deal with him and who knows what would have happened. At first I didn't want to tell him what I had found. Also God showed me how the laundry drain where the clothes are rinsed and where I bath my dog was filed with chemicals. The Holy Spirit "who else" had me watch the clothes as they were rinsing. Normally while the clothes are washing and rinsing I find something else to do but not last night? I went to the laundry room early and waited because I wanted to make sure all those tasks were completed before my departure and that's when I watched and the Spirit hit me with the thought that this may not be the best place to wash my doggie. Needless to say I was able to leave with my fiancé and dog walking me to the train station and my little boo boo trying to jump on the train.

SUPERNATURAL FAMILY PLACEMENT

You know I was just thinking about my Aunt the caregiver and about us all getting sick. She made the statement about how she's blessed with a good family and I thought how the saying goes we can choose our friends but we can't choose our family. It's funny because sometimes it seems as though God places us right with the family that we are meant to be in. Now I know many reading this are like what you must be crazy but think about it God provides us with choices! Now if you are born into a family that is dysfunctional and abusive you can rise above it or become a victim of those circumstances. Look at Oprah who was from a poor family who was molested but asked the God within to help her rise above. There are countless stories of those that we consider successful who have risen from backgrounds of poverty, child abuse, neglect, drug and alcohol festering homes who decide this is not going to be me. I remember a close friend of mine was telling me because he was raised in poverty he would go to school in the dead of winter freezing with windbreaker jackets and be teased. Or because there were too many siblings to get regular decent haircuts and many of them would walk around with long hair and again be teased! As a result he loves to get his haircut because it makes him feel good! He wore the best quality clothes because he knows what it is like not to have; or sneakers and shoes are a treat because he remembers going to school in busted shoes with cardboard to protect his feet from the weather elements. His adult behavior is a molding of his circumstances!

Then you have others that fall into the victim mentality and feel as though the entire planet owes them something because of the screwed up situations in their upbringing. As a result many are cold killers, thieves, manipulators who truly feel they deserve to get over and bully others. This is where Christ steps in. It's like how this young Nigerian woman I interviewed once said that men cannot change men only Jesus can change their hearts. I've researched other religions and incorporate some practices but FOR ME Jesus is the only name that has transformed my life and countless others. For example I once had this tenant who seemed nice but was extremely regimented and claimed he was a Buddhist monk at one time but as time went on he revealed who that inner layer was, selfless and cold. See you can only mask for so long, a true monk is the total opposite. I always ask what if I were a Buddhist monk living in Tibet and died where would I go? For I really don't think I would go to hell. Well no one is yet to answer. Monks, Muslims who are transformed in prison often function within confinement.

Most beings on this earth are a member of a religion based upon their birthright, or they were forced to change because they were enlightened during a confining moment or moments in their life journey. Some feel that it is necessary to belong in order to reach a desired result. They may desire being a more productive member of society or wanting peace and balance in their lives. Others may serve so that they will receive certain things in the next life. And the list goes on. Well I know that all religions require sacrifices and constant practice and most ARE NOT AFRAID TO SAY I'M X Y Z. But for some reason many especially in the creative industry of music and film are in hiding for Jesus. It's as though if we don't blend in then we are seen as odd and are denied a place. I know without a doubt that Jesus is real and the Son of the only living GOD.

Many can talk about serving God but who are they referring to, is it the living God, Jehovah? You know the one who will allow confirmation when you read it in a derivative of the Word (the Bible) and then you turn on the television or radio and it's the same message or you are listening to a sermon and everywhere you go there are the same words. My friends and I were joking one night saying when this happens it's as if every minister, teacher or writer must call up one another and say hey let's put this forth into the universe and saturate the planet earth with this message. When I was having my seizures and my Aunt would tell me to say in my mind plead the blood of Jesus or cover me with the blood of Jesus I'm telling you it was the hardest thing in the world to penetrate my brain and come into alignment with these thoughts. Now remember I couldn't speak humanly anyway but the moment I said the word JESUS there was a release and I could begin to speak!

During my latter bouts I would struggle to look in the mirror and watch my face; and the moment I said JESUS my facial expression changed. It went from being contorted to becoming relaxed and peaceful. I often say my life should be on screen so that people can get visuals. I mean you had to be there to see it. So when we talk about being in the right family it isn't just the natural family that you were born or raised with but the supernatural family. The family of true Christ followers. I and my baby consider ourselves true 'keep it real" Christians who live in the reality of this world, aren't snobbish trying to live above our fellow brothers and sisters and doing our best to reflect the light in situations. After all Jesus was amongst the people, socializing with every type of being that was discriminated against with the sole purpose of reflecting His love and thus making positive changes. Too often we witness self proclaimed Christians who snob their noses at the poor and broken hearted. They drive right past fellow congregation members, do not offer to lend a hand and if so only do it in front of others with titles, you know what I'm talking about!

Wanda n Les

with Uncle Bunny standing

with a favorite cuz LaShawn

Les Lynnique n turtle

parents Teller n Idell

Ny n Diego

with my bestfriends Mom, Aunt Es n Aunt El

with mentor Bruce Hawes

With Mom at Antique store

at prizegiving my sister n my niece n nephews

Aunt Es with cuz Deb n Me

Aunt ilene n David

my adopted family The Eddy's

me and Daddy

LA N Myrtle Edness Christmas 07

EXERCISING "HOLD UP" MOMENTS FOR CHANGE

I stopped smoking because I thought I was going to die. I tried everything from the patch to smoking cessation classes to cutting each cigarette with scissors. The joke is I would carry these small scissors around for the sake of cutting the cigarettes in half and I ended up smoking more. It started from the occasional tea leaves with my cousin's neighborhood friends to the menthol Newport then I heard they had fiberglass in them which could cut the lungs so I switched to Marlboros and boy was I hooked. Now looking back the irony is that I wanted to protect my lungs from being cut but I could care less about the fact that I was charcoaling them with tar! I remember this guy telling me that his father had quit cold turkey and teased me saying that I wasn't strong enough to do that. Well I quit years ago January 16th, 2005 and he still smokes. It is not that I'm so strong on my own for the Lord stepped in because I made a pact WITH Jesus late one night . . . I smoked so bad that I remember being in London with my Aunt and smoking a cigarette with a family friend and we had to search all over to find a place to go and smoke and in the process we lost my Aunt who had looked for us and got tired so she had our baggage sent with her to the airport. She figured we would catch the vibe which we did after we were frantic that she had left us but the lesson was definitely learned! Now getting back to that awful but rectifying night which turned everything around, it went like this:

I smoked my last cigarette at 6 p.m. then climbed into bed and at about 11p.m. I AWOKE and COULDN'T BREATHE I felt LIKE A FISH OUT OF WATER. I banged on several of my neighbors doors in that condo complex and not one person would answer. However someone did answer my cry for help. I couldn't talk so in my head I said Jesus if you let me live I promise you that I will never pick up and smoke another cigarette. I went for a

$500 ambulance ride literally around the corner to a nearby hospital where they diagnosed that I had phenomena in my left lung only to find out five months later that I had systemic lupus on top of the remainder brain cancer. The fluid would engulf around my heart and guess what from that night on I've never smoked another cigarette. In fact months later someone asked me to light a cigarette for them and without thinking I naturally picked up the cigarette to light it for them. My Savior reminded me and I said, "No I don't smoke" a and that was my first outward confession as I proclaimed boldly that I didn't smoke anymore. That Satan would have tricked me into smoking again but my Lord and Savior was like "Hold up!" And many times in our lives we have to allow for those "Hold up and hold off moments in our lives if we truly want change!"

SPEAKING IN TONGUES

When I was younger my childhood friend and I would pretend that we spoke another language. We would be in Disneyworld and other places and speak this natural babble language and my Mother would tell as to stop acting silly but we continued. Later I found myself speaking in this same babble talk to my twin nephews and in my mind I would say look at me or do x y z and they would do it and smile.

Now that they are older I sometimes speak that language and they remember. You know I've always asked why would every single human being on this planet as a baby speak the same language. This question was answered yesterday by my Asian Minister who explained how we all derived from Adam and Eve. We all spoke the same language before God scattered us with different languages after the building of the earth's tallest tower and that being the Tower of Babel! When I get filled with the Holy Spirit and start speaking my prayer language it sounds similar to the babble which I understand was an ancient language from when they tried to build this skyscraper. Well I just know that in the midst of my chemo storm when I was alone with my dog because my trusted cousin had run off with some of my chemo money I felt my lowest! It was at this low point that I spoke with Mother Barlow and she birthed my prayer language right there on the phone in my favorite chair as I held my pug. Yep it was no longer babble to me because I realized that this was my natural language from young. Deep huh? After all we are spirit first and flesh second so it makes perfect sense to be able to speak in spirit right? Feast on that concept and let it marinate!

HANGING MYSELF HAD A DEEPER PURPOSE

You know the way God has me writing this book or should I say account of my journey with Him is absolutely phenomenal! Some areas in my life I didn't want to go back to because those experiences take a lot out of me emotionally. I love the Lord with ALL my heart but going back sometimes I literally have to ask him to hold my hand as I travel whether it is back, during or forward. Speaking of holding my hand last night I watched an award show where they mentioned live on the air with one of the music award presenters putting up a symbol of horns and praying to Satan for the music. Several in the crowd did it and one of the music groups who boldly showcased the simple to pray to Satan actually won. Now I don't know if anyone noticed but that was illustrating the power of Satan. There it is, put boldly in our faces but yet when we go to talk about Jesus on the air we are shut down. We can talk about another teacher but my Savior, the Son of God is like the new cuss word. Why are we hanging ourselves when we should be standing up for Christ?

Getting back to last night the last episode I watched was a show on how a music celebrity shot himself by accident and how the bullet was a mere centimeter from his heart. Now this music icon has proven that you can try to take your life and make an impact but I was thinking man if you used your testimony to promote the power of God, the living God, that would set the world on fire! I'm going to pray right now that Christ infiltrate this popular individual's heart and have him become an instrument for Christ.

Last night after watching certain performances and one in particular it disturbed my spirit so much so that between those images and the Satan prayer I couldn't sleep. It got so bad that I literally had to repeat the few scriptures that I fully committed to my heart over and over and ask Jesus to hold my hand. I demonstrated to my fiancé how I had turned on my stomach and held out my hand and guess what the Holy Spirit allowed my hand to rest in His. Just like when I was a little girl and my sister and I we were in the backyard on the swing-set and my Mother had to stop pushing my sister to go do some things in the house. She could see us out of the kitchen window and as my sister whined for her to come and push her so my Mother told her she was busy so ask Jesus and she did. Guess what my sister started to swing without anyone visibly behind her but it was evident that she was being pushed by another. Therefore from young the belief was so strong that now as adults we can't discount the power of the Holy Ghost or Angels. Thus when I felt something hold my hand I went to sleep peacefully and I awoke to a feeling of internal joy.

On another occasion I had a severe seizure after I had taken all of this herbal mixture from this lady's son who I may add was not licensed. I knew it must have knocked out all of my anti seizure medication out of my body so I passed out after struggling and when I came to my left side was holding and comforting my right side. I always said that it felt like someone was comforting me but it was me holding me. I know now that there was someone present, Jesus a powerful presence that you could tangibly feel. And as I'm writing this I have on my XM Praise Gospel station and a song entitled "Endow Me" is playing and they are singing about the power of the Holy Spirit and how it will make you live right. When I clicked on info to see who was singing this song I'm surprised but relieved that they are mainstream celebrities such as Coko, Faith Evans, Fantasia and Lil Mo. And here my partner, Mr. Holy Spirit and I just mentioned how powerful mainstream celebrities would be if they were to deliver such a song. Talk about the flow of the Spirit huh?

Angels have always encamped around me. When I was on drugs and was being bombarded with negative spirits and energy blaming me for mishaps of a close family member's life. I was told that it was probably my lifestyle that caused them to try and commit suicide for the second time. Well that spirit of suicide jumped onto me and the next thing I know I was wrapping a sheet around my neck and I jumped out the side window and proceeded to hang myself and out of nowhere I felt a force lifting me back up to the ledge so that I could climb back inside. Now the side of the house was all flat brick therefore I couldn't humanly grasp onto anything so the force that pushed me back up was an angel! During that exact time some friends of mine drove from Washington DC because I was on their minds super strong. I literally felt that force push me back into the house and there they were. Even writing this I still can't get over the fact that the side of the house was nothing but smooth brick so I couldn't have climbed on top of anything. God you are just too much! I just know that even back than God had me. The Trinity was and is still in effect you all, so DON'T EVER doubt the power for that force was my Lord and Savior saying not this one.

This morning the Holy Spirit prompted me to start studying Ephesians and while I'm writing this particular sentence I'm listening to Tramaine Hawkins' song "What shall I Do" where the lyrics talk about letting the Lord guide you to make decisions, and steps in life that will lead to eternity. She cries out that she'll wait for the answers because she knows the Lord will come through.

Well in Ephesians 1:13 and 14 it talks about once we believed in Christ, God claimed us as His own by giving us the Holy Spirit as he promised long ago. And the Spirit is God's guarantee that He will give us the inheritance. He purchased us with the ultimate price by sacrificing the very life and blood of his ONLY son Jesus. That's deep for me, which would be like sacrificing my dog for you. Not going to happen, the days of rituals and animal sacrificing were ceased when Jesus died on that cross. The only sacrificing we have to do is our lives, our thoughts, our actions, our words that is our sacrifice. I always pray that we would allow Jesus to shine through our lives.

It's funny because many are drawn to horror films but when the human body becomes possessed with an evil spirit we freak out! Well what about making a film where the person willingly allows a good spirit to take over; you know the reverse, um that is it another thought for a project thank you Holy Spirit after all this is your book I'm just the instrument, the vessel to depict your works, the testimonies for it's all about a more defined assignment!

THE AWARDS

You know it is joyous but painful for me to watch the awards and other shows where I know I have either worked with the individuals or was in their company sharing a word time and time again and then they disappear and bam there they are on television, the radio or a magazine. I'm personally tired but then again maybe God places or better yet positions me to be in individual's lives for the premise of providing hope in some way or a seeded word that will remain with them so that they may go onto their next season. But does it hurt, heck yeah. I have to wait on the Lord and just remember that He will never leave me nor forsake me and He knows the pain in my heart and He will carry me through. God knows our deepest desires He knows and I believe in the word Psalms 13:12 'Hope deferred makes the heart sick," and that's how I feel when I see all the manifestations around me, I feel sad. "But desires (longing) fulfilled is a tree of life" and I have to hold onto that. You see this scripture is twofold for me. One being that the Lord has used me to help to make others longing fulfilled and two; God will make my longing fulfilled in His Divine timing! Lord I see you turning things out for my good all around me and I have to be more patient. For I know the visions and manifestations that lie ahead of me. Thank you for being my partner for you are my greatest award.

My Essence is Hope

I was in a church meeting once and we were asked what our essence is? What do we feel we were placed on this planet for? I responded in front of a crowd that 'I felt that my essence is Hope . . .' What is your essence and do we truly live out our purpose? I know within my every cell that I'm born to bring hope to others via the media formats music, film and writing thereby using all formats such as the eyes, the ears and the mind being transformed to believe and feel hope. Now sometimes I get trapped and feel in my heart that there is almost no hope but then I have Jesus as my Lord and Savior and I'm reminded that He is the rudder of my ship. I prayed that God would allow me to memorize scripture because this was something that I had a hard time doing and then it happened. I was at a friend's house and she had this booklet on her table and my eyes went upon the scripture Proverbs 3:5, 6 "Trust in the Lord with all your heart, lean not on your own understanding. Acknowledge him in all your ways and he will direct your path." Well later I was speaking with my mother and she shared that one of the scriptures that she holds close to her heart is "Acknowledge the Lord in All thy ways and He will direct thy path." Well that is confirmation for my partner Mr. Holy Spirit had me memorize the same scripture and it is the first scripture I was able to remember and keep in my heart. For me that was and is hope to follow through by trusting God for often we can not see what lies ahead of us and many times it doesn't make sense. But if we are driving to Florida and the Holy Spirit tells you to take a longer route and everyone is screaming at you because you took the wrong turn well it's for a reason. The reason could be simply to avoid a negative or to get you at the right time at the right destination to encounter a positive! It is that simple and that is how the Father works. Or should I say Daddy which is what I hear so many people calling him these days.

You know years ago I wrote the lyrics to a song called "Father, Thank You" and I wrote Daddy but I was afraid as to how people might interpret the intimacy of it so I rewrote it as Father throughout the song. Now all I hear is Daddy and one time we were in service praising the Lord and my hubby broke out screaming "That's my Daddy!" This one guy who my baby looked up to turned around and said sternly to quiet down and everyone could see the embarrassment and those around him told him that he was not to let NO ONE steal his joy . . . . so the point I'm making is that our Daddy takes care of us even when we can't see our way through the muddled waters. God can, He knows what's best for us . . . . hence the song "God's Got It." God is in control even when we can't see it.

DREAMS ARE REFLECTIONS

You ever had a dream that was so memorable that you just kept on repeating it? I used to always dream and I mean I would dream deeply. One time I had this dream and there were all these people I knew who were dead and an older cousin of mine was driving them around. Come to find out in real life that she has never driven in all her 80 plus years of being on this planet. And now that I think about it she was driving her husband and a few others from that same Parish. I saw her husband when he was on his death bed in severe pain and he told me he saw his predeceased granddaughter and she was asking for her Papa but he wasn't ready. I believed him because I was told by a sincere individual and somehow I knew that I was connected to the dead. One time I showed up at a friend's death bed and I could just see his handsome smile and I tried to call other acquaintances and friends to come to the hospital but the majority did not but I knew his time was near. I whispered in his ear for him to let me know he was alright when he passed over. Well later that night I was at a favorite local nightspot and low and behold I saw him flash before me and then an eccentric well known cousin of mine smiled at me and said, "Oh you saw that too?" That was my first experience since seeing my great-grandmother in my sleep all dressed lying in her coffin the day before her funeral. Apparently she was wearing exactly what I saw!

Well getting back to the story I saw that same granddaughter the grandfather had seen the day after she passed and my dog was barking and my mother called while on a cruise to see if everything was alright and my mother never calls while on a cruise however this time she felt something wasn't right. That grand daughter was a cousin of mine and my partner's niece who was killed in a bike accident. When I think about my ex partner of almost a decade, we went through so many deaths together but this one was so close. This was a child I took under my wing, a child who lived with us, amongst us and around us and today her memories will forever live within us. I was so obsessed with how this child died who broke her neck when the impact of the bike made her fly onto the rigid rocks by the ocean. I wanted to know did she feel any pain and that night for the first time in my life I ended up sleep walking and walked right off my stairs and landed onto the lower level. I heard clear as day a voice say, "As quickly as that happened is as quickly how Aly spun into the air and landed onto the rocks in a flash." That was something I tell you with my partner screaming her name "NO Aly" and her sister on the phone and then her two nieces begged me to come to the funeral but I remained abroad. It was a blessing that they included my name amongst the family in the newspaper though. After that I would often see her in my dreams and her many look-alikes everywhere. I even kept calling my goddaughter her name for a minute whose name was close mind you.

But you know out of ALL my dreams the one that stands out the most is the one that made me look at myself for who I really am and not how others view me. It was based upon the following:

They had this pyramid scheme that I joined one time and then we got my sister involved on the back end and then she won the money something huh?

Any hoo I went to sleep and dreamt were I saw some money sticking out from underneath this car. I went to pull it out and all of a sudden it just kept coming I mean dollar after dollar and I was looking around because I felt embarrassed that I was gathering all this money and it wouldn't stop. Well eventually it did and I went on a spending and carousing spree. In this dream I was a man and the place reminded me of New Orleans with all the brothels and outside verandahs and stuff. After a period of time my friends and I decided to leave this particular city. It was like a scene from the classic movie the "Sound of Music" that my mother took me and my siblings to see every summer during some of my formative years. Well we left this town and I think we were escaping because I saw nothing but flames. We were climbing this huge green hill that was on the side of a sparkling lake. As we were climbing the hill I started to laugh at my mates because they were all gray and older looking and I said to them, "Where have the years gone because I still feel super young." They told me to look in the water at my reflection because obviously the way I was acting I had never stopped to look at myself, like the Michael Jackson song says, "Take a look at the man in the mirror." Well remember I'm in heavy dream mode here so I look into the water and there I was; the face of a lion . . . You talk about spooked and that woke me up immediately. I was so stunned that this is the only dream to date that I have ever written down! What do you think it means? For all my readers I would like to know so email me your views at **hismultimedia@yahoo.com.**

I strongly believe that people enter and interweave in each other's lives if not for a season, a mere reason that may or may not lead to a lifetime. Some relationships are meant to be nothing more than a time flash or as I just told a friend a "space saver." You know the ones that were a big wow for that moment. Others are links to draw us closer to the purpose that we are designed for. That is why we must seek wisdom and guidance so that our paths are truly directed. I've learned that life is simply lessons learned so nothing is a waste of time. Now for someone out there God has given me a word and that is for you to marinate on this, "You know at the end of the day it's all about God and our God is not of laziness or confusion so if that is the case in your life than reevaluate." Just saying . . . Live the dream, don't be a dreamer!

I JUST GOT IT (SCRIPT)

You know I pride myself on the fact that obedience is better than sacrifice and now I'm living it. I mean it wasn't just not having sex with my husband before we got married and doing it God's way that was so great, it is my daily living that makes it the right way. I have a girlfriend who stated on this television episode that we have made wrong and sin so glorious that doing right seems wrong. It is one of the greatest but must truthful lines on any reality TV show. Yesterday I spoke with one of my sisters who is Muslim and we talked for a good two hours and our lives parallel each other. We talked about doing a film and writing our stories into a script and you know what it was exactly what I had envisioned eight years prior. Now I had to go through all the crap before any script would be complete enough to make it into a movie. But now with Christ within me I'm being molded into the person that I'm capable of becoming!

Recently I kept questioning as to why I keep attracting people with borderline personality disorders or are emotionally unavailable and I just got it. I'm being made aware of it through counseling so that I can recognize all of what I've been through as a child. The physical, emotional and sexual abuse has all played a part in who I have became and what mistakes I have allowed myself to make as an adult. The glue to all of it is the Christ that lives within me. That's the trick to holding all the pieces together. Otherwise I'll be emotionally defrayed as well with all that I've been through. You know I always tell others that children are like computers and what we put into them largely determines what types of individuals they will become. I have the opportunity to constantly plant positive spiritual seeds and examples into my stepson. I remember one day he asked me where was I going out to and I told him to a service and he said, "Why you are already holy." Now is that cute or what? Talk about a compliment that means that he has been watching me through the good and the bad; it makes a difference as to how he views me and I don't ever want that to change! The other day when I was going out I said to him and my nephew, "Can you believe it, I'm going out dancing!" and they both laughed. It was these same two who saw my wedding dress first and I asked them for their opinion and they gave me the thumbs up. I strongly believe in creating positive imprints for people to draw on for future references even when times are glum.

With Christ in my life there is a constant positive and joyous imprint and we can reflect this in the way we treat people and the things we do. My Muslim sister and I draw on the commonalities in our lives and our faith. We are not trying to outshine or judge one another but display the God within us. She calls him Allah I call Him all the names of the Trinity along with Jehovah and do not hide that Jesus Christ is my personal Savior. I believe He is the Son of God and she sees Jesus as a great prophet. I respect her and she respects me. The other day when we had a disagreement I told her that I was going to love her through it. Being a Christ follower is about actions not deeds. Like I stated earlier we have to live this thing! It's true what they say you have to stand for something or you will fall for anything. I personally recognize the same demonic spirit that has been traveling on my journey when it comes to my personal love life. I told my same Muslim sister back then I would get so upset because I couldn't fix the depression in the people I loved so I turned to cocaine. Today I've made the choice to turn to Christ and through counseling I have both spiritual and positive reversal tools to change me and love me better.

Out of this life choice concept has evolved motivating and powerful message songs! However it was early this morning when the Holy Spirit was telling me to get up and of course I was saying, "I'm still tired" but because I was obedient I got it, I just got the revelation as to why I dated the same types. As one of my best friends put it, they are all the same both men and women you've dated. Thank you Lord for awakening me not just physically to arise this morning but also spiritually for as you showed me in Philippians 4:7 that true peace comes from letting God be in control and than it clicked. If I just keep my mind on Christ when I'm being distracted the answers shall be revealed. All my life I have been attracted to people that I've been trying to fix, trying to show them about unconditional love when actually they were just doing the best they could with the examples that they were given. I reacted to their behavior; I got caught up in their world! I gave them the power when ultimately the moment I began to seek God more; the more I gave up trying to handle circumstances on my own and asked for guidance from my Creator. I hope you readers are following me. I am learning to be transitioned and that is what WIT (Women in Transition) teaches us, to transform our mindsets. Like a baby being taught, our conditioned minds are being reprogrammed to do things differently because we think differently! God aligned me with my counselor who believes as I do beyond positive thinking but the belief within that created the entire concept of light. Yes the light bulb was just clicked on when it came to me and I know by seeking Godly counsel I'll be alright for I'm actively proving God as my Bishop G would say. By me asking the Holy Spirit what to say, or what to do in my circumstances is displaying that light shines through ANY darkness whether it be debt, murder, molestation, abuse it doesn't matter. God is able!!

LAST NIGHT IT BEGAN (REST IN PEACE MY BROTHER TAMEL SIMONS)

Last night a meeting was held and a group of ten showed up. I had prayed that whoever was meant to show up would in order for positive change to occur. My one requirement was that we all came from a spiritual place and therefore knew that there is a higher being, a God that reigns supreme over our lives. The result was that it was all agreed that our country was broken and we needed healing. The cross section consisted of those that the Holy Spirit led as instruments to share the vision with a mission statement in place and consequently a meeting of the minds manifested itself. We exposed ourselves and took off the masks and became real and a 'Keeping It Real' movement for Christ was borne in Bermy. Brother Tamel I don't know why you didn't turn to me for you knew my fight. You always brought the best out of me, such a pure spirit. I remember at that prayer service in the park with the Premier and the Spiritual leaders in our community you told me to get up there with my camera with the big boys. Yep you and Trevor, I will do my best to be a trooper but when I return home I will miss your smile but I feel your presence as I write. Gone too soon.

RESCUE MY HEART

We just came from an intense weekend spiritual retreat where we looked at our hearts. It was called "Journey of the Heart" and just this morning I was listening to a favorite song of mine "Rescue My Heart" by Michelle Williams and my partner said alright let's start writing again. Don't get it twisted I love the Lord so much that I literally entrusted my life in His hands. And thinking about it that is a joke statement after all I only gave Him back which I already was, His! Now I'm not talking about getting saved, reborn or baptized I'm talking about my entire life. I got married to a man where it all began as a spiritual journey of the heart. We didn't fall in love based upon physical attraction but spiritual love and it's a journey believe me. But I answered the call from the moment my partner, Mr. Holy Spirit told me to go and speak with him to days later making that first call. I heard it clear as day after I went to witness to him that he would be my husband and I said, "What? Oh really." But deep in my heart I knew that was the Lord and I had to obey no matter what. It is like the lyrics and melody to a song God gave me "no matter what comes your way please don't stray just listen to his voice. People come and friends may go but

God's love remains the same." You know when my partner the Holy Spirit gave me that chorus I said okay but I didn't appreciate its full meaning until this weekend when I met with my Pastors in the early morning by a lake with him strumming on the guitar. It was the three of us and we were feeling the presence of the Lord singing chorus after chorus and I told them about the chorus God had given me but I couldn't fully remember it that time but I had Holy Spirit boldness to mention it and the next morning I sang it with a group.

FEELING IN LIMBO

I attended an event last night and let me just give you the set up. I've been working everyday with my parents on my house and I put in a few hours and yesterday I felt this sudden peace so I laid down after a quick shower and went into this heavenly sleep. I felt so refreshed when I awoke after going into a deep ram sleep for forty five minutes that I just wanted to call people but then I remembered that the phone didn't have long distance so I scrolled through my US phone and came across a friend of mine's name and local number so I dialed it and left the message that I was going to a whale watching film. You see earlier I saw in a Bermuda newspaper that they were having a film screening at the college and I knew I wanted to go to meet some new people. I pray every day that God will direct my path because as my line goes we can only see down the street or road but it is God that sees around the corners of our lives!

Well getting back to the story which if you haven't noticed by now is that I can be long winded because I want to get every point across.

While I was getting ready to go see the film a friend called and asked me if I wished to attend an event with her so I accepted the invitation and guess what? I was able to meet new people including those who I felt had done me in so to speak, but they greeted me and said I was glowing but that was the beginning. The real purpose was when we started to talk about God at this scenic bar setting on an open patio overlooking the ocean, it was simply breath-taking! Then to my amazement there was a former neighbor of mine who I forgot had his roots in singing and a few wondered why he chose to sing with an older non colored band instead of using numerous musicians of color that were everywhere. My response was that they can open doors for him and are people too. I spoke to the young man and told him I was proud of him and thought he was quite smart. He said, "I've gotten so many gigs with this band and I'm at peace because they are the most disciplined set of individuals that I've ever worked with." Then I don't know how it happened exactly but I think I must have said that we have to thank God for all the blessings that are being bestowed upon you and he looked at me and said the unthinkable, "I've given up on God, I've denounced Him."

Well it was at that point when I knew why I was there. I talked to him and lifted my shirt to show him my arm and told him how earlier that morning they couldn't get blood out of my arm and they told me to pray and I remembered to call on Jesus and repeat the name out loud and instantly they were able to tap into my vein after having tried for almost a hour. I discussed the galaxies with him because my partner the Holy Spirit showed me that was where he was at. You know from my close relatives, to my friends on face book and others in the generation just under me there are so many that denounce God. I ask how is that possible in a country where God is so prevalent, just how? But there is definitely a gap between those who are in ministerial positions who have been bitten by the power bug and those that are in the next generation that will lead. Ironically the function I attended was based upon the concept of networking and supporting each other's endeavors so that when they become the next leaders certain principles will be in place. It is time that we place the reverence of God back where He belongs, the foundation!

WELL HERE WE ARE

I'm home once again and my parents are one of the few on the island that do not have the internet. Now everyone has cell phones and hi-tech blackberries so the guys in the house don't need a computer and my parents have no need but this is killing me pardon the wording for those that take every word literally! This morning I realized that while I'm here I have to make myself explore the side of my brain that has creative options. With the computers and easy access when I'm in Philly, technology has become a necessity for me. However here I realize and respect that my parents truly keep it old school, literally. I mean they dip and transfer water from tank to tank, heat up water on the stove because my dad unplugs the hot water heater to save money so that in the morning there is no hot water. They do so many things old school and you know what I'm looking this morning at the positives of that. However when we have to plug in lights, watch my dad who is getting up there switching the water, opening the tank my spirit is saying, "I have to make some money Lord to take care of them and make them comfortable in their own home." My Mom said when I arrived two days ago and slightly complained about some things that she is on her way out of this world so she doesn't need the luxuries that I and others take for granted.

Now my parents have traveled the world and stay in the best locations not to mention my home next door is quite modern so I may not understand it all but the Holy Spirit my partner is telling me not to complain about the little things but enjoy and appreciate the big things such as the enjoyment that I get from being with my parents. I think in their minds they enjoy the basics because it reminds them of how far we've come. I can see why they are meant for each other and have learned to listen more. Now my Mom may drive a car that's computer operated with no manual winding down of windows etc but she'll tell you that she doesn't know how to work a computer. I feel the lesson for me this week is to appreciate rather than trying to dominate but at the same time hold my ground.

Therefore in a world that is spinning out of control I seek God's face like David did more and more in order to hold my ground. I chose to seek wisdom and direction for without Godly direction this world seems to have less affection and love. Everything seems to be microwave and rushed and as a result many souls are slipping through the cracks. I strongly believe during these end times the message is about ordering our steps because when we become out of alignment the enemy can position against us. Now many of you reading this might say what on earth is she talking about, has she totally lost it? Well how about when I arrived home to see my family a few days ago the moment I got off the plane I felt dizzy and heaviness. When I went to get my bags the only words I could get out was yes to the question if I needed assistance. I couldn't believe that I was having a partial seizure in my brain!

Here I am writing on a Saturday morning, a weekend not my usual Monday journaling. But this evening I will be giving my testimony for the first time at a women's conference. Now the past couple of days have been hell and heaven. I say this to say that I went to inquire about a process whereby I could become more permanent for my husband and family. Well I had been given this number and lost it a few times and then I kept putting off the date until the week before I was to go home and have a life changing meeting amongst my people. I was accused of certain things and my heart was saddened because I knew the truth. I knew God had it when I asked Him who should I share with, who Father. Abba who? Around the same time my computer became infected, my music that I composed suddenly disappeared and it looked like someone had gotten into my system. I knew it was the enemy and I said, "Oh Satan not today" and proceeded to get my laptop when I banged the top of my head where my tumor cut is. You talk about pain well I had this lump that looked like the incredible egg. I knew I had to go church, not the regular Bible training but church. My soul cried out for worship, nothing more nothing less! I said to my husband later that day after our supper that I felt like going to our church. Now remember I just said I didn't feel like going to our church's Bible training because I needed church. But the Holy Spirit said, "No you go to your home church" and when my husband was getting ready to take me I thought he was just going to drop me off as he usually did but he said the Holy Spirit said for him to come in. Now when we got there we expected training papers but no one was in the narthex. Let me tell you the Holy Spirit had instructed my Bishop to have just that, church. That was some worship service were the presence of the Lord just filled my every cell. The singing, the praising, the worshipping; now that is what I'm talking about. There is no drug on this planet that can fill you like the presence of the Lord can.

CHERISH THE MUSIC OF PEOPLE'S HEARTBEATS!

Artists Jels n Monte 1st trip in Times Square, NYC

my babies Markus n Markel n niece Sky

my adopted Showell Family took me in

AJ enjoying nite after Grammy
event in the convertible

friend Gary

Mom, Mother Bobb, Joy n Daphene

Franz playing in concert

Godson Jordan Keith

Dez Ganier n Angelica

my friend Bob who is a brain
tumor survivor

My genuine good friends
Mike and Deneen

SISTERS having fun

with Goddaughter Teshay n
her mom Shawn

with Goddaughter Alae-jah

with brother Dean Carlos

with Jels n Diego

with Godson Kirk

with NIECE SKY

with the T-360 music crew

Barbara n Diego

Diego's birthday party with friend
Charlie n mom Barbara

You know how the saying goes I thought I'd seen it all well this applies to what happened to me last Saturday. I went to visit a friend after not seeing him for well over a year and it was great. We both had the brain tumor thing going on and had originally connected by residing in the same apartment building. Well we were supposed to go on a walk but he informed me that he had to help out at his school and if I wanted to help out as well so I said yeah. Now keep in mind we went from living in the same building to different sides of the city what a long drive but my hubby drove me there.

We walked and talked and it was like old times, just a new section of our lives. We both had purchased houses and still had the same bond despite our circumstances. They say you know you are true friends with someone when you haven't seen them in a while and when you do see them it was like yesterday and you never miss a beat. That's the music of genuine friendship never missing a beat never pausing as to what to say next. I prayed to God for that since so many friends had been taken out of my life I prayed for replenishment but only those with true hearts.

During the past few years I had so many people in and out of my life for a season that I felt like my life was paused on the spin cycle in a washing machine. So many lives had been taken from me that I now felt empty when it came to people including family. I mean in the past five years I experienced a lifestyle switch where so many I thought were my friends just stopped speaking to me no matter how many times I left messages. I was cut off for going "to the other side." Not to mention there was the break up or the subtraction of my long term partner of nine and a half years as well as her family. In addition there were the two murders of cousins, the disappearance of my spiritual family, my long term music partners, my spiritual group and the breakup of my favorite uncle and I. The straw that broke the camel's back so to speak was when the cousin I trusted and had taken in blatantly stole my chemotherapy money. Just writing this makes me weep and cry out Lord I need you. The song from Reverend James Cleveland "Where is Your Faith in God" is playing in the background and all I can do is have faith in Jesus and continue to work towards my purpose like it says in James 2:17. I need faith to save me from losing my mind, faith that I will live and not die and faith that this book will touch the lives of millions. If I wasn't journaling and having my private worship services with God every morning I would have certainly perished inside. That was a blow I'm telling you. It's been a heck of a ride you all! I asked God to clean my house and that's what He has been doing. I left my dream condo in the city of seven years and moved to an apartment for two years. I changed my life so I could meet new friends, left my church so I could find a new one and it was there that I would meet my husband.

You know the saying let go let God truly means just that. God has been oh so faithful and has given me not always what I wanted but what I needed. You know one of my favorite lines, 'we can only see down the street but God sees around the corners of our lives.' Many times we have to let go of the wheel and let Him do the driving for He knows what truly lies ahead. And that is where trust comes into play and even as I write this I just want to cry out, "Lord I love you, Lord I praise you for holding me tight." Sounds like a song right? Just maybe I'll go and write one after I finish my journal entries on this fantastic morning. You know God is truly about connecting the dots and this morning while I was in the bathroom I heard in my head "You are cancer free, you are cancer free!"

Switching gears I watched a show last night and one of the characters said that she was cancer free and was so overjoyed by the results. Well earlier on face book I responded to someone's prayer request and stated that I was a brain cancer survivor. That was the first time I had used those words. You see earlier this weekend when I was working with those junior high school kids I told them that I had a cancerous brain tumor so I could relate to their teacher/counselor; that friend who I originally met in the apartment building that I actually resided in years prior as a student. Upon hearing this they looked at me in amazement and I said, "Yeah it's been ten years." During those years there have been many complications but it could have been worse such as the paralysis my friend has on his left side and yet he still enjoys life.

Despite his weaknesses my friend Bob runs miles every week and is even a part of a runner's club. I went with him one time and all I could do is walk while he and his mates kept running past me. Now remember he has a partially paralyzed left side and therefore walks with a slight limp dragging his leg and has a curved left arm. The scripture that comes to mind pertaining to my buddy Bob Lutzick is one I heard three times on three separate occasions in three different venues. Somehow my partner, Mr. Holy Spirit gets that message across to us . . . . In Him I live, in Him I move and have my being . . . .

That is it as I often say, "I'm walking in my healing and destiny. I claim victory in Jesus that I am cancer free . . . for in Him I live, I move and have my being . . . Thank you partner Mr. Holy Spirit for being my director. I love you so much."

I've been so concentrated on the circumstances recently in my life that I forgot the excitement of life. The other day while my friend and I were walking through some of the former streets of my past life I had flashbacks of cocaine places, past relationship drama but at the same time there are the sweet memories of walking my baby pug to his first vet. "My little pooshka." Then in the midst of my mental reminiscing suddenly there were three guys who resembled bikers from a movie walking the largest canine I've ever seen. I asked if I could touch their dog and rubbed its back. It looked like a large Alaskan husky and I only knew that because I had recently watched a documentary on Greenland and the Arctic Circle. The "dog" was friendly but then I asked the guy was he some breed of husky and he replied as he strolled off "no" it was some word he used and I said, "I've never heard of that" and he said, "Oh it means a domesticated wolf." I was excited and felt fulfilled that I shared a moment of nature. I stood there in amazement because I remembered that a few nights ago I saw the similar "dog" recently in the movie "The Wolf Man" with my hubby. It was huge but beautiful and I couldn't believe I encountered it on the city streets. I had rubbed its back without the fear of knowing what it was. You see if I knew what it was I would have never touched it and that is the text message I sent out to friends and family.

This brings me to how we view life for if we knew what struggles and challenges we have to go through to get to that place of fulfillment we would never go there. And God knows this so He just connects the dots. But we have to be willing spirits to allow Him to move and position us; just like chess parts until we finish playing the game of life!

We must recognize that people and places are often for the seasons in our lives that once interconnected make up the parts or sections that we call our lifetime. Seeing and touching that wolf makes me feel that only the best is yet to come.

ANOTHER MONDAY COVERING

With a new week comes new problems to tackle. The enemy loves disaster and hates to see us moving forward in peace and unity. It seems that when problems come my way I don't have man to stand on I've got my true consistent everlasting comforter and partner the Holy Spirit to lean on. Every time something bad or let's call it a negative shifting occurs I can feel it in my inner core. As a matter of fact I got down on my knees in a church bathroom and asked the Lord to cover me in the blood of Jesus. This is something I learned from my Mother, well the covering part not the kneeling in public part!

Needless to say last night or should I say some hour this morning I felt like I was just laying in God's bosom. I'm used to walking with God and I would grab His hand ONLY when I really need Him. However I recognize that I'm starting to hold His hand more like a child does with its parent; sometimes letting go but now I find comfort in Him wherever I go!

WHEN FRIENDS DECIDE TO TAKE SUDDEN EXITS YOU KNOW GOD IS SWEEPING

You ever have people come into your life and the moment you put your trust and hopes in them then bam out of nowhere you get shot in the heart. It's a feeling were your very core becomes so beaten and bruised that you have nothing left to give. It's like the song says when you feel you can't go on give it to the Lord. You know within a three year period God literally swept my life. He swept everything from the people to the places to my practices. It may hurt in my flesh but over time I've learned through much prayers and tears that it is for my good. He removed me from all kinds of toxic relationships, some more personal than others. I was in counseling to empower myself, to learn to make changes and to stop being a doormat. Well let's see it He began opening my eyes when my music partners who I had invested heavily in both financially and emotionally decided to show their true colors once my cousin was murdered and they realized I couldn't give them anymore. Then there was the lady that came into my life through another friend when I was doing some filming for them and we bonded. We would talk about everything and she was there for me just as I was there for her including supporting all the legal advice for her personally and her music career and then came the big bang. She called me out of nowhere telling me she can no longer be my friend! What type of childhood garbage is that, especially the line were she said people are waiting in line to be her friend, I flipped. Then there was the girl who came to me about music and her woes and I invited her into my world and then she made the statement that she felt that she was more of a friend to me than I was to her. Now remember I'm still in therapy learning handles on how to stop being a doormat or letting the guilt trip get to me.

There were friends that were in my life for almost a decade and the moment me and my former life partner split they made the announcement that they were never really my friends despite the fact that I put them up not her and had helped them extensively from my heart but hey I guess I was no longer a part of their world. Then there were the close uncles who broke my trust. One sexually abused me and "I had to learn to forgive him and forgive myself. Then there was one who watched me get assaulted by these AIDS and HIV Infected transgender tenants who I had befriended. Now that is a story that deserves its own pages!

I felt so betrayed and again the issues that I HUMANLY STRUGGLE WITH are Abandonment and Rejection! I had to cry out to my partner, the Holy Spirit to guide me and ask Jesus to cover my heart and again I had to forgive. Then there was the one uncle whom I couldn't see living in caves or cars and begged to have him put in our apartment and he abandoned me by leaving me stranded at the airport. And the last one to date was the one whom I looked at as a father and he sacrificed our relationship and manipulated me by taking my trust and saving a voicemail so he could have his way to win my Mother's sister's heart; most would call that blackmail. Luckily my Mom listened to me leaving the message where I and he talked about how deep I felt about no one taking my deceased Aunt's place in my life so it was nothing bad. Then there was the spiritual mom trip and the list goes on from family to friends to business . . . . The bottom line is "people change" just like the song my former music partner and I wrote decades ago. And with him I guess I was taking too long to make anything happen despite all the thousands and he made off me in the interim and all I wanted to do was have two hours a week to write but hey time does reveal just as our buddies "Debarge" wrote.

You know there are seasons and for every being that comes into your life there is always a reason. I've learned that despite the fact that we are all human beings does not make us the same beings with the same spirits?

As long as we live on this earth there will be lessons to learn and the majority of them involve other people. I truly understand the Bible when it talks about guarding your heart. It is just as my counselor speaks about guarding your core, your inner being. I understand that most of my work has to do with relationships. My expectations may be too high. I'm not perfect but I'm learning that as long as I have a tight personal relationship with my Lord and Savior and allow God to control my life I can experience a peace that does pass all understanding and this is for real not just another cliché.

When people that we trust, love, share, and endure precious moments with do a 360 on us it's as if we are sucker punched in our inner core. We can't function, our insides feel as though they are being extracted from within and yet we still manage to survive, well most of us. Unfortunately there are those who have given themselves away once the silver cord is severed and they feel that they have nothing left to live for. My friends I'm here to tell you when friends, family or colleagues let you down there is someone who will never leave your side, His love is unconditional, and you can talk to Him about anything at anytime and don't have to worry about hearing it again. He truly is a friend that sticks closer than a brother, one that doesn't keep a check list as to what He has done for there is only one and as I'm writing this I can feel the anointing. I can feel the joy, the peace that passes all understanding as I journey this long train ride. That friend is my boo, my baby, my all, my main man, my protector my everything and never get it twisted I'm not talking about my other half(my true earth love) I'm talking about JESUS.

STILL RECAPTURING BLESSINGS

I've had time to consider how God felt, my family felt and what would Jesus do? So I'm officially inviting my uncle. And we'll see what else God lays on my heart to do because weddings are supposed to be happy times not times were we keep watch on those family members like my other uncle who represents bad vibes. Well like I said we will see I still have ten more weeks.

You know many things happen in a course of a week, lives change in a twinkling of an eye. For example on Saturday morning I was walking my dog and the Holy Spirit said get down and pray. I was fearful since the last time I got down on Walnut Street when I went to get back up my back cramped. Just imagine a Charlie horse in your back! Nevertheless I obeyed and got down openly on my sidewalk and said Lord you know if I get down I may not be able to get back up. Well the Holy Spirit guided me to applying a new method to getting down on my knees on that concrete sidewalk and when I told my sister the story she screamed, "What, you get down and pray IN PUBLIC!" I once heard this artist say to the people you have to declare Him in public because He died on the cross butt naked for you . . . Kind of deep huh?

Anyhoo I guess I was down on my sidewalk for a minute and this lady three doors down saw me and asked if I was alright so I told her that I was praying and she said, "That is a good thing." Then I said, "Actually I was praying for the neighborhood" and she said, "That is also a good thing." Shortly after I went to this amusement park with my new family and when we returned home all I could see was television news trucks and cameras with a crowd lined up with candles at the far corner of the same block in the same direction the Holy Spirit had guided me to pray over earlier that morning.

And to think earlier on in the week I found myself wondering what would the block be valued at if there was no corner store, would the value go up or down for when I purchased the house this was pointed out as a concern for people may loiter outside of it. Later I learned that it was a blessing and is run by Christian Koreans! So getting back to what had happened, one of the storeowners went after a shoplifter with her loaded gun to scare her and keep her there until the police came but they ended up wrestling with the gun. The result was the shoplifter shooting the storeowner four times with the owners gun. Now that corner is where a bus stop is located and trust and believe there are always people present.

That was such a beautiful sunny July 10th day. That morning I saw people walking their dogs as well as children riding their bikes on the sidewalk. Those four shots fired could have been four lives taken instead of the one. See how my partner, Mr. Holy Spirit works and how God intervenes. I know for a fact that God used me to pray on that sidewalk for the saving of lives and the interruption of the Accuser's plans of a massacre that day. And this happened for another testimony of how God shows up and shows out. To this day I have never seen that woman who I thought lived three doors down. I don't understand it but other people live there and apparently always have; long before I moved onto that block. I assumed she lived there because she was standing there. I guess she was an angel! I ceased questioning just like the vision God shows me with me holding an award shouting out, "Jesus is real you all." That is what my journey is about illustrating to the masses that Jesus is real you all . . .

A couple of years ago my cousin who is known to be a prophet called me up when I had just got of this train after having gotten of at the wrong stop due to being caught up negotiating a music contract for my singer cousin. I couldn't believe that they didn't want to include a monetary disclosure clause, even my lawyer thought that was odd. Well they later proved to be on the crooked side but that's who my cousin decided to flow with. My company wasn't even included in the original pertaining to a finder's fee or for advising since they said we could just trust them but time always reveals. Getting back to my point my prophetic cousin called me and told me that he just had a vision of me receiving an award in a formal gown with longer hair in front of many and I told him maybe it was the award they had in my name in Bermuda but he said no he saw this happening here in America. Well years later the crooks proved to be just that a stepping stone for my singer cousin who now works out of America with her new music celebrities. As for me the awards keep coming and I'm waiting for that huge award my prophetic cousin was referring to and the one I repeatedly see in a vision. But in the interim I'm doing my best to keep representing my Lord and Savior. And the lifetime achievement award goes to *Jesus Christ! (Clap, clap)*

THAT TRAIN RIDE

I just returned from my cousin's funeral who was senselessly murdered, yet another one. Now I find out that a family friend died worrying and you know the saying "you are going to worry yourself to death" well it applies . . . its real . . . Within that same week we lost two other family friends. During this year I have lost seven more and we are only into the month of July. Seventh month and more than seven deaths of persons that were a part of my journey and have been physically erased. It's almost like when we read how in the last days people will disappear, well that's how my life seems to be with people vanishing around me and to tell you the truth I'm not even that old and it's been happening for a while now in spurts. We may have some good years with very few deaths and at other times like 1989 I had twelve deaths in my family. Actually it was to the point I had to drop out of school.

On another occasion I specifically remember bringing in the New Year at Times Square and despite how intoxicated I was I had this need to go and see my Uncle Melvin. Now if I could have that strong desire when I'm drunk imagine how the Holy Spirit works in my life now that I'm clean! I just thought about that "Thank You Lord." Any hoo I was partying and saw some acquaintances one of whom passed due to not following doctors orders a few years ago . . . . Yeah continuing to smoke and drink while having a hole cut in their throat. Like hello! Are you not paying attention? But then again I continued to smoke like a chimney after I was diagnosed with cancer until I couldn't breathe that one night.

Ok getting back to Times Square it was lovely from what I can remember I was with my Aunt El while my Mother stayed in the hotel. After the ball dropped I left with those acquaintances who were going to a party along the Van wick and I knew this was close to my Uncle Melvin so I was breaking my neck to go and see him; something was pulling me. I convinced this handsome gentleman to drive me there and told him we could return to the Van wick party spot later. Well we got lost and despite my clouded head God knew where I was going. And let me pause again; isn't it true that many times in our lives when we are in a cloud and our flesh can't see its way out God ends up pulling us out. Just like a lifeguard jumping in to save that child that is drowning. Just as the lifeguard oversees that designated swim area looking out for those who may be in trouble so does our Father, I'm telling you we may think we're getting over but God never misses a beat you feel me . . . .

Point in case we finally reach my Uncle's in Jamaica, Queens and I hugged him and woke up my first cousins who tried to sober me up. I told him that I loved him and the rest of my family which is where I was partially raised. And as I'm writing this I just reconnected with some of them twelve years later at our cousin's funeral. Um boy I love my New York family! Whilst at my Uncle's we called my mother, she was still in Manhattan and didn't feel like making that train trip.

Mom said she would see the Smiths that following March after my sister's graduation which was in the next three more months. I returned to school and I was studying in the library and had told my parents to pray for this major exam I was taking. I can see the scene right now; while I was in the library studying a cousin of mine suddenly walks up to me. Actually I went to that school because that particular cousin was there on a soccer scholarship and despite the fact that I got into other prestigious schools I chose this particular one because I wanted a familiar face.

Getting back to that Philadelphia college library scene; like I said I was studying minding my own business when my cousin approaches me saying "Aren't your parents here?" and I said, "No I just spoke with them night before last in Bermuda." And he replied, "Well isn't your Uncle dead? I responded and yelled, "What that's impossible I just saw him a couple of weeks ago." Well the next thing I know my parents and my Uncle Donald and his now deceased wife, my Aunt Elaine were there to pick me up. My family scooped me up in a van and the next thing I know we were driving to North Jersey and they told me how the same Uncle I broke my neck to see that New Year's morning had passed from leukemia. You can imagine how devastated I was! That was my first death experience of someone close to me. It was also the beginning of me recognizing my God given gift of sight, some call it being a seer.

My parents were so sweet in trying to shield me from the sudden news because they knew how I felt about my Uncle but that big mouth cousin got to me first knowing I didn't know. But I guess somewhere in our lives we all had that experience of secretly wanting to be the first to declare something. It's human nature but some get out of hand if you know what I mean? You have those friends or family members that rest assured you can count on to be those special news report bearers! It's almost as if we silently appoint these individuals and eventually look to them to receive whatever news. And on a serious note you know readers writing this today was a breakthrough for me in accepting my favorite Uncle's passing. Wow my first cousin and I used to hang tight with stayed up until dawn just crying and reminisced about her dad. Yep my Uncle Melvin. After all these years I still miss his lively presence.

WHAT SET THE PATH OF BEING OUTSIDE THE BOX

I attended a semi-private high school were I was the only one other than this much older girl who came from my primary school. Everyone else went to schools with familiar faces. When I was presented with three top schools to attend were I knew I wouldn't know anyone I accepted the challenge to go outside my box!. My second mommy Aunt felt that Warwick Academy is where I should go due to its strong discipline and high success record of academic achievements. Something inside of me told me to go DESPITE the fact that I wouldn't know anyone. I went beyond the familiar and this has set the course for my life. From the point on I've lived my life outside the box. Thanks Guys . . . .

Recently one of my spiritual leaders that I looked up to called me weird in front of a bunch of people and I had to call her to let her how I felt in order to release it. I explained how I felt the familiar feelings of being hurt and embarrassed because I was always seen as being different. We discussed it and moved on. As I'm writing I'm crying because I know God called me and yeah I'm special. The Bible does say that we are a peculiar people. The Holy Spirit just told me to also let go and be the bigger person and extend a wedding invitation to my Uncle so I made sure that he was the first invite that I mailed out. Now whether he comes or not is on him.

And guess what he didn't attend my wedding I'm sorry to report!

A Time to Reflect

Here we are a New Year, a new season, a new reason, and I have a birthday tomorrow wow. So I get to reflect on not just the last year but the last decade and how I plan to use all that I've learned to move forward. I mean so much happened in the last decade of my life that I could write a thousand books. I fought cancer twice, went through four clothing sizes due to the discovery of my systemic lupus, went through clinical trials for brain cancer, lost all of my female reproductive parts so I was told, and as a result felt de-womanized if that is a word . . . . hum. I quit smoking cold turkey and all drugs which is a story in itself. I brought and sold a few properties and took care of my heart. Went from being in a long germ relationship with a woman who I married and divorced; to falling in love with a man and marrying him.

It was a decade alright and I got to travel and do missionary work as well as documentaries. Let's see I've owned a record label, a publishing company, a multimedia company, had newspaper columns, started CD reviews, two television series, assisted artists in their quest for fame, produced CDS, written songs and after all of this my greatest accomplishment that I'm proud of is falling in love with Jesus! There I said it for I was on a quest for the joy that my partner, Mr. Holy Spirit fulfills me with. And as I'm writing this I'm thinking about all the people that have been in and out of my life from family to friends to tenants to artists to "frein-enemies" and who has always been there? God has always been a constant in my life. The one thing that I haven't completed is this book.

Now I'm feeling a bit sick but at least I got to go to the parade with my immediate little family as they are referred as and show my husband what family life is really about. I'm in a new season of my life and with God at the head I can't go wrong. Of course there are always snags but with a son always correcting you about every word that sounds vaguely familiar to his sense of cuss words how could you do anything less than want to be the best. God granted me with additional years beyond the time medical doctors stated. I feel blessed and thankful for all what God has allowed me to go through in order to strive to become the best. And you know why because my Lord and Savior deserves the best and I was created by the best. So may God bless you as you reflect on your journey for without the pitfalls there would be no hands to grab onto and wouldn't you rather know which hands pull you up and which ones are there to bury you?

This is why we need to go to our Father and ask our partner for that Holy Spirit guidance along this life's journey. Trust and believe the enemy of darkness never sleeps so neither should we! We can rest in the comfort of knowing that our Father goes before us but we can never become too complacent with anything in life other than knowing that you know for sure that Jesus Christ died on the cross of Calvary and shed His blood for our sins not His but ours. Now that is a deepie . . .

IN THE MIDST OF THE MOTHER OF BLIZZARDS THERE IS OUR FATHER

You know God has a funny sense of humor and His ways are definitely not our ways. Two days before Christmas I kept reciting the scripture Romans 8:28 "All things work together for the good of those that love the Lord" and Jeremiah 1:8 and 1:19 where He adamantly states that He is with us and rescues us. Well I had been begging God to show up and show out especially to my husband. In addition my husband was stating how I needed to mend a broken relationship with one of my uncles and I stated that I had given him so many opportunities but if he decided to call I would act like nothing happened. Anyhoo with all that being said we drove five hours to spend the Christmas weekend with my cousins and their extended family in Massachusetts. I wanted to share this moment with my hubby and after much prayer God made it happen. Our drive to Massachusetts was smooth until we took a wrong exit and once we realized we tried to turn in one of the state trooper turn points.

I had just told my hubby how I knew someone who got stopped over the George Washington Bridge in New York for going too slow in the fast lane. Now here we are driving slower than normal looking for one of these illegal turn points and all of a sudden there are flashing lights behind us with a muffled voice over the bullhorn. None of us could understand what he was saying so we stopped the car. My phone was ringing at the time and I recognized that it was someone calling from Bermuda but I didn't recognize the number and as the state trooper got out of his unmarked car I dropped the phone and without even looking at one another we both instantly raised our hands in the surrender signal. Well the trooper said he flashed us for our safety because we were driving too slowly in the fast lane. How ironic is that with the story I had just told my hubby? Now imagine if we had actually turned in the illegal turn point we would have been fined because he was right behind us in an unmarked car. Now I know I prayed with our Reverend friend the morning we were leaving for the Angels to go before us and surround us but hey . . . . I actually posted on face book that you know you are from the city when you raise your hands when stopped by the state trooper only to find out that you were driving too slow in the fast lane. And that was just the beginning of our Christmas adventures.

We had a great stay with my cousin and her husband at their incredible home. My husband enjoyed himself so much that he wished he could have stayed for one more day and I guess we should have but then we wouldn't have experienced God in the mix beyond usual circumstances. You know hen little things happen and you say that was nobody but God who prevented me from going here or doing x y z. I just knew within my spirit that I had to get to my cousins because it was a divine appointment. I didn't know what or why but everything in my core was craving to go like a smoker needing a cigarette! My husband couldn't understand the importance but I knew there was divine significance and told him every time I feel like this something always happens and it's a lesson that needs to manifest.

After enjoying ourselves we looked at the news and they said they were expecting a blizzard and twenty six inches of snow so we agreed that we would leave two hours earlier than the time we had set. Early that morning I looked out the window and saw some snow swirling and everyone was saying, "Oh that's just snow flurries nothing heavy." Therefore we took our time and left a half an hour later then scheduled.

As we left Massachusetts the snow came down harder and the further we drove into Connecticut the weather went from calm snow falling to roads being filled with so much snow that you couldn't differentiate the side markings of the highway. The highways turned into backstreets and cars began swirling and sliding. Out of nowhere you couldn't see and there was almost zero visibility. The snow started looking like a tornado moving rapidly in circular motion with high winds. Of course you had some larger and higher vehicles overtaking and speeding as if they were really going to get far. Some of those same cars we saw further down the road stuck in the snow or spun out. So here we are driving slowly, almost creeping to be honest. We got excited when we saw the occasional snow plough in front of us and then everyone started to follow them. There were moments when we saw single drivers swerving and my husband screamed for them to get out of the lane. Then there were those who would suddenly stop because of a pile up due to everyone sliding on the slush ice. We had to keep putting the window down because of the ice buildup and my husband simultaneously scraped the windshield on his side and drove. At one point at the suggestion of my cousin on the cell we began looking for the lodging signs. However when we went to find them it was almost as if they disappeared in the snow since the roads were barely drivable.

Thank you Lord that before we left Philadelphia we anointed the car with oil and prayed and did the same before leaving Massachusetts. For some anointing yourself and objects may be a ritual but when you know that you know that there is power in the blood of Jesus there is no norm. Every time you anoint there is purpose. If you readers don't remember anything else from this book please remember to anoint with purpose, we believe for there is no greater name than that of Jesus and when you anoint in the blood of Jesus believe like never before. There is without a doubt protection when you trust Him literally with your life NO MATTER WHAT . . . for you were created for His purpose for His plan for we are merely instruments to be used and played by our Heavenly Father, Lord God Jehovah!

Now getting back to the adventures of God we could just about see so my husband said he would be the look out for street markers on his side and I would do the same on my side. When he asked me how was it on my side I would normally respond covered. I could see the tips of the black railings on my side when we crossed throughways and then I took a minute break literally and my partner Mr. Holy

Spirit had me peak over and when I did I couldn't see any railings for they were completely covered by the snow. I rolled my window down and looked over and there we were heading straight into a ditch so I started screaming, "In the name of Jesus we plead the blood of Jesus" and asked my husband to move to the other side. He got mad and told me to stop being paranoid and I told him I was just calling on Jesus and the Angels to go before us. I didn't tell him about the ditch until later and that was the only time that I blurted that out loudly. Nobody can't tell me that Jesus isn't real or that Angels don't exist!

Then was the time we were turning to follow the service and lodging sign and I felt in my spirit like giving up and then my church called on one of those programmed calls and when I saw my Bishops face I became excited and listened to what he had to say about protection and immediately my spirit calmed back down. Talk about calling at the right time! That is what I refer to as divine timing. After that we came upon some signs and didn't know whether to take a left or right so I tried to call others but there was no answer. I realized later that no one was meant to answer just like we weren't meant to find the lodging area.

When we couldn't get in contact with the cousin who gave me the original directions it prompted me to call my other cousin who told me to take the highway I 95 and then I spoke with her mom on three way and her mom called my estranged uncle. The one who my husband had said was getting older and it would be nice if we made amends. Well that same uncle called me and like I said earlier to my hubby that if he called I would act like nothing ever happened. So when he called that's what I did and he guided us from New York into New Jersey and to the gas station since we were almost empty. Now remember what I said about that scripture Romans 8:28.

Earlier while on the phone with my estranged Uncle when I saw the whiteout with the tornado snow showers, I cried out to God that I didn't want to die like this. I'm smiling because who am I to tell God how I should die but I cried out anyhow and my Uncle heard me desperately pleading to God. As far as I knew he didn't have that type of Jesus/God relationship thing going on. He did however see me transform my life from my lifestyle of drinking and smoking to a renewal of my mind. Umm I must get that song recoded again, "It's Time."

Here is another kicker; while we were waiting to get on the George Washington bridge there was so much snow that none of us knew if we were on it or not. We were so disillusioned after waiting for three hours in traffic only to find out later that we were stuck on the ramp. While waiting we had to use the bathroom in public and my boo put coats around me while others were patiently waiting and shaking the ice of their windshields and wipers. I know that memory will stick in my hubby's head for that made him laugh. Now while waiting I went to dial my Aunt Jan who lives in New York but somehow my partner had me dial my other uncle a respected Reverend in Georgia and as soon as he answered I smiled at God and asked Uncle Darius for prayer. You see I was subliminally instructed to have prayer for it says when two or more are gathered He is in the midst and it gave my husband the hands on opportunity to see how the order of God works.

That prayer went before us and we praised him in advance. I know that was no accident but a divine call literally. Immediately when we got on the New Jersey turnpike oh my gosh I was so tired that I wanted to snooze and my husband said, "Go ahead babe I got this" and when I did bam we started to slide and I started to pray in my head so guess what I couldn't go back to sleep. Somehow we ended up going to two service stations and at one of them the car got stuck in a snow mountain and people there had to help us get out. Forget the fact that I no longer driver since my brain cancer; my hubby told me to jump behind the wheel and steer as he pushed and that's what I did with no fear, no questions for we were in survival mode! Unfortunately the car wouldn't budge so we had to get a shovel and my baby dug us out while I jumped out and asked a service attendant for directions to the Pennsylvania turnpike. Thank God we were only thirty miles away. When we reached the highway my hubby started driving in the wrong direction and my wife mode asked, "Babe are you sure this is the right way because when I travel by train we pass that area and it's the wrong way." Anyhoo it was and he admitted that he had a bad sense of direction and we got on the right path. He became excited like we were driving in the 'Grand Prix' and said, "Babe we are almost home" and I said, "We aren't there yet." I wasn't being pessimistic but I knew that our adventure wasn't over and that accidents normally occur close to home. So here we are close to home having traveled through the eye of the storm against sixty miles per hour winds with snow coming up to our knees when standing. Then we get on the curve ramp and the car just spins and he looks at me and calmly steered the wheel away from the side guard where there was a serious ditch and we both called on Jesus. Then we reach literally to the opposite side of our house and the car gets stuck on a snow bank as we try to turn the corner. And what is behind us at 4:30a.m? A Septa bus with two drivers. The drivers got off and helped us get out of the snow bank. Really how did that happen at that hour and where did they come from?

The Bible speaks to us about entertaining Angels unaware. At first my husband was saying that they better drive around us and got a bit frantic but I kept praying saying, "Lord you brought us this far" and remained calm. After they helped us I said to make sure that we toot the horn and wave. We rolled down the window and shouted out thank you! The strange thing was that there were two helpers but as the bus drove past we waved at only one person, the other had disappeared so I know that was an Angel! After hearing my mouth the Lord probably said let me send one of my boys to help them out.

About eighty percent of the time someone is always parked in our spot in front of the house but God had it laid out until the end and NO ONE was parked in front of our house. Snow was piled all around us but God held our spot so we would not have to drive around in the snow or walk any further. Not to mention that the neighbor had dug out our spot out so we didn't have to shovel for it was already done. God is a God of order and we cannot forget that. When I entered the house at 4:40 a.m I called my former estranged Uncle so that he could tell the rest of the family that we arrived home safely. That was my partner guiding me so that all of the family would now know we were communicating. And more importantly he said to me, "Thank God He brought you home safely" and I said. "That was nothing but Jesus!"

I found out later that my family was even more concerned because my cousin's friend had just got killed by hitting a tree and when they went to look at the tree, it was not split and the car was not smashed and those who were there were puzzled over how could this have happened. My response to my cousin was when it is your time, it's your time! I foresaw us flipping over, I saw our older car dying, and there were no ambulances or police to hardly rescue anyone in the numerous car pile ups. As a matter of fact the Mayor of New York was pleading on the radio for people with bobcats, trucks etc to come help the frozen city. But we had the greatest helper of all, my partner Mr. Holy Spirit who steered us on command in the name of Jesus!

Tell me that wasn't an adventure and a lesson in endurance, team work, mending and most of all a 'God show yourself series.' I had prayed for my husband to have one of those intricate "Only God can" moments I just didn't know that I would be with him. This actively taught me family togetherness, forgiveness, the power of the name Jesus and the power of prayer. My hubby always says that there is a lesson in it for all of us and believe you me it was definitely that, a divine appointment. Fourteen hours, sixty mile per hour winds, drudging through knee deep snow was truly the mother of blizzards for 2010 on the east coast. Now look at God for only He has power over Mother Nature!

UP JAMMING WITH THOSE CHRISTMAS VIBES

Been up for about two hours and I'm supposed to write in my journal but got caught up on my face book and emails . . . you know how we do let's keep it real! And in between all of that I was trying to get my baby D taken care of for the Christmas weekend. Well here I am journaling and I have to get ready for church in a few and now the computer is about to shut off. What I love about this season is how happy everyone is until they almost get ran over by the shoppers and even then everyone's pretty cool. I love the fact that no matter how commercialized Christmas has become the essence of Christ is still being carried out in the way we treat each other. There's respect, laughter and joy even in the midst of the rush.

Yesterday my son and I just learned something new about the candy cane. I was at the studio and our engineer's wife gave out candy canes and a Jesus loves you button. I went to give my candy cane to my son when I got home, you know being motherly and he announced he didn't like peppermint. What a shocker since he eats every other type of candy. Check the God moment, it caused me to start reading what was on the card attached to the candy cane and I read it aloud to him. We both learned that the shape of the candy cane is a J for Jesus. The card said how the candy maker wanted to make sure that people didn't forget the true meaning of Christmas so I guess the Holy Spirit give him the idea, sorry partner it was you . . . The Holy Spirit inspired him to make the hard candy in the form of a J for Jesus and then color it white for His purity and red for the blood He shed for our souls. As a result we have the original J shaped candy cane with the red and white stripes. We learn something new every day and yes that was a God moment that we shared. Ok got to rest a bit before getting ready for service, can't wait to get my worship on. I'm wearing my red . . . . oh yeah . . .

IT'S A NEVER ENDING BATTLE

This morning I was just sharing what happened to me yesterday with a mother of a very famous family. I was telling her how her family is a living testimony and that they will have to reshape the world. First she was ministering to me than I was to her and then my partner said you need to write this in your never ending book. Well this book does seem to be as endless as my life. I first started three years ago and prior to that I was making sixty minute tapes and then my partner, the Holy Spirit pointed out that 'No' God wants me to do it another way and start typing an electronic journal of my life's journey. As you may have guessed I'm longwinded so I said, "Really?" Anyhoo here I am and I know that God will give me the finish point for part one. Getting back to what happened yesterday while I went to clean out one of the apartments that the tenants left in the most deplorable state and a lesson learned was not to sleep on anything. Just because a tenant pays their rent on time doesn't make it okay for them to destroy the property. Therefore it is important to do notified inspections at least every few months!

As I was looking for my keys I saw this beautiful neat lady walking up and down the street so I immediately thought she was from the outpatient house and was going to talk to her but my partner said to just observe. Then I saw these two guys pull up in their car and then she was passed a package; she immediately turned around and happily walked quickly up the street and around the corner and I mean she was moving you hear me. In my head I felt something say you remember how that tastes don't you; why not see where the drug dealer went. Child I couldn't believe I had that thought after all these years of being clean and then I remembered my illness and the effects and then honestly I was negotiating in my head when suddenly I started to sing the words to a worship song my partner had me write and I had happened to record it the night before. As I was singing the lyrics and melody in my head the feelings left! I said to myself and to my partner "Wow this song must be going to be a hit!" You chose me; you delivered me, healed me and transformed me. Well if that wasn't enough of Satan's game I went inside the apartment that was deplorable and while I was cleaning I came across a bunch of straws and some still had caked cocaine in them. Then the whisper said, "Just taste it" but you know what I rebuked that in the name of Jesus immediately. I gathered all of the straws and left them in a container so my husband could see them and I knew that God would cover him. The beautiful part was that I was able to go on cleaning and know that I'm delivered and walking in my healing. Gosh I love the Lord now I just have to work on some other issues for I know that I am a work in progress but my Daddy's got me.

God's Always in Sync

This morning the Holy Spirit, my partner woke me up suddenly only to find that my dog had vomited and pooped. I just got up like a robot and began running back and forth cleaning up the mess. This was 4 a.m and my husband doesn't get up until 4:40a.m. I tried to go back to sleep but couldn't and the Lord had me turn my XM Satellite onto the Gospel channel. At first I wanted to listen to the soft hits station but couldn't. Then my partner reminded me that you can't dictate to God are you insane? So I obeyed and it soothed my spirit.

I got up while my husband was in the bathroom and started reading the Word and my partner had me turn to what I thought was the book of Solomon and I began reading about his general observations and how there is always a time for everything. The Spirit had me look at this particular chapter and it was Solomon the author and the book was Ecclesiastes Chapter 3. I kept reading and couldn't wait to share on face book what I had learned but realized there wouldn't be enough space so here I am writing to share it with you. When my husband came out of the bathroom and had finished praying with me I told him to read the chapter and he told me that last night in his personal studies he wanted to read something else but the Holy Spirit had him reading the first two chapters of Ecclesiastes. Then it was brought to my memory how this Prophetess who is in our lives had told us to study certain books and one of them was Ecclesiastes. We may not be studying physically together due to physical restraints but we are studying together in spirit. It is all good for the prayers of the righteous availeth much for God knows I've been harping about us not studying the Word together. Like Solomon wrote having been God inspired that it's not about our timing but His timing after all who are we to dictate to the one who created the moon and the stars . . . . hello?

SIMPLY TUNE IN

Much time has passed since I last wrote in my electronic journal. Gosh I've revisited an entire countries and have come back home. I strongly believe more than ever in Christ manifestations along with Holy Ghost guidance and it is no joke, it is quite real. I guess that is why it was originally termed ghost because you can't visibly see it just feel it. And as I'm reminded by my partner it's also termed 'Ghost or Spirit' because no one on this planet has ever been able to draw it, paint it, or sculpt it. We have no tangible reference of it like we have of Jesus and other Biblical characters to prove their existence. All we have with the Holy Spirit is the proof of feeling, synchronicity, and manifestations of events, people, places and things. It is sought of like having the invisible man as your 'Seeing Eye' dog. But I'll tell you this my partner guides me to write, compose and produce as He comforts me, guides me and provides for me with a new found confidence level. I love it but I realize that I must tune in and recognize Him.

Today is Wednesday, December 1st, 2010 and my Dad has to get some more tests and all I can hear on my XM satellite station is Kari Jobe's song 'Healer' and "How nothing is impossible for Jesus for He holds my world in His hand and Jesus is all I need." Well how fitting is this being that I couldn't sleep because I have so much to finish. I keep feeling that I'm getting older as are my support team. I need to get this book completed as well as the songs, films etc that God has downloaded in my spirit before my family passes on. It is a lot of pressure, so much to do and so little time, "Lord I'm becoming more desperate for you." Um what a great song idea. I seem to have so many fires in the iron and all I can hear is a friend of mine saying "finish something!" You know the saying of how you may inspire others and motivate them to do but when it comes to myself well the only person I was told who is blocking me is me! I need to flow more with my partner and be guided in not just some actions but all. I need to follow through so here I am writing again after a month away from the pages that constantly turn in my head. I know that time reveals all but I can't just keep things locked in my head that need to be read. I write in lyrics but speak in parables and document reality for these pages are not just my stories but those of many of you. I apologize for walking away when I have so much more to say. So much for you to feed upon, for in Jesus the fountain never stops flowing and you will never go thirsty.

With God I desire more for myself, ideas never stop and it's because as I learned last night in Bible study that it is in our DNA to want what God gave us from the beginning, dominion over the earth. He gave this to us from the very start. Before I went home I asked that God continue to place in my life those He desired not who I desired. I prayed that He remove from my life all of those that are not meant to be and replenish me with those who are meant to be. When I was home I reconnected with some friends from my past and my buddy Carol Anne O'Mara who is now a mother of two sons told me how she remembered years ago how we sang in this group and I was the lead singer and they were my backups. I had forgotten that I sang after being around people that can really SING! I was constantly told that my voice wasn't good enough so I stuck to the demos. She brought this to my memory and I saw it as we were all singing together there were no backups. Ironically the name of the group was, "The Young Inspirations" and we sang throughout the country. As we reminisced she started singing a song I hadn't heard in years but tuned in with her like it was yesterday including our harmony parts. It went like this "I'm a new creation, I'm a brand new man, all things are passed away, and I'm born again. He is my comforter and friend." Well here I am just tuning in and getting reconnected with what God planted inside of me a lifetime ago. Holy Spirit, my partner thank you, you are my comforter and friend. And oh November 11th, 2010 made it eleven years surviving with the cancer or what I like to call it the "C" and I feel more alive now than ever. He is a restorer of everything, you just have to believe and follow through. It is worth the effort, trust and believe! Well until next time.

JESUS IS THE ANSWER

Did I ever tell u about the time when I was in a domestic situation and the police came and asked that one of us leave. I decided to leave with my friends. While outside I sat on the sidewalk of the popular South Street about one block with my beloved pug Diego and asked in my heart, "God what I'm I going to do, what is the answer?" Well the response was written on the back of a moving truck. I looked up and there printed on the back of the truck was 'Jesus is the Answer.' I said to myself "Okay I know this but how does this apply to my situation right now" and then went on walking down the street with my friends.

Here I am a decade later and ready to do my morning tasks when I hear Michael Smith on the satellite radio station singing "Jesus is the Answer" and get this I was in the closet getting a jacket when my partner said, "Oh no you have to write about how God revealed that answer to you way back in the midst of one of your storms when you turned to man rather than me and that didn't turn out too well did it?" And you know what He of course was right for I had become more dependent on man and my life ended up in a whirlwind of disappointment. But God was always right there no matter what, even when I couldn't see that it was always Him with the entire Trinity acting on my behalf, saving me from myself. Like the songwriter wrote 'If it had not been for the Lord on my side, where would I be.' Jesus is my answer!

COMING FAST AND FURIOUS

This morning I was up when my husband left and we prayed but prior to that I was having a few conversations with the Lord in my sleep. So I got up after he left and said ok partner what are we learning today? Well the Holy Spirit took me to Job 28 and there it was all unfolding. I was like ok Lord I could do this I get you! Now there was a musical track I partially composed entitled my life is a movie and at the time when my partner and I were going through the tracks for the Worship project this one didn't fit and I was a little sad but cool because it was so stunning that I knew God would have me use it down the line. Now this morning I could see and hear quite clearly that He wanted me to recite Job 28 to this track and record it for the Project. When I looked at the translational break down I just had to share this and put it on face book. After I did that I went back to sleep and said I'll sleep for an hour.

Well in my dream we were all at one house and I could see the faces of certain family members. There was one man who I saw running around the house and I followed him and then he defecated behind a couch and I cleaned it up and told him to remember he is living in a house with humans for he is not a dog! I asked him if he knew how to use a toilet and he said yes but he wasn't comfortable with it. I figured this was in my dream because I watched my dog have attacks yesterday with his body cramping up intensely to the point that the gentleman I was having a meeting with I asked to pray with me while I ran and got anointed oil. I rubbed the oil over my baby's body and asked the man to pray for him and then my doggy relaxed and was healed. Imagine this guys first impression of our meeting but it sealed the trust God wanted to instill. Finally getting back with my longwinded self I thought this was the reason but I never had my dog in my dreams even though he has had attacks before. With regards to this dream we were all on this roof top and as I looked into the sky I could see these vehicles with airplanes passing underneath. I tried to get my mom to see them but every time she looked up she saw nothing.

Now a few weeks prior while waiting in line at the movies I kept seeing this opening in parts of the sky. There was this orange colored moving object and my husband who is a skeptic on many things saw it and still said, "Oh it's probably a jet." I told him there is a **greater invisible presence than a visible one**. I showed him a plane flying by in the opposite direction and it was obvious that no plane could fly as high as this flashing object. It disappeared and moved and then another opening flash moved and reappeared at such a swift speed. If only you could see the awe on his face even though he didn't say anything, that look was priceless! I said to him, "I'm just saying there has to be other life forces because you know what we've just experienced" and then I changed the subject and we went into the movie theater.

Now my dream/vision had me seeing either missiles or ships in the sky but they were surrounding us and finally my Mom looked up and saw it. Suddenly I heard from the sky a voice that told me to suit up. Then it said very clearly "Your talents can be taken but your gifts can not." God continue to steer me in your direction despite the many distractions!

THE ONLY OPINION
YOU HAVE TO WORRY ABOUT

Transformation

My dreams are becoming visions of reality. On Thursday night I had a dream about a family member of mine needing a make-over. She wore her hair back and had on glasses and a bunch of us laughed and when she looked in the mirror she had a makeover but it wasn't her in the mirror it was me I was her. On the Wednesday night I attended the Spanish Choice Awards at the Kimmel Center and didn't like the way I looked in the picture I had my hair pulled back and to me I looked old. I felt underdressed and said to myself I need to change my wardrobe and let go of the old and comfortable and make room for the new me. After all I changed my personal life and gave up my past way of living only to answer and obey the voice of God and marry my baby, my boo despite all the challenges I know my husband is who God created for me.

In addition if I could have that trust in my brain surgery, and my personal life why not my new look. My partner is telling me to wrap it up and get to the point. Here we go, I had the dream Thursday night, told my husband Friday morning and Friday night there I was at a girlfriend's house at her friend's bachelorette party. She was getting a makeover so they asked me if I wanted one and you know what, I did. The result is that I looked exactly like I did in my dream. When I looked into the mirror I had the same hair color that I had with the dream makeover and just like in the dream when the family member looked into the mirror there I was.

Now when I look back I remember a dream I had years ago where I found some money under a car tire and the more I pulled on the dollar, more money just continued to flow and I was embarrassed because I didn't want people to see me pulling all this money I mean it just kept coming. In reality I had just joined a pyramid scheme and we got my sister to join and even though she joined at the end she actually got $13000 a short time after putting in her $1000. Now in this dream I spent the money recklessly and partied with all sorts of people in what looked like New Orleans and then years later I visited that same location in New Orleans for the first time. In this same dream at the end I was walking up a hill or mountain overlooking the water and was laughing at my friends because they were all gray and had gotten old. They told me that they didn't know what I was laughing at and that I should look at my own reflection. When I looked into the water I was startled because what I saw was not what I felt I was. All those years I thought I was like everybody else when in actuality I was not! The reflection I saw wasn't a human being at all, but a lion. All those years I thought I was something else; I felt I was something else all because no one ever told me anything otherwise!

For years I never truly looked at myself. I remember in college when I got in trouble and I was linked with these prominent lawyers and one of them told me that everyone else may have been Volkswagens but I had the engine of a Porsche. Back then I wanted to be a lawyer in my country but they told me that by the time I finished my schooling there would be too many corporate lawyers and here we are decades later and Bermuda continues to flourish internationally and needs more corporate lawyers. As a result for years I felt cheated but I now know that was the hand of God. I look back over my life and can see all the dots connected and how He has always been there protecting me. He has allowed me to live through many facets such as homosexual relationships, drug addiction, molestation, suicide attempts, abuse, esteem issues, cancer, and all sorts of afflictions. God is good and now I'm learning another lesson and this time it's the music and media, the explosive instrument that I was uniquely created for.

Last night or should I say early this morning around 2 a.m. before my computer shut itself down to recharge I was able to complete the first part of this Transformation chapter. And here my partner and I are three hours later letting our readers know the lesson that was revealed. Through all of my musical challenges what I felt in the flesh was people not wanting to be a part of this special life changing project! One minute they said yes they wanted to be a part and then bang its avoidance and excuses as to why they can't be a part of it. I started to take it personally but my partner allowed me to see motives and reasons for connections. This project is not mines but His! I'm simply the vessel that He has chosen to use and for that I say "Thank You!" He pointed me to my lesson in Job 38 to 40 where He speaks directly to Job and what my partner had me extract into my spirit was that although I may feel that people failed and cheated me as far as loyalty my ONLY option is to totally submit to His authority and trust Him. This includes Him placing the new tenants that we need.

Like God said to Job can he explain the concept of the formation of the universe and nature? Just as all nature is beyond our limited human understanding we must rely on God's unlimited resources for He knows what is best for us. I know the hard part is in the waiting or just going through and trying to figure out human motives for it makes no sense. But humans are complex and lie and God is not a man that He should lie (Num 23:19) so why not trust and be loyal to Him who has always been there and has gotten me through. We have to just praise Him through every circumstance! "Lord I'm just waiting and resting in your care while keeping my eyes fixed on you and enjoying this inner peace that I have because my assurance is in YOU and not man. You are teaching me so many things including forgiveness and mercy. Just as you have mercy on us Lord Jesus I worship only you. For you are my Savior, my Healer, my Deliverer and Best friend. I am yours and you are mine for you chose me first. And because of your love and new mercies everyday my mind, body and soul is constantly being transformed into who you want me to be." Here lately I keep hearing, and reading confirmations of the lyrics and lines my partner has placed within me. I say, "Thank you for the Trinity!"

TRY A NEW WAY!

This past week God had me rewriting some songs I had written with melodies and lyrics that gave positive messages but not His messages. You see after my prophetic weeping or break down as I like to refer to it. I've become even more sensitive to the voice of my partner, Mr. Holy Spirit. Not only are we writing this book together we are now writing songs together in sync. It is no secret that I enjoy all kinds of music styles so last night before I went out to an award show I had said in my mind while listening to some music that I would love to have that type of music on that channel and then I heard a voice say, "Do we need another weeping?" and I said "No Lord I get it I'm doing it your way."

I started to tell my husband that if people were in my head they would think I was insane and then I told him what I heard and he was like what? So I said never mind after all I figure he didn't understand when I tried to explain the prophetic breakdown or let me correct that my partner says prophetic break through, thank you my precious one!

Anyhoo he didn't understand my prophetic breakthrough when I told him that God asked me would I give up my music for Him and he said God knows how much you love that but anyways I didn't fully understand it either until now. I'm listening to "Reunited" by Peaches and Herb and I just got it. There's one perfect fit because we are reunited. This station has music that I love so much and it's the music that I long to write to but I have to do it God's way. Eventually I went sleep to it and He showed me glimpses when I awoke to His messages mixed with a particular radio format. Then I asked my partner for a quick word before starting my day and He showed me 2 Chronicles 33:17. Although the people loved God alone they worshipped Him the wrong way. God had them make their sacrifices in certain places and this was to protect them from the influences of subtle pagan worshipping. He stated that mixing can be dangerous for we have to be careful not to let the secular influences distort our way of worship. Therefore I understand my personal sacrifice and the reasons as to why God took over the Worship Experience Project "Lesson 1". And the glimpses He showed me were of Him taking back that precious gift and ministry that He gave and administered to Satan! God is the original Creator and everything else is a duplicator don't get it twisted!

CELEBRATE THE TIME

God has appointed a timetable to every one of our lives. How we live life throughout that time is ultimately up to us. We have to take the pains with the gains and remember that we are not on this journey alone. Our partner is there the entire time, that's right the Holy Spirit. Right there beside us, always there to guide us, that is the line that my partner gave me for one of the songs. This morning my husband prayed with me about someone who is so dear to me, my Aunt. My Aunt has been more than a regular Aunt she is my second Mother. From as far as I can remember she took me to dance class, paid for my braces went to every dental visit, every recital, every play, every graduation, every accolade, my divorce, my suicide attempt, and my red carpet and Grammy events, she was always there. Now I love both of my Aunts the other one has been there as well but had her own child and this Aunt had none so I was like her daughter. As I'm writing tears are flowing as I reflect on our memories. That's why I try to tell my Husband that creating memories is so important especially with the son God has entrusted us with. I don't take any of this for granted. We must try our best to celebrate our time on this planet earth!

IT ALL MAKES SENSE

A few Saturdays ago I had this dream which I've learned was more like a vision. You see when it is a dream it rests in my spirit but when it's a profound vision it stirs my spirit. I can't stop talking about it I searched for various interpretations. The vision went like this; I had to go downtown for something and on my way home I ended up at 30th street station a major train intersection and I heard them say the train is leaving at x time so I ran up the stairs immediately to catch the R8 which is the train I used to take every day back and forth when I lived in the East Falls section. Anyone who's close to me knows that my heart desires to move back to that region of Philadelphia I mean that is where I developed my history. I attended school there, that is where I got hooked on drugs, that is where God brought me back to the same building to look at the Projects where He showed me you can choose to go left or right but I have brought you back 365 degrees so you have a choice and I chose Him! It is where I searched and I mean searched for a church home. It is where I experienced my divorce, my new life. It's where I stopped traffic in the snow just to get to church, it's where I first started dating, it's where I first was introduced to music, it's the area that my dream house resides in. It's the area that I foresaw in my dreams while I was overseas. It's where my journey in this city began when I went to school, simply put it's my HOME. So now do you get it I was catching the R8 because it was familiar. I know I'm long winded but you get the picture. As a matter of fact every time I drive past there I'm homesick but getting back to my dream/vision I rushed to catch the R8 and as I'm writing this my heart longs for that area, Holy Spirit help me get out of my head please!

Okay I get to the platform and I miss the train by a hair and I become anxious because all I long to do is to get home to my husband. Well the train rolls back and they announce that it went off track. I and others rush to try and get on it anyway. Now tell me that is not the craziest thing rushing to get on a TRAIN THAT IS OFFTRACK hello . . . . Well my spirit shifts to another mode of transportation but this time it's a bus and I'm in Bermuda. For some reason when I dream of Bermuda I'm often at Parsons Road which is near where I partially grew up. So I'm on this bus and I'm about to get off because my main concern is to let my husband know where I am. I get up and then remember that part of that area has been taken over by gangs so it would be unsafe for me to get off for it is no longer like when my grandmother lived or when I attended the Newlands Salvation Army church, none of them no longer exist. However the impact on my life is obviously so great that I continue to retreat there even in my sleep.

Therefore I didn't get off the Prospect bus and went to get my cell phone to call my husband. I realized I forgot it so this girl who I often see at my church, New Covenant, is there and she says she will sell me a call for fifty cents. I go to look for my money and realize I have the wrong purse and have my traveling purse which is this oversized bag that I used to carry. Everyone would say, "Oh that's a nice bag but Lord it's so big, you don't hurt your neck or back with that?" And of course I would say no and then I realized it was one heck of a large purse so I started using it to travel with. When I noticed I had the wrong bag it caused me to look at my feet and I had mismatched shoes, one was a pump that I wasn't that comfortable wearing and the other was my trusty flat shoe that I was very comfortable with. Now here I was catching the wrong train because where I had moved in the natural I would be catching another train not the R8. I was just all wrong from the start going back and retreating to my familiar. When I awoke the next morning I purposely wore the pump shoes and made it comfortable.

That same day I went to a service at a shelter and was delighted that my husband came for I had been trying to get him to come for the past two years. It was the result of going there that all sorts of things started to happen, I publicly repented for my sins known and unknown. I've never done that openly and the part about repenting for sins I was unaware of, wow. Later I discovered at a friend's church at the feasting of the tabernacle celebration that we were in the Jewish and Christian custom period of repentance. Well in the natural I didn't know this but in the supernatural my spirit was quite familiar and that is why my partner prompted me to openly repent. But check this, after I repented and my husband and I gave our testimonies God asked me would I give up my music for Him. Well I was blue I said to God, "You know that got me through my illnesses but of course after you Lord." He said, "Oh no it was me and me alone. The music is what I placed inside of you but it ALL comes from me for I and I alone are your God!" I used to make the statement well you know music is my life, wrong!

The Trinity is my life, the Father, Son and Holy Spirit. I feel so blessed to have a lifestyle that has three in one watching over me, in me and beside me . . . . Wow!!! Well I continued to cry and from the outside it looked like I may have been having a nervous breakdown I mean the more I would negotiate with God about not giving up the music the more I cried and I mean boohooed, gutter snot crying You would have thought I lost my baby. Well this went on for a good forty five minutes and the Lord asked me one more time, "Would you give up your music for me?" I replied "I gave up so much already, my career, my being a mother, and Lord you know how much my music means to me it is my identity!" And He said, "No I am your identity first" and then I said, "Yes Lord I'll do it if that is what you want." He responded with, "Because I want it all I want all of you!" Well when I said "Yes Lord." He said "Ok we are going to do it my way" and the WORSHIP EXPERIENCE PROJECT BEGAN!!!

Just Want Something Profound

You ever go through something that you know is only a season but you want a profound word or confirmation? You don't care where or how it's coming you just desire something profound from your Lord and Savior, Jesus Christ. Well that's me this morning weeping; stomach churning and I just need another breakthrough. The money coming in won't be enough to pay the bills. It seems that every week I'm negotiating with utility companies and every week I'm always given some false promise. I'm tired of being treated any kind of way, people giving me whatever they feel like and expecting the same result. I'm tired of carrying for it has been a year and I'm tired, in fact I'm sick and tired. Again I know now where that saying comes from because I've experienced being physically sick and tired. I just lost my friend, I'm fighting to keep my illnesses under wraps, I'm trying to keep the bills in order, I'm tired of being alone with no affection, I'm tired of always being the one to strive for intimacy, I'm tired as a woman of not being given that little something that makes you feel appreciated. As women we like to receive more than empty words, how about a manicure, a pedicure or massage, some romance beyond the movies! That's when my partner, Mr. Holy Spirit showed me that I have Him and He has me. As a result many times it is He that is my date, my constant companion and He has made a way for me to pamper myself.

As I'm writing this I'm listening to Kurt Carr's "I'll tell God" and he sings about no more crying, no more worrying, if I tell God about my problems He'll work it out for me. And He is working it out for me. Now I'll tell you if that is not a direct word or something profound I don't know what is! I instantly feel better after letting it out by writing it out. I'm listening to a song that my Mom and her former singing group, the Newlanders used to sing "This is the Day." This is the Fred Hammond version but I clearly remember when my Mom's friends came back from Israel singing that song . . . . "this is the day that the Lord has made, we will rejoice and be glad in it." My mind is shifting to how a girlfriend of mine lost it all and ended up in a shelter and how it was the springboard of change for her new beginning. I'm listening to the late Rev Timothy Wright's song "Jesus, Jesus, Jesus" and I just finished screaming and weeping which led to me lying prostrate on the floor. In this song he sings about the testimonies of the people in Katrina and how no matter what they preserved the song which focuses on this old lady who consistently kept crying out to Jesus. She sang that His name is above all names especially when this man had a seizure in the temporary shelter because he couldn't get his medicine she called on "Jesus the Healer!" When she saw the baby, and all the tragic results of the storm she called on Jesus and could see Him clearly as a Savior, a Deliverer and when the tractor trailers came with food, clothing and medicine she started crying more and the people couldn't understand why and she cried tears of joy and just started thanking Jesus. People we need to call on Jesus and thank Him through our circumstance!

This reminds me of the fact that this too shall pass and I need to start praising Him through in everything! After all He keeps me, He heals me, and He provides for me, He is my comforter and friend. Like a friend of mine said on our radio show, "If He never was to bless me with another thing, He has already done enough!" Only my partner could have brought this to my mind, I tell you the Holy Spirit isn't a joke. He'll remind you of every blessing even when you're broke. And that is why they call the Trinity, the only living God, why ? Because He is three in one and I'm telling you as I type from this bed I have went from crying to getting on my face on the floor to having my stomach in knots to experiencing such a peace; if only you could just see me. I'm dancing and grooving in this bed typing away listening to ready for this "There's Hope" by India Arie. I tell you talk about a musical line up that only God could have orchestrated the order of. All of these songs are being played on my satellite TV and now I'm closing out this chapter listening and rejoicing to my man, Hezekiah Walker's "Faithful Is Our God." I'm telling you Hope fest will happen with lineups who have testimonies, those who have been through the storm and are proof that only our living God can bring us through. Songs by Hezekiah, India Arie, and Tye Tribett keep popping up so I close with the lyrics "I will reap the harvest that's promised to me and take back what the devil has stolen from me." Unfortunately when I had finances I didn't know how to appreciate the value of money, or the value of who I am but I'm telling you I have Answered the Call.

God dialed and I answered so although I may weep I know that joy has never left my soul. You see once you have the tools of how to cope and work that faith Jesus will see you through. After all I'm medically not supposed to be here when the maximum stated time online for one of my stated afflictions is ten to 15years . . . holla and I want to say thank you to my readers for putting up with my craziness! Like another girlfriend of mine stated in an interview, "God must look and say well there goes my children again" and that's what we are His children. We whine, but we have to learn our lessons, be disciplined sometimes when we are ungrateful and be reminded that our Father loves us with unconditional love. We will get it once we give up the wheel of our lives and get over our human control freak selves for we are constantly trying to take it back. Imagine the visual, you give the keys of your life to God to drive and then you are fighting trying to put your hands back on the steering wheel, and eventually you will crash if you don't let go. Well I'm on a roll now so let me go for I have a God filled weekend planned. Oh and my partner, Mr. Holy Spirit just said as I was saving and scrolling through these pages, "Is that Profound Enough For Ya?" God bless you my readers.

LORD CONTINUE TO TEACH ME

Every morning for a week I've been grieving the death of a good friend of mine Minister Ron and I had the privilege of just sharing a spiritual connection with him where I would know or see things with him beforehand. I felt survivor's guilt of having had the great C and why God has saved me to remain on planet earth and not Ron. I think of all the positive memories and by going through the footage for his family of our time in Guyana makes me cry more. I feel guilty of not getting his full testimony that we talked about. We let life and people's opinions get in the way and I'm telling you when God gives you an assignment you should do your best to carry it out. God knows the end to the beginning but we don't. We cannot see around corners only down the streets of our self absorbed lives. We need to listen to that inner voice more because it is the Holy Spirit prompting us. Pray about everything. For example yesterday I was going to catch the train home from downtown and I said, "Lord should I go to my right on Walnut and Locust or should I go my usual route on my left to City Hall? Then I said to myself "If I turn to the new route I may come upon someone that I'm meant to see or meet." And I started to walk in that direction and then my partner said, "NO go your usual route through City Hall." So I stopped on the sidewalk and stood there for two seconds and for that quick moment I was saying to myself that these people probably think I'm crazy.

Check it out I don't know these people on the street passing by and they don't know me so why was I caring about their opinion. In that split second there was the space that my friend Ron preached about from his hospital bedside about how Satan can slip in and that he did to cause doubt. It was the voice of God that said NO and stopped me in my tracks literally. I now know where some of these sayings come from like "in a split second" or "stopping in my tracks" because I was allowed to become aware to experience them. You see when you know and listen to the voice of God all things become new. For that quick moment I allowed the enemy to whisper in my ear but I allowed the Holy Spirit to rise up a shout in my spirit. You know what I'm talking about the shout that makes you say, "Heck no I'm going this direction because I know it's right!" I'm trusting God and will walk in faith to follow His directions not mine I'm just a walking talking breathing vessel. Like the song says, "I'm His and He is mine." For when you make that commitment to Christ you commit to strengthening your relationship with the Trinity just as you would work on your human relationships. After all we work hard at being committed to our careers, jobs, family, spouses, friendships; you all know what I'm talking about! So why can't we commit to our relationship with Jesus why is that so hard? Why do we give Him the short end of the stick?

Maybe the answer is because it forces us to walk by faith and just as we breathe the air that we cannot see but yet know we must rely on it to live than so must we live in Christ. We cannot always see in our human comprehension but we must live our lives like a living testimony. In Him I live, I move and have my being. And you know something this is the first time as I'm writing this that my partner, the Holy Spirit has allowed me to experience this very scripture. In fact now as I'm thinking about it in this context I can see how a lot of scriptures that we may take for granted come to life. For example Psalms 37: 4, 5 "Delight yourself in the Lord and he will give you the desires of your heart. Commit your ways to Him, trust in Him and he will do that." Numbers 23:19 "God is not a man that he should lie" Proverbs 3:5, 6 "Trust in the Lord with All your heart and lean not on your own understanding. Acknowledge Him in All your ways and He will direct your path." Psalms 119:105 "The word is a lamp to my feet and a light to my path" Psalms 18:32 "God arms me with strength and makes my way safe." Man I'm on a roll, okay

Holy Spirit let's get back to the story of traveling downtown . . . hello oh my spirit is speaking in tongues, hallelujah. I'm jamming to "They That Wait Upon the Lord" with Fred Hammond and John P. Kee . . . Wait on Him . . . . I'm worshipping on this computer yes Wait on Him . . . and hey you who are reading this will get your breakthrough, Lord knows I just did!

Okay getting back let's recap, zoom in folks. I was downtown and didn't know whether to turn left or right because I just knew I was to meet someone. Started to turn right and walk and heard a voice and there was a quickening in my spirit saying, "NO take your usual route" which was on my left. When I reached City Hall they had my usual side blocked off so I had to go further down and I dropped to my knees and prayed; then I caught the elevator and went underground and stopped for a donut. As I was walking I heard various people singing and then the last corner before catching my train I heard a song that was so familiar. It was a worship song that the Prophetess kept playing literally over and over last Sunday and my Husband would sing it loudly. I heard it loudly with the keyboard and normally street musicians are playing guitars, the drums, and handmade instruments or singing to tracks. The song was a worship song "I give myself to you" and right there at City Hall underground I stopped and harmonized with this man and all of a sudden I knew all the right words, all the right harmonies and people started listening. The man whose spot it was said "You two should sing together. I normally don't go to church but I would come just to hear you two!" Now he kept saying and hollering that we two should get together so we all exchanged information and I gave the street musician my card. You see the guy who was playing and singing just happened to stop by along his way home and knew the street musician.

The Lord had him stop at that exact moment to sing and play that exact song for exactly when I would come along their path. When we worshipped I felt the presence of God and could care less who was looking at me. One lady said she loved that song and put money into the street musician's hat. Now imagine here I was about twenty minutes earlier wondering what type of people I would meet.

God positioned me where I would just let it all go for His glory in His perfect pitch. Now the guy who was playing has a praise and worship group and get this they are called "The Anointed Ones." I had just told him about the Praisefest we had and we wanted only anointed people. And you know who was looking at all of our unity and excitement, the street musician. He witnessed the joy of the Lord firsthand. And as I'm writing this there is the revelation of the street musicians concert that I wanted to have and it will be used for God's glory. Don't know all the intricate pieces but I do know that the particular street musician plays a vital part. I guess that's ministering Ron's style or should I say Jesus style for he did take His ministry to the streets.

So Many Similarities

This morning at 2:45a.m I awoke because I found myself crying in my sleep and I was weeping reflecting on the memories of Ron. A friend of mine who was being ravished by cancer and this is his third go around. You know the saying three strikes you're out well the number three is significant. But it seems like my life has always been connected to death and that's where it hits me. As I was looking at my outline I read where I was to write about my friend Michael who passed but there was a time I didn't feel like going into it. But Ron brought it all back. As I go through my personal challenges and fight I cannot not understand the whys over the simple things in life like creating memories and why some people want to detach themselves from that; I now get it.

As I was crying my head off or like we say in Bermuda balling my eyes out I felt Ron's presence clear as day and then I felt him slip away. I reflected on our memories and most recent how we would talk over the phone and he became my first trainer. He trained me so that I could get in shape to fit in my wedding dress and my family would tell you I was so proud to know I had a trainer and they would tease me. Then I hired him to cater my wedding and boy did we have a time dealing with the stove issues but he was dedicated that's for sure and made it happen even though we had plain white rice instead of seasoned. We talked prior about how I wanted to film people's testimonies and have them aired on television. Today I see where God is going and has gone with using me within the media. What comes to mind is the scripture "His ways are not our ways or lean not on our own understanding" well I'm paraphrasing but this is so true.

I reflect on the order of events from driving to get table cloths for a fellow church brother to talking about what his Grandfather had told him and what he wanted most out of life such as a family. As I'm writing this I still hope in my heart that he gets the chance to have his own family and start his ministry but that is what my will is not God's will and we must subject to His will not our will. We were spiritually connected and I would literally feel him; for example one night I had a vision of all these stoves somewhere in his house downstairs like a basement. Now keep in mind I had never been to his house. I called him and told him what I saw and he screamed and said to his friend Norman, "How would she know that is what I'm planning on doing, starting my catering company and I was going to get these stoves." Then I go to this venue to discuss business and the result was me telling this person that Ron was sick with colon cancer and the guy said, "You know what we went to barber school together" and then we all decided to visit him later. Well I had this life changing vision and I ended up back at that venue on a Sunday morn and found that the venue was holding its official first church service. The same guy who is now a friend preached about how he values life and how he found out about a friend being sick and now he may have to enter hospice.

Eventually Ron passed but I had the chance to film him and let him know how I felt about a few things before he transitioned. That taping is now all over the world on the internet with him ministering with a congregation at his hospital bedside!

IT DOESN'T END AT
THE FUNERAL

Yesterday was my friend Ron's funeral and for the most part it was genuine. But last night as I was going through footage I was trying to figure out what other footage could I place in his short film to make it more effective. I came across all sorts of testimonial scenes of not just his life but of others that ran through my mind as well. So many thoughts are running through my mind and this morning I asked God to show me and naturally my partner did. He showed me Ezekiel starting with Chapter 5 and then I asked Him who was Ezekiel and He showed me that he was a prophet who was so faithful to God that he obeyed the most dramatic requests of God and then he showed me that was me with the kneeling anywhere God asks me syndrome. Even fellow Christians are sometimes embarrassed with my kneeling in public as was I at first but not now!

Then as I read on it showed me that Ezekiel was a street preacher just like Ron. I sought of had a clue but it was when I was instructed to read Chapter 5 and it began talking about the barber and how he was told to shave his head and I said ok Ron was a barber and so is my friend JoJo. It also confirmed a conversation I had yesterday with a friend of mine about how I just have this passion to film peoples testimonies and I want to do it with reenactments. I began thinking about Ezekiel doing the dramatic to get God's message across and how we can be creative in our approach to spread God's Word! We can look at allowing ourselves to be creative instruments to get the message across. Like Ron did when he preached from his hospital bed to several and now even though he is gone physically he is preaching to millions via the internet. Now that demonstrates creative passion for the Lord and Holy Ghost boldness.

Aunt Ilene and Uncle Henry

deceased friend Jo Jo

deceased Bob Pop Barlow

deceased best friend Michael

deceased adopted sister Sharon Showell
n dog Dee Dee who both passed after
book was written

with deceased Aunt Sarah

with deceased Aunt Lydia

deceased friend Ron playin ard using the water bottle as a mic

deceased inspiration Dana who fought cancer in several locations

with deceased best friend Nate

KNOW 4 SURE

You know in the morning I literally asked my partner, the Holy Spirit what are we doing today. Lord what is it that you want me to learn? Each day I learn something that's exciting and purposeful in my life. This morning He led me to another level where I learned about this Biblical hero Ezra and how he led the people back to God and was so humble and publicly wept before God. It was through his example and the encouragement of the prophets that led the people from exile back to Jerusalem. Now Bible scholars out there don't get caught up on my every word but the message is what's important. Ezra changed lives through example and ushered in a new way of worship. The church that I sometimes attend has a leader, Pastor Dion who reminds to Ezra. This revelation is pertinent in the fact that we are holding our first Praisefest at the Ark "It's A New Day" tomorrow and it is our first collaboration with my company that God entrusted me with this church. Right down to the very name God gave me just like the company names, record label etc.

During my morning worship I got on my knees and face and laid before God and wept as I saw children in India with their sweet spirits and faces. Even thinking about the vision while I'm writing this brings tears to my eyes. And you know what, I'm scheduled to go to India at some point and my company "Hismultimedia International Inc" has formed a partnership with an Indian venture "Vision and Mission Ministries." All I'm saying is God is God and if you give your life to Him he will fulfill your purpose and you will travel along the journey of who you were created to be. At the end of Praisefest I would like to have everyone singing a song God had given me called "Meant to Be." In one of the verses says "Even prior to your conception you were born with a global purpose" and that is what it is all about, being who you are "Meant to Be."

I remember when I was young I would always read books about other places and imagine that I was in them, like living on a fishing boat in Norway. Or living as a Bedouin in the desert. Even to this day I enjoy watching shows about other countries and I joked about being a missionary but you know what that is what God wants for my life. My parents were in the Salvation Army and I always wanted to be an officer to help people in the world. I even remember gathering all of these people together with their bios to assist a lady who wanted to do a movie in Bermuda and she had top acclaimed producers on her team that had produced some known feature films but the powers that be let that fall through. I have always tried to get my country involved for free, I never used to charge just promote! This one guy that I was helping said to me "You are like a Mother Theresa that's who you remind me of" and I got angry because people would think I'm stupid for doing things for free but in my heart I always knew my gifts and generosity and compassion came from God. Now I can see where that part of my journey has prepared me for today. I guess you can say I look at my life as the song He gave me "Meant to Be."

IT HAS BEEN A MINUTE

It has been a while since I've gotten the zeal back to talk to you guys. So much has happened I don't know where to begin so I won't; let's just say that my WIT sister featured all of her Women in Transition sisters in her newly released book "Abuse behind the Badge." This is such an accomplishment for not just Rosa but all of us. And for me it couldn't have come at a better time. It was during my separation period not by my choice mind you that I needed that healing and by meeting with my sisters at the opening of the book signing gave me a spark. As a Christian woman who walks with Christ I was distraught but not defeated. Again I ran to church not the world and this

reflected on my WIT sisters. I'm proud to say my faith has sparked them as well. I believe there is a saying but during my separation I learned who truly was in my corner and that no matter how alone I felt God proved again that he never left me. I had to just break away for a minute and get on my face and knees and just bow down on the floor next to my dog and pray. Lord you are my Savior and best friend for there truly is none other like you for You are truly the living God. Now check this out;

Something terrible happened to me so I turned to reading the Word when my flesh wanted to call another being. It was early in the morning so I said to God as I usually do "Where do I turn?" And my partner had me open up to the book of Isaiah 58 and then

I highlighted verse 11 where it says "The Lord will guide you always he will satisfy your needs in a sun-scorched land." Then I read chapter 59 and I looked at the translation for verses 16 and 17 and you tell me was this a direct answer? It said paraphrasing "He would also rescue His people from sin because this is an impossible task for any human. God himself, as the Messiah, Jesus would personally step in to help." Now is this not a direct answer from God for my on time situation.

I as many of you keep forgetting that we are vessels it's as simple as that. A vessel for good or bad we are like drink containers and no matter how fancy the container what we fill it up with determines the taste of whether it will be sweet, sour or refreshing. What I'm trying to say is that God created the container and gave us the choice as to what to fill it up with and we can either refill it every day or let it sit and go stale. If I never believed in the Holy Ghost and that the Bible is a living word, I believe now. It realize it is through my trials that I'm made stronger like Kirk Franklin's song says "Hello Fear!"

2 THROUGH

You know today was the last straw all I could do is cry out to God and ask why???? I'm so tired of sacrificing and feeling just defeated. All I could do is get on my knees and beg Jesus for his healing touch. I mean for the first time I didn't want to come back home to my family. This lawyer made me feel like an alien and all I can ask the Lord for is his mercy. I know I have my health challenges and now these financial woes. My apartment at home isn't rented still and we had to do so much fixing up because the last tenant's husband deceived us. Last night I was at a revival and Pastor Paula White talked about seasons and I left there feeling so empowered. Right now once again I was looking forward to attending a movie screening and my husband just didn't stick to his word, not a phone call so I could make other plans.

Earlier a friend of mine in the industry disappointed me and I'm just asking God what does he want from me, I'm tired of broken promises from everywhere. I'm feeling so disgusted but then I turned up the music and Vickie Winans was singing "How I Got Over" and I feel much better because I know these are only distractions from the enemy. I have to ask God to literally guide me as to whom to call, what to write and I'm literally at the mercy of His feet. You know folks will disappoint you time after time, say one thing and mean another but I know my Lord and Savior will never forsake me and that is why I'm writing this to let you know no matter what comes our way we must listen to His voice. I mean I don't want to seem ungrateful for I know He speared my life for a reason time and time again. I know that I have to maintain a peace because my health will spiral out of control. Now I may have been diagnosed with brain cancer, systemic lupus, have a titanium chip in my breast and osteoporosis but most of all I have the love, the unfailing love of the only name that I could utter JESUS CHRIST!

Now these proposals for Hopefest, Praisefest, the songs, films and even this book shall come to pass. But the pain, the chaos, the broken heartedness, the strife, the grief, the underlying torture, emotional abuses are all for the reason of showcasing who God truly is. You see in the midst He'll show you bliss. I now realize that is why so many people that I trusted have disappeared or removed themselves from my life when they don't see any more money or I'm no longer available to them so they may think but God has another plan. Like Pastor Paula talked about the separation from the wheat and the shaft time will show you who is worthy and who needs to be in your life. It's not about what we want but about what and whom we need and we need to continue seeking after Jesus especially when you are feeling so low that you want to give up and when things are going so well that you don't have time to seek after him. That's when we need to seek Him more. As a matter of fact we should always take out the time for His acknowledgement.

Can you imagine if God decided "Oh well I don't have the time to give you another breath, then what?" I had fluid around the lungs so I know what it feels like to resemble a fish out of water.

I felt so out of control that is when I cried out to Jesus and made the pact to stop smoking cigarettes and I did. Imagine feeling that desperate for wanting life so much that all you could do is cry out! Emotionally that is how I felt today and now I'm looking at TV and I see a girl I met who dreamed of music and there is her CD "Hold On" and she's ministering to me so I'm sharing this with you. Just keep trusting and holding on to His steadfast hand! He will give you no more than you can bear.

JOY COMETH IN THE MORNING

All I could do is get on my knees and pray, or sit on the toilet and weep, get on my face in my bedroom and cry some more and listen to inspirational music. I love the Lord so much that even writing this my face is streaming with tears because not only has He done so much for me He has set me free, free from myself and has been there in my dark cancer moments and my award winning moments. I complained last night to a sister of mine about the pain I'm feeling with being married but lonely. The moment we said I do the devil said I don't. But as a prophetess said at a spiritual retreat because the Holy Spirit put in my heart to create a wedding ceremony that wasn't about me but about God so our marriage would be attacked even more. My partner, Mr. Holy Spirit had me gather people from all cultures and religions and those that would not normally attend a church and experience the God's direct presence. It was not my ceremony or my husband's but a sacrifice to God to plant seeds and ultimately wins souls and presents a taste of our faith. As a result we became a direct target for the enemy. If I didn't know for sure well my dog confirmed it by doing the same behavior that he carried out when with my former female partner.

My Diego would want to share his love so he would sleep with me downstairs at night and every morning when I would go to the bathroom he would run by look to see if I was looking and run upstairs to her . . . (That is for the record two relationships ago) and sleep in their room. Now all before I got married and we slept in separate bedrooms I thought it was because of the covenant we made with the Lord not to have sex with one another before tying the knot and you know my baby never went out of his way to sleep in there. Now because my husband snores he was sleeping with me sometimes and other times he would sleep in the room that is really my stepson's. Now during the times with the atmosphere is clear my baby wouldn't be affected. Also the other night my baby kept wanting me to go downstairs so I thought he wanted to go out to the backyard or wanted something to eat. The little boo ran ahead of me downstairs and when I got into the dining room he was there sitting on the floor between the legs of my husband as he sat there with his head in his hands. Don't let anyone fool you animals know they just do!

Last night when my husband picked me up from Bible study I was so excited talking about what went on and he just looked at me. My heart became saddened and I told him you see this is what I miss talking with you spiritually and he just nodded. I feel that the reason as to why I'm in so much emotional pain is because I experienced what it was like to fall in love with the spiritual man but the natural man I never knew. I fell in love with the better man and not the beast that lies within. Lord you said you would never leave me nor forsake me and you are not a man that you should lie so I put my trust in you. I know this is my assignment to help save souls and it starts here in my household.

You know we learned in WIT that once you have been awakened to what you deserve and what true love can be and what abuse really is then the light is on, you will always know and the choice is yours. I had to pause as I'm listening to this famous pop group sing a gospel melody with the music. Wow . . . that's all I can say you know when music hits you and it's from the heart for you can feel that in your soul. Now I'm listening to "It Ain't Over" by Mauretta Brown Clark where the lyrics say "It Ain't over until God says it's over, so keep fighting, fasting, praying, progressing, reading, interceding, believing, trusting, blessing, it ain't over until your victory is won." How fitting are these lyrics? It's as if they were speaking to my soul so you know when things like this happen, it's nobody but the Holy Ghost. And it brings me to the point that we hardly hear the title Ghost anymore and now it has been replaced with the term Spirit but they are the same thing. Right partner? You can feel it but you can't see it but you know it's there!

WHEN IS ENOUGH ENOUGH?

I don't get it? They can lie to you, disappear on you, spend up the money and still you take them back once they show you a little affection and then it's the chain sea saw act again. At this point in my life I just want peace and know that I have someone who has my back emotionally, financially etc. Tell you the truth I've learned truly that what comes out of a person is their true heart. I have to ask God why do I keep running into cold hearted people when mine is so tender that it bordered once on the sidelines of a doormat. They say insanity is when you keep banging your head against the wall expecting different results and I've asked my partner, the Holy Spirit to guide me in a new direction one of healing rather than suffering in silence or sharing with the wrong individuals but to guide me into a new realm. Of course this realm of healing is writing. Like I once wrote in my journal how I used to run to cocaine to numb my brain when in distress but now I run to Christ and my life is so much clearer.

Lord I know I answered the call but does it have to be this hard, I know there is a lesson but I need to hear from you someway somehow either in a dream, vision or anything! I want to hear clarity just like the day I felt the pulling towards my husband and then I heard you speak those words," that's going to be your husband" and I said yeah right. Now that I'm writing my partner, Mr. Holy Spirit just brought to my attention that it's the same spirit. The one that caused me to feel funny and as a result I tried to avoid my ex prior to us getting together. I mean one time I literally was trying to hide so she wouldn't see me and I almost tripped at that Cup Match game but she saw me anyhow! The same spirit that had me talking for hours and everything seemed so surreal. I knew there was selfishness and darkness but somehow that's what I'm attracted to. That spirit just follows me.

Some run to the light and I run to black holes in hopes that I can shed light. I'm a fixer not a savior. Man if it weren't for my faith and my unquestionable belief in having accepted Jesus as my Lord and Savior I swear I would have sunk on this wavy ocean a long time ago. However Christ threw me a rope and I grabbed it with both hands and shouted "Lord save me!" Now I'm shouting "Lord save me once again from this horrible nightmare. Lord save me from this emotional tidal wave." I'm emotionally drained and as I threw the clothes down the stairs I did so with no emotion the moment I could see that he planned the whole thing by taking his overnight eye care and I knew I had enough. Now he decides to text me where he is and then tell me to give his stuff to charity that he doesn't need it.

I need to sleep and not allow this spirit of drama, confusion and complexity to get the best of me. Now I'm receiving texts with the suicide game. I'm going to rest and the sad part is if they decide to kill themselves I know I tried after all enough is enough!

THERE IS NO WEAPON FORMED THAT CAN HINDER GOD'S PLAN

You know being back home everything seems to be status and materialism. Everybody has a blackberry even the kids. Certain cars and boats are a status symbol as well and I ask myself will I ever measure up. In the past ten years I've never worked a 9 to 5 and God has helped me manage my health. I've squandered an easy 50,000 and this time around God is showing me how to do things differently. I've had successful events but have had many ideas stolen and put into place. But this time around it's all about Him and not the world. I know that I could never measure up to the world because truthfully I am not of this world. Every step, every signal is there to show me that I am a child of the light so those of darkness can't stand to be in my presence!

I've lost countless friends in both places, people that out of nowhere just stopped returning my calls, what the heck is that? And you know over and over in my head I tried figuring things out why is it that once I left "the Life" people that I had been there for, partied with, was there through thick and thin just evaporated. It was so bad that some people didn't even consider me enough to return my wedding invites or face book now that is cold. And I'm not in a pity party but some would visit the city where I'm at and say they will call me and then always lose my number. Now my cell phone number never changes and neither has my parents which have been published in the telephone directory for the past thirty years. The bottom line is if you wanted to reach me you can for I don't know when or where someone's head is at.

The one thing I learned from counseling is to place my energy where it is appreciated and I must admit I missed this point in my past with my last female relationship but with hindsight we learn. And like the book I read after my tumor surgery stated that lessons are repeated until learned and believe me I'm not trying to repeat many. I woke up this morning and said, "Okay Lord I got it and Mr. Holy Spirit can you hold my hand." I'm a stickler for Proverbs 3:5&6 "Trust in the Lord with all your heart and lean not on your own understanding. Acknowledge Him in All thy ways and He will direct your path." As I'm writing this my hands are flipping around like dying fish but you know what, "Satan I rebuke you! I rebuke every attack on my body, my mind, my family, my finances. Jesus You are Lord and ruler over my life and I stand on your Word that No Weapon formed against me shall prosper, NO WEAPON.'"

So I MADE it to my ten years with brain cancer and no more chemo. Once I told everyone I made it, then I experienced hand tremors, arm tremors and the occasional head tremors and then it hit me. What hit me I was beginning to live out my purpose so the enemy was going to fight me more. I realized that certain past politicians had taken my ideas right down to the nine and I was to meet with this prominent musician who had my family up early discussing my shared ideas but then said they didn't have money in their budget. Soon after the politician and the musician had this fabulous show which was so similar to what we had discussed that it was frightening. How could anyone be so cold, so callous but that is where my lesson in discernment comes in. God is only showing me that while my ideas on paper will work and have proven themselves in the past; it is time to move on. My health is at stake and my finances are dwindling and I have work to do for His glory not men's pockets or fleeting fame!

I realize that time is a gift from God as well as its captured moments. I just left the bank by the peaceful water and all I could think about is the last time I walked those steps and how I had our family friend Rosie with me who had just passed. I almost felt a longing to go on the ferry to reminisce with others on a Friday afternoon. It was my upbringing to be family oriented and oh so much has changed. Rosie was waiting in the car with my Mom for hours when I had that last meeting with that musician as well as the politician. I told my Mother you never know what could happen I mean within six months Rosie passed, I got married and developed hand tremors you just never know do you?

IT'S BACK

Within the past decade I have gone through medical hell but God was in control. And is in control. Someone predicted that I would only live to my early fifties. Well right now I can just about hold a phone. Even sitting on the toilet my arms have tremors and my head occasionally jerks and I know its seizures that are being suppressed. I called my husband and let him know what time it is; boy do I love him ! I asked him to pray for me and I'm growing despite the circumstances.

I don't know, maybe I just know that it's been hard for me to write but the Holy Spirit just showed me something. Just as I was inspired by him to write" Praise Him through the Circumstances" well this applies to my life. He is my salvation, my dying to self, my obedience to Him that's what this is about. I just celebrated 10 years of surviving with the remnants of an inoperable brain tumor. Right after I was telling everyone my testimony I started having tremors in both hands and arms but as I write this, tears are rolling down my cheeks and I'm trying not to cry on the computer but the God that I serve is so awesome! He is my Father, He is my Daddy there is none other. Lord knows I can't turn to others. Lord you know giving is what gets me through like the first time after my surgery I had a walker and I was shopping everyday for everyone else.

Every country we've visited I'm always shopping for everyone else. However I'm learning to recognize this game of resistance. It's the same game, different faces and you know what I'm not giving in to it. I celebrate life as long as I have breath and NO ONE is taking that from me. Many times its about the power that we give to people and today I choose to live, I choose to give what I can . . . Now I can praise through the circumstances for it is my choice to be obedient and stand through all the trials and give up all the dinners, shows etc. I'm asking God what are you doing? It's about me and my covenant to you first, I get it. Dying to self means praising through, confusing the enemy as my spiritual friend said yesterday. I realize that I got married to Christ not my husband. As my stepson says "Got it!" **Like George Huff sings there will be "A Brighter Day."**

I can't look at all that I've given up on a human level because it will consume me, all the money, all the materials. I can't allow NO ONE to change me unless I want to be changed. I'm a giver, one whose natural instinct is to share and that's who God made me to be so to go against that grain is again very hard. I now have no other choice but to rely on my partner's guidance and ask for discernment. I cry out to my Lord and Savior asking Him why and then of course He had me pen the lyrics to "I Just Know" but actually through all of this God is remolding me. When I take it to Him in prayer He does not say, "Oh Les stop your complaining or this is drama." He says, "My child hang in there for the lessons, hang in there for the classes because my child this lesson and program is designed for you and how you react to being molded and guess what, you are about to graduate!"

THERE'S NO ONE LIKE JEHOVAH

Well that's the song that my partner the Holy Spirit had me wake up to this morning, we're back at it; the duo at work again and it feels good! For weeks I wasn't feeling the urge to write anything with a flow. It was always a forced thing but this morning I woke up with my mind staying on Jesus just like the song says. Yesterday I went to church and my baby sang for the first time in the choir. He had been nervous but it was something God had showed me in a vision so I was proud but not surprised. After all this choir director reminded me that I had told him almost three years prior that he should take him to sing in the men's choir. Well that was our first date out of town and here we were almost three years later married. But that's how my God operates He'll make a way out of no way!

Yesterday the Minister talked about us exercising what God has put in each of us the power of being into potential. Then he called for all of us who have the spirit of fear and my entire group for the radio show went up. While I was up there the Holy Spirit said get down on your knees and it was hard and I said to Him that it was easier for me to do this in the street than in the church and then I said, "Okay Father I'm going to step out from everyone and lean on the alter before you." At first it was hard because it was out of my comfort zone; as a matter of fact it was out of the Sunday routine but no matter how strange I felt due to pride I remained obedient and I did it!

In addition to that this guy who I had worked with and had some issues with; well I grabbed his hand hard and I prayed you hear me I'm talking about I wept. Now that I think about it on my way to church this Sunday morning these ladies who I enjoy riding with told me about Jeremiah. One of them Sis Lil had taught intense Bible study for seven years and I was pleading with her to start again for I'm so desperate for the Word. She told us about Jeremiah being the weeping prophet and how he sacrificed his personal life for his purpose. I was saying to the ladies, "Oh isn't that the one where the wall came down?" They smiled and said, "We are talking about Jeremiah not Jericho!" So you see how bad I need to know the Word. And yesterday morning the Minister spoke from Ephesians and that is where the Holy Spirit said to me to tell my husband to start our Bible study. You know it got so deep yesterday morning that I went to write something down and I had already written it! My partner, Mr. Holy Spirit is letting me know now that it isn't Alzheimer's but supernatural timing!

LUPUS IS ONLY TRAVELING ON THIS TRAIN IT IS NOT MY DESTINATION!

Yesterday a friend of mine who is a miracle himself by living on a partial lung told me about a friend of his who was having problems moving her limbs and had just been diagnosed with lupus. I feel as though I was assigned to this girl on the phone for that split second for up until now I have yet to hear anything so I assume she is doing well. My friend has passed on so I have no clue if I saw her at the funeral or not. We shared pain stories and I told her about the medications they had me on and then we discussed the side effects. We shared stories of not being able to sleep and she told me how she was afraid she would not be able to work and use her hands again. My partner, Mr. Holy Spirit had me assure her that she will not be able to manage this condition without Him, the sustainer of life! We than assured her that the connected phone call wasn't by accident but a part of God's plan to remind her that there is so much more to her going through and getting to the other side. In order to encourage others that lupus can be managed we have to remind that there is hope. Although we may have to make adjustments there is always a plan for our lives and how we choose to deal with it is our choice!. Yeah there will be rough days filled with pain and pity but it is truly up to us to see our journey through in a positive light. And I can say this because as I'm writing my eyes are still painful from a recent flare up but like Phil 4:13 says "I can do all things through Christ who strengthens me!"

Now I was told that she was a Muslim so I shared my faith with her and only told her what works for me and my faith healing. Stories like how my Asian pastor had prayed over my knee and I felt a fierce heat and then my knee was alright after it had been prayed over. I told her straight up that I am a keep it real Christian and my faith has kept me and brought me through! In addition to conventional methods I practice holistic methods. Therefore I didn't beat her over the head with my beliefs but shared my experiences as well as other ingredients that my very spiritual Bermudian holistic Doctor Alma has given me.

Lupus is only a condition that I was diagnosed with years ago. It moved into my space so I carry it, it does not carry me my Lord and Savior does the carrying. The young lady told me how she couldn't walk down the stairs and often had to slide down on her behind! She talked about being in excruciating pain and I told her that's what I used to deal with. In fact last week I had a flare up and my knee bones started grinding with bone on bone so it was painful to walk. Now this lady had sounded hopeless but once we started talking there was a shift in her tone from blah to "oh yeah!" I pray that is what my survival through my trials bring others hope. I'm a living testament of what God can do and is doing. Don't get it twisted just because I may not always say it, my heart rings songs of gratitude, all glory goes to God!

I started to relive the nightmare that my body went through prior to my systemic lupus diagnosis I told her how I remember crawling because I couldn't walk and as a result my dog thought I was playing with him until even he knew something was wrong and started barking intensely and trust and believe my baby isn't a barker! I recall swimming in a public pool and my whole body getting cramps, talk about a body Charlie horse. Strangers had to rush in and carry me out of the pool while my then partner was on the sidelines wondering what was going on. One night I had it so bad that I was afraid of my body cramping up while I was asleep. I'm telling you there's nothing like awakening from your sleep to the reality of your body being cramped up after you've experienced the nightmare in your sleep. I was afraid to sleep so I slept sitting up, needless to say I got no physical sleep. But I had to go to church the next morning because of all that God had done, like saving me in that pool the day before. I asked my former partner to go with me but they refused saying they were tired from being up all night with me when I actually watched them sleep for hours. I began feeling queasy but I went to church anyhow. When I called for them two hours later they were gone so I kept calling and no one was there! I didn't wish to be alone so I went to the studio because I was afraid to be home alone in case the intense cramping started.

One night after smoking my last cigarette at 6 p.m I woke up at 11 p.m. and could not breathe. I felt like a fish out of water. I got my partner up and she wanted to walk to where we had to go and I'm telling you I banged on all my neighbors doors on our floor and no one answered. Take note that once again I was looking to man to help me, to save me, to rescue me rather than the Creator of all men! So as I was knocking on the doors in my heart I asked Jesus to spear my life and if he did I promised I would never smoke another cigarette. Well we ended up at a nearby police station and they thought I had been smoking drugs such as crack cocaine. Really why would we go to a police station? Once they realized this was real and not drug related they called an ambulance and I was driven to the hospital around the corner. Mind you there were no apologies. I had no insurance and that ride of four blocks cost me $500. My former partner stayed at the hospital and I was diagnosed with having phenomena in my left lung. So I had to be on medical house arrest for two weeks, meaning I couldn't go outside period! And I never smoked again.

Now I was a medium smoker and could easily smoke a pack and a half a day with some help from my former life partner. She would smoke all of mine and save hers, even hide cartons and we smoked the same brand. Needless to say I would buy a whole lot of cigarettes and I believe she is the one who got me to switch from my previous brand to hers, deep huh? Anyhoo getting back to the story, it was many weeks later and I remember being asked to light a cigarette for someone and when I went to put it to my mouth to take a puff the Holy Spirit reminded me that I had made a pact with Jesus and I didn't smoke anymore! This was deep since my former partner and her brother would always taunt me that I would never be able to stop smoking cold turkey and bragged that their dad did. They said I didn't have the willpower. And hey they are both correct. I didn't have the strength on my own because trust and believe I had tried the patches, cessation classes, teas, herbs, even carrying scissors to cut the cigarettes in half which only made me smoke more . . . so no I couldn't rely on my own strength because I failed over and over. But once I made a pact with Him, my strength was renewed. So when people ask me for a light or a cigarette on the street, I feel good about saying sorry I don't smoke anymore. And when others inquire how I stopped I boldly tell them that it is not because of me, it was my pact with Jesus. Now let's not get it twisted here we are years later and if I'm stressed and smell cigarette smoke it brings urges and then I laugh at the enemy and say, "Good Try Satan!"

God allowed me to go through the circumstances to stop cold turkey! Seven months later I was diagnosed with fluid around my heart and the reason was that I had systemic lupus that was raging out of control! At that time my former life partner who wasn't the most attentive person would leave me or watch me go through pain but now looking back I have to believe they couldn't handle it because that is what I have to believe in order for me to continue to be on the path of forgiveness. Now I do recall when I would spend all of this money on these guys who worked downtown in the plush section of Philly with wealthy patients so I thought in my former mindset that if it works for them it will work for me. Right?

I had fruit diets, sound and vibration therapy you name it. I even took special pills they personally manufactured and at first I was getting better. Later they had people chanting in circles on the beach for me and things got real bad. My former partner and my dog would stay downstairs while I spent weeks in my bed hobbling to the bathroom. The guys I hired put me on a vegetable and fruit diet consisting of pineapples, mango etc. Then one time I had to visit my neurologist for the tumor and the guy I had hired took me to the hospital to meet with her. Well I couldn't even walk by myself, I was that weak! Just thinking about it makes me realize how many times the enemy has tried to snuff me out so God has something planned for me beyond all I could ever imagine.

Getting back to the story my Neurologist of over a decade apparently didn't like what she saw so she called behind my back to a friend who was the head Cardiologist but all my poor doctor could do was to plead for me to hurry back to see her. She recognized that it wasn't my brain cancer but something much more. Imagine that? More, like my body hadn't been through enough. I just didn't know how rough it was about to get.

Well about two weeks later it got so bad that I could just about roll the toilet paper to wipe myself and that was a huge task. One day a friend of mine, Nyeah was on her way to school and something told her to stop by and she told the taxi to wait for her for she felt something was wrong. They had to lift me out of bed and carry me to the taxi and we went straight to the hospital. Once I got there I asked for the test that I remember my Neurologist telling me about. I did this and it was like a movie the next thing I know I was holding my friends hand and they were rushing me through the hospital so fast that all I could do was pray and say, "God you got this!" When I look over my life He has gotten me through so many things that I should never doubt him but the flesh in me sometimes still gets a bit agitated.

After the Cardiologist did some tests they rushed me through the halls like some "E.R." movie and I was admitted to the Critical Care unit. They couldn't get blood so we went through the feet thing again and this time they ran a heart pick because I had developed so much fluid around my heart that if the outer lining didn't peel off I would have to have heart surgery. I was born with an enlarged heart so my heart being bigger than the norm was no surprise but heart surgery, really?

My Mother and nephew Meko stuck by side. All sorts of friends visited and sometimes my partner would spend the night. I remember she had to do a catering job for the United States President and couldn't be with me but my cousin who worked with him directly came to visit me with secret service. Talk about a hospital uproar. I received all sorts of extra special attention that I thought was for me but actually they were trying to meet my cousin. I'm so clueless about the groupie thing. However my Mom always tells the story of how this girl brought in a demo and recorder for me to listen to her friend, I again clueless thought she was just coming to see me and eventually had to send her away. After all we had to make a decision about having heart surgery. Do you think I was interested in listening to someone's song or talent?

The doctors had told us that if my heart's outer layer didn't peel off or shrink I was headed for surgery. They said that if I couldn't walk they would have no other choice. Man I told my Mother that I would rather have brain surgery again than my heart. I prayed to God and my partner, Mr. Holy Spirit to get me out of that bed and with tubes attached and heart pick in I got up and walked a few steps and then back and forth. Now ironically my Rheumatologist at that time was Doctor Maldonado. I told him that I had my Mom's birthday cruise to attend and I wanted to have a massage by a man on that beach in Barbados while drinking my virgin Pina Colada. I CONCENTRATED ON THAT PICTURE. Later I was released and when I went back for my check up the doctor couldn't believe that my heart shrunk and there was no scaring. I said, "Do you believe in God healing you?" He nodded and said, "That could be the only explanation." Now six weeks later I went on that cruise but before I got on in Florida with my Aunt I toppled over and they found that I had an ingrown toe nail that was so embedded that they wondered how could I have possibly walked with it. I kept it in a bottle for it was that long. Not letting that slow me down I boarded the cruise and my own family didn't recognize me for the steroids had me gain almost 70 pounds! In fact they passed me and I was hollering "It's me Les!" Too funny, but losing this weight over the years has been difficult as well as paying off that cardiology bill. Between the brain thingy and this I had to go through four sets of clothing sizes now talk about expense I praise God for my Aunt Es and what my anonymous Uncle K did for me. And check this five years later I married my boo who ironically had the same name as my former rheumatologist. Now Just look at God!

I was so supernaturally protected that after all of this trauma and drama we discovered that the main guy who I hired as my alternative medicine man actually had flunked medical school and only pretended to be a doctor. Now in his defense **many things he did like the sound and vibration therapy worked** but the fact that I had lupus unknowingly, he could have killed me. Apparently they said he should have picked up on certain things.

For example all diseases flourish in acidity so we need to become more alkaline and what he was instructing me to eat was acidic! We found out soon after that he had some mental disorder of delusions so when my mother threatened to seriously sue him we received word that he and his alternative medical partner had fled to the San Francisco region to set up shop.

Excuse me I need to say this. "Lord please forgive me right now as I'm writing this I may get agitated but I never doubt you for that is the spirit of fear that I allow in. Lord you have brought me through so many trials when the doctors said, 'No' you said, 'Yes!' You have always had your Angels encamped around me and I just want to say thank you from the bottom of my heart! Thank you seems like not enough so I've given my life to you as my sacrifice."

Wow I just had to go there people; be humble and reflect and most of all as I prayed with Mother Barlow this morning it's all about gratefulness! This will truly keep you in check. Especially when the storms come to rattle your cages. As I'm writing my partner, Mr. Holy Spirit is ministering to me at the same time. One of my Mom's favorite sayings keeps on popping in my head "Faith without works is dead." And I'm telling you without any hard work you wouldn't be reading this book today. Trust and believe my friends! And getting back to the story, you have to keep up; it's a spiritual protocol here! (Smile)

When the young lady on the phone shared how sometimes her lupus got so bad that her family members had to carry her I was able to reflect on how it took two people to raise me out of my bed and I knew God had allowed me to go through it in order to share this testimony with someone else. That's what it is, the pyramid effect! Jesus used this method to get God's message across. It is our duty as human beings to pass on our stories of how we made it through!

ON THE RADIO .... OH OH

Yesterday morning I was in a perky mood and then I went on my computer to check my emails and as I was on the phone there it was .... on supersonic blast! I was asked to work on a commercial for a brother in my church that I had assisted before. We believed in and still do in his cause of spreading the word despite our differences. Words can't express how my heart felt to know I was assisting not just him but the Lord. Well Any hoo I read his email and there it was he was having an event with the exact name of the events that God had given me. Just as I clearly heard God's voice say HISRECORDS and I followed suit and incorporated it back in 1999 a few months before I was diagnosed. A well established label's vice president asked me to go home and come up with a name for a label that would assist my people and other rising artist in my homeland and that's how my God appointed record label began. Well God was always giving me names of festivals, shows, and films etc. even when my walk wasn't that tight with the Lord, the Holy Spirit continued to honor the fact that I would turn to God first before making major decisions.

One night I was asking God to give me the name of a festival that would honor Him by assisting others, my plea was that simple. Being in music and film I or should I say we, that being my partner the Holy Spirit and I completed a documentary entitled WE R 1. We showcased it in a venue and had other inspiring artists, musicians and testimonies from a variety of amazing people. In addition we asked for cans of food, books, and clothing to assist the less fortunate in Africa. We marketed that show and as clear as I'm typing the name of the event was given to me by that same voice, the name God literally gave me was 'HOPEFEST.' So when I read the emails and how this fellow church member wanted me to assist with Hopefest 2009. I freaked and I still can't believe it. He had written two letters telling people about this event. Another thing is that I made it known that I would have Hopefest 2009 after my wedding in October to celebrate my 10th year of what God has done in my life. That's right sweetie it's been ten long years since that diagnosis. Like Alicia Keyes song says lesson learned and something about being burned so after asking the guy to change the name of the event he said God had given him that in 2004 and he held an event similar. But I wasn't buying it, my core didn't feel right.

Logically my spirit tells me that wasn't the case until a seed was replanted. You know this discernment stuff just resonates in my soul and you know when you know! I'm reading a book by Melinda Ireland and it talks about heavenly holding patterns and I needed to read that after I cried my eyes out to my fiancé and mother yesterday about being burned. I had no choice but to wait on God. I actually told the guy oh God gave u x, y, x, and b and now you are telling me this. Do I believe him well to a point but were seeds planted? A definite yes, I mean there it is on my website and my space page that he claims he never saw . . . So today it's about where he wants my feet to go.

I dedicate myself to projects and right now my main project is my wedding and trust and believe I'm asking the Lord to direct my path on that; as well as my new potential tenants and my fiancé's job and let us not forget song placements. In the words of my Uncle Bunny's song, "What would we do without the Lord" which I intend to walk down the aisle to. Now let me go and add Donna Summer's song On the Radio to that DJ play list for the reception . . .

LISTEN TO YOUR CORE

Hold on to your dreams, well that's a line from Yolanda Adams' song Hold On that is what I heard on my XM radio when I started journeying this morning. After a night of being stood up by friends and going from club bar to bar. That's right bar I sat there drinking my club soda, I wanted to go dancing at one of them for it gave me the opportunity to hand out business cards and for me to readily admit that I am a keep it Real Christian and I wanted to promote inspirational music. I guess I get that from growing up and having a Dad that passed out 'Warcrys'(global testimonial newsletters) for the Salvation Army in the bars or bingo halls at home. I feel that the world is filled with so much pain and strife that we need uplifting. One thing I noticed at the bars was that everyone was seeking and searching for joy. Now despite the fact that I was going through my own inner turmoil I still did not turn away from Christ.

At this one spot believe it or not when I was bringing back chicken wings from the store to the bar the Holy Spirit said get down and I said, "Really here outside on the sidewalk of the bar" and the answer was a yes so I did it. I got on my knees on the concrete outside that bar door and prayed. Afterwards I proceeded into the bar with the wings and then my Mother called long distance and I was speaking loudly over the music so she could hear about my inner turmoil and one of the things we talked about was the Word. I said "Momma I have no other choice than to believe and stand on Proverbs 3:5, 6. I have to Trust in the Lord with all my heart and lean not on my own understanding. And to Acknowledge Him in all thy ways and He will direct my path. And another one Mom is that I stand on is Psalms 18:32 God will arm me with strength and keep my path safe. Mom I truly have to believe for God didn't spare my life for pain and I know that He will not leave me."

Now imagine if you were sitting at that bar trying to drown your sorrows in booze and you overheard this, it's a seed and a direct hit on the enemy! And you know as I'm writing my partner, the Holy Spirit is giving me a revelation that when the Bible talks about going out amongst them that is what I'm doing. Another example is when I got into "the fight" we will call it and I used some cuss words and then put my hand over my mouth. Well a young lady who was present said, "Oh it's okay to cuss I do it all the time." I didn't respond then but the Spirit convicted me. I had partied with her and a friend and demonstrated in living color that I didn't need alcohol and danced for nearly two hours straight on one glass of club soda. So the next day in casual conversation I said to her, "You know yesterday when I swore please accept my apologies; I should have said something then because for me as a Christian it is not okay to swear it says so in the book of Ephesians and you noticed last night I danced my butt off without a drink." She interrupted and must have misunderstood and said, "Drinking a club soda is not drinking" and I responded, "Precisely that's what I was saying some people need a drink to get over their shyness but with the Holy Spirit that is all I need and as you saw I could dance the night away!" I'm being transformed before your very eyes, no more alcohol so the same needs to go for my speech.

Even in the midst of the storm God is still doing His thing. Had I not been involved in "the fight" this planting of seeds would have not occurred and I'm telling you even though I'm getting married in less than a week with me and my intended not speaking I'm trusting and believing that God will intercede and I'm practicing being still. Like it says be still and know that I am God. One thing I know for sure is that this wedding is bigger than the two of us for it is about allowing the Holy Ghost to do His thing. It's about God showing up and showing out! I've consulted God right down to the program words, music choices etc. It's about all of those individuals that will never normally attend a church to feel the presence of the Lord. It's about Him not about us but I don't know if my intended understands that so I'm trying my best to stand still so that God could do His work. Like someone told me, "God doesn't need your help in this situation dear. If you gave it to Him why do you keep taking it back?"

HOLDING HEAD ABOVE WATER

Not to complain but the wedding occurred about a month ago and I still have no tenants and Alex has no job. I have had identity theft and I'm being harassed by my former tenant who moved in for three months and was deployed to Iraq and not to mention they messed up my drain. They left tall of this metal stuff in the toilet and I specifically told them not to flush it but to take it out of the toilet for I foresaw a blockage. The bills are piling up and the unemployment isn't enough so as I'm writing I'm praying for divine intervention. I just turned on the TV and they are talking about divine instructions for financial solutions. They are talking about the sowing of $100 as a covenant between you and God. Here I'm telling you about me having limited funds but the Holy Spirit is telling me to do this.

Now the joke is I was scanning for Bet Inspiration and here I am being bombarded with broadcasts of divine financial solutions and faith on healing. On top of all of this my hands have the tremors so "Lord I need a healing please! Lord come and takes control of my finances, my life, and my body. Lord take control and direct my path Lord, direct my every footstep along with my thought patterns in Jesus holy name!"

I watched the program and the Minister was talking about once you accept Jesus and allow God to take over your life you begin to walk in your rights. Now one of my favorite scriptures is Psalms 18:32 "God arms me with strength and makes my path perfect and safe." **I'm reversing my tears of sorrow and fear into tears of joy and positive tomorrows!** With God before me who can be against me. Even as I'm reviewing this manuscript my lupus has flared up in my eyes so I can just about see but the big 'but' is that I have hope. I continue to believe that scripture Psalms 25:21 "May integrity and uprightness protect me for my hope is in the Lord." I have received countless prophesies and they all point to prosperity and success even though right now it appears that I'm in the desert with droplets of water! Lord prepare me for the rain.

CAN'T SLEEP

I've been up since 4:30 a.m. listening to spa music and sweating the remnants of my cold out. I talked to God and the song by Toby Mac rang clearly within my head. "I don't want to gain the whole world and lose my soul." So much is on my mind such as my Aunt's surgery tomorrow, my Mother flying in today and how will we get around without her walking too much, the wedding, my boos perspective job, my hormones considering in two years we have never been intimate, my nephew getting knocked down by a truck the day before and the list goes on. My church family who I once was so close to and now through tragedy seem so far apart. My Mom's former client and longtime family friend is in her last stages of cancer, my adopted aunt in her stages of breast cancer, my tenants moving out to fight the war in Iraq and again the list goes on. You know the war never hit home for me personally until my newest tenant whom had only been there for less than there months informed me that she has to go to Iraq. Not to mention two houses over they were deployed as well. The funny thing is that I asked God to put the right tenants into my apartments and He will.

So you see so much lies up in the air and according to the book I'm reading by Melinda Ireland "Divine Delays" these are heavenly holding patterns, up in the air that is.

Do we ever stop and think of our words and how powerful they are. It's like the saying be careful what you put out into the universe, or be careful what you pray for, you just might get it. All of these aforementioned scenarios require faith in God no man on earth can determine the outcomes. It's a God thing! When I think about it my entire life has consisted of scenarios that only a greater force could have connected my "journey dots" my points of visitation ultimately leading to my destination! You see just as I play with words, write lyrics, plays, melodies, scripts, articles, this book, and documentaries they all are considered creative works stemming from no one but who, don't all shout at one time, our Creator!

Right down to my marriage I've given the creative control over to my Father. The direction of this book, my entire life. Too often we as humans have this natural ability to hold on to control ourselves especially when we indulge in drugs and alcohol. Often we give our inner control away to a higher substance so just imagine once you turn it over to Jesus. There I said it **"Jesus"** and when you make him your personal savior you don't have to worry too much about negative consequences for the Word says it will all turn out for the good. And the one thing I've learned is that my God does not lie. Like His Word says He is not a man that should lie. Within our human brains we can only fathom a snippet of who God is and what He can do. Parting of the red sea or speaking from a bush for he was God of eons past and He still performs miracles at present. Take for example my little nephew getting struck by a big truck. My mother was driving and in traffic when there was an ambulance, fire truck etc up ahead. In her mind she was thinking it must be a bad accident and then she saw her granddaughter and grandson and immediately knew it was the other twin. No it wasn't coincidence that she was on the scene. And when I spoke long distance to my little man I asked him if he thanked Jesus and he said yes. My six year old baby boys.

As I'm writing I'm crying because NO ONE can ever tell me that Angels don't exist or that God isn't real. For all that my family has been through we still rely on that Higher Presence for like the song says "there is Somebody Bigger than you and I." My Mom pointed out that on my last requested wedding date my oldest nephew had gotten in a bad accident the twins' brother. He too survived after a handle bar was almost plunged into his brain. Again my Parents came on the scene and he as is written, had been indulging in Wine and Spirits. There is a reason for that title people, do not sleep on it. For the spirits really had a field day until my Mom and Aunt Q started pleading the blood of Jesus. The doctors were about to perform surgery but God performed it and today my nephew I'm proud to say has a small visible reminder scar on his face and now drives. Wow he actually has his license thank God no more motorcycles!

What I'm trying to say is He will make a way out of no way just like the song says. And through writing this recount I realize that this is therapeutic for my inner person. I'm learning to fall in love with me and who is inside of me that makes me tick! My partner, the Holy Spirit confirmed this last Sunday when my Filipino Pastor pointed out that when Jesus ascended to Heaven he left us with a comforter, that being the Holy Spirit. And today you will hear many public figures talk about the Spirit and it needs to be pointed out that the Spirit has a first name just like you and I. His first name is Holy . . . (Gee I guess now I know why they call me Nevida, my transcended prayer warrior Grandmother). Now that I think about it the Prophets K who I met with at a Holy Spirit Conference said that I was carrying the prophetic mantle and that I already knew that. I and my family come from a bloodline of Prophetess and Prophets. Prophets not always in title but definitely in action, you know Super Powers! Even when my little nephew got knocked down yesterday both brother and sister said that they felt something was wrong. They have it and we will teach them to be more in tune with this hereditary gift which stretches wide on both my parents sides. I had Church Planters and staunch Prayer Warriors and Evangelists such as Grandma Any Simons, Grandma Nevida Joell, Aunt Lydia Furbert, Captain Ruth Benjamin, Major Albert Benjamin, Aunt Sarah Lee, Cousin Eloise Simmons, Conway and Joan Simmons, Cousin Nona, Cousin Lois and Madeline Joell. My DNA is injected with strong women of God and we won't get started with the male Bishops such as Uncle Eugene and Darius Joell, Uncle Henry and Cousin David Joell and the one who my Grandma passed her spiritual government mantle to, Uncle Vernon Lambe Sr. and so many more. There have been so many in my blood family that have had an impact on me. Even my adopted Uncle Bunny Sigler a fighter for the Kingdom. I was once told that I come from "Spiritual Royalty" and I guess if there is such a thing I most definitely do. I can see why the attacks would be so severe and often. My entire family is saturated with God's equipped army.

WAKING UP WITH A SONG!

"Lord I love you with a grateful heart, each time I think of you the praises start. I love you so much Jesus, I love you so much . . ."

This morning this is the song that's ringing from my heart. A song that is so appropriate to a fresh start. How many of you wake up with a song in your head but even more so what about that song being in your heart. There is a different feeling, one from without and the other from within! Every day I walk amongst my block's tree lined street and look at my house and I know God is the answer to the impossible. When I went through my legal separation I knew that I would only be in my apartment for two years, that's right that same apartment I had seen in a dream. The one that I resided in years prior and used to get high in. This time God had placed me on the top Penthouse floor surrounded by windows and every day I could see the same high rise building and neighborhood where I used to get high at years ago. Amazing but don't get it twisted my Father said, "Here's an opportunity I've allowed you to turn 360 degrees and you can either go backwards or move according to my direction!" Now I could have chose to go backwards because I was coming out of a divorce situation and believe me the drugs were still available or I could use this position He had placed me in as a testimony to let others know that He is able and that we can do ALL things through Christ. I'm not saying that there were never any thoughts of getting high but they were few and far between; fleeting thoughts that I rebuked in the name of Jesus! Now nobody can EVER tell me that there isn't power in that name **JESUS**. NO ONE.

THE HUSBAND AND WIFE CON TEAM THAT MADE ME RELY MORE ON THEE

I once had these freeloading tenants who worshipped all sorts of things and had built an altar with an Indian Chief Head, Mother Teresa, an Indian yogi, Jesus and others. They would put fruit; money, weed and incense on this alter and kneel before it. Then they would smoke pot all day and transport people in order to fulfill their needs. Well with all the things they saw happen with me one of them said "They say there is power in that name." My warfare with demonic tenants is a book in itself. I had met this couple at a friend's meeting and they said they were screwed over by their cousin and had to be out of the house that they had put $20000 into and fixed up. They shed tears and were so convincing that to this day I don't know if that story was real or not but I do know my reality with them was a living nightmare. I was going to rent my apartment to students but listening to them week after week my heart cried out and I could not see these people on the street in the cold especially around Christmas time. It wouldn't be right and what would Jesus do? So without ANY credit checks I allowed them to move in and they gave me some upfront funds, one month's security, first and last month's rent which they had received as grant money.

They gave me a photocopy of their social security card and drivers license. They had a reference from an old man who said that he catered for them . . . So I felt hey maybe they are legit. Then the money problems came so I had to sign papers and had to call them a few times to get it all. In fact I still had a heart for them and told them they could have a hundred of it since they had fallen on hard times. I had another property that I made arrangements with them that they did not have to pay rent in the interim as long as the husband would fix the minor repairs to this house and I would provide him with the money for whatever materials he needed. Well this job went well for a while and then I went driving with them to get materials once or twice so it was no reason to question them right?

When I evicted the transsexuals from the house I paid the husband and a friend of his $1500 to clean out the place. So long story short they didn't have to pay rent and received hundreds of dollars every few weeks to work on my other property. Sounds stupid right?

Eventually I went to the property after a few months and hardly anything had been done. You can only imagine how used I felt. I had this couple over for Christmas dinner, had gotten them jobs by having them pick up folks, and had shared laughter and sorrows with people who I considered as friends. Big mistake . . . My Mother and her prophetic self could see through the "dynamic con duo" from the moment they picked her up from the airport she knew they were con artists. I've found that con artists often talk a lot about what they've done and what they can do for you. They are fast talkers or they can appear as these immediately deep spirited individuals were everything is about God, the universe and injustice! That's their game talk, all to reel you in and before you know it you are caught in a mental and emotional trap.

The only way I got out of all of the traps was through Jesus and allowing the Holy Spirit to literally guide my movements and of course professional counseling. You know this couple even went as far as informing me that my new fire alarm system wasn't working. They watched me call electricians, and spend countless hundreds of dollars on trying to find out what was wrong. I can't believe that they watched me go through mental torture trying to figure out the reason for the fire alarm failure that was almost new.

After I kicked them out I found a new fire alarm company which I paid thousands of dollars to install a new system and they discovered that the line had been cut in the ceiling. There it was clear as day the husband who was one of three people that had access to the building's basement had taken the time to deliberately cut the lines. Talk about straight up evil! It was only my trusted grounds man of over a decade; me and the husband who had been cementing some walls in the basement that had keys to the locked door. He spent hours in the basement high and when I look at it doing very little cementing. I later found out for sure that it was them for months later I was notified with proof that they had taken out personal fire insurance from a New York based company to cover themselves.

God speared me from these demons that were plotting to cause a fire in the building and then they would sue me. Now what a scenario! I put them out because they revealed themselves about taking the money and not upholding their end of the deal so when the time got near they did something else that would take me off track. But as the song says "Through it all I've learned to trust in Jesus, I've learned to trust in God." It was none other than the Holy Spirit that led me to discover all of these things that were hidden from me in the natural. From the right timing to visit the other property, to having the deal with them for the right time, to discovering that once again demons come in many faces but in my life if you take a look it's the same patterns. Always in relationships with people whether it is in music, tenants, church or personal. You know the enemy knows you just like God knows us. The enemy knows what appeals to us, and our weaknesses. Satan's job is none other than to steal, kill and destroy. Anything that is chaotic and filled with confusion, pain, guilt, and shame and has a lack of true peace and inner joy is not of God! We need to recognize this simple but realistic principle that when there is no peace then we must get on our knees and demand that God take over, and ask the Holy Spirit to order our steps. Cry out, "Jesus you win I'm helpless; you drive this vehicle that has been termed as the physical me."

You know we all have that inner voice both believers and nonbelievers which as I'm writing this I realize is a term that I'm not so fond of because Satan and his imps are believers as well. The demons obeyed Jesus so they believed right? I like to use the term as of right now non-followers and followers of Christ. Now getting back to what I was saying we all have an inner voice and with animals it's instincts. You ever hear someone say, "Man I should have followed my first mind." Or "I felt something telling me not to or to do it." Well once you accept Christ as your personal Savior, hence the word "personal" because you allow your mind, body and soul to be renewed. You have a new outlook on life and the way you think, act and talk. We as humans are not perfect but we strive to be more like Jesus. So what I'm saying is in my life I've found that the only way to do this is to rely on the Holy Spirit, the comforter that Christ left for us. Basically it is that inner voice and guide that needs to be recognized as a source of strength and enlightenment!

When you have accepted Christ you have the Holy Spirit to rely on, guide your footsteps and protect you. That husband and wife team only caused me to strengthen my beliefs based on seeing once again the Holy Spirit in action. They say everything in this life's journey is about learning lessons. We learn lessons from the simplest to the harshest moments in our lives. Just when we think things can't get worse they often do but we must hold on and remember that this too shall pass. These are the times when we must as the song says "Have a little talk with Jesus, tell Him about your problems" this is scary because we all love some form of control. We must take our hands of the wheel and literally ask the Holy Spirit to guide us! I get on my knees in public sometimes when the Holy Spirit beckons me too. I sometimes say, "Here, now, what in front of all these people?" I remember one time I was on a busy city street and I was beckoned to show humility and get down and pray. I tried to negotiate with God saying "Right here Lord? Can't I walk a little further to a less crowded spot?" Well I negotiated all the way until I reached inside a train station which was even more crowed and God said, "Now!" I was like man come on but I obeyed and got on my knees and did a quick thank you and guidance prayer. When I got up a little boy said to me, "Miss were you praying?" I said, "Yes I was giving thanks I figure if the Muslims can do it why can't we as Christians?" He smiled as his mother dragged him by the arm and he just kept looking back at me. Well from that moment on I may negotiate a little but I don't question God. How could we be unfaithful or ungrateful to our Creator, our Father? Yes we falter but we must keep on and get back on track. We can never allow the enemy and its sea of naysayers keep us down.

Tribute 2 My Uncle Henry

I have an Uncle who had suffered with Parkinson's for years and his son prophesizes just like our Grandmother and great Grandmother and Evangelist cousins. Time and time again my Uncle would go in and out of the hospital. Up and down from a walking, singing man to a man being fed by tubes and eventually on life support with the doctors giving up hope. His son prophesied to me about his dad receiving a blood transfusion and his Mom said, "No he doesn't need that." And days later that is what my uncle needed because in addition to his Parkinson's his blood was contaminated. My cousin and I prayed for another miracle of God stepping in and showing out in the name of Jesus. The result was my uncle being taken off life support, breathing on his own and today only has the Parkinson but it is controlled.

A decade later my Uncle passed with all his brothers and sisters at his bedside. They all sang a melody of traditional Joell family songs including their anthem song that Uncle Hen taught his sisters "I Saw a Man." Check the lyric "Last night I dreamed an Angel came, He took my hand and called my name . . . ." When he passed I didn't know in the natural but I was lying on my floor next to Diego hundreds of miles away and all of a sudden I felt him pass me and I immediately called my cousin David to see if he had heard any news but he hadn't. He remained hopeful since his only sibling his brother Paul had just been murdered in cold blood months before. I always tell my Aunt/Godmother that she needs to write a book on faith and survival after losing a son and then her soul mate and best friend all within the same year! That couple set the standards of marriage quite high but with God leading them and Jesus being the glue how could they not survive any storm. I miss them for they were so in sync and encouraging as a unit.

God gave my Uncle an additional decade after the doctor's grim prognosis. He was able to relocate to their dream home in another state. He lived to see his grandchildren and was able to spend time with his son chatting in rocking chairs on the front porch only a couple of months prior to his son's untimely death and then his own. I personally believe that the Holy Spirit gives us premonitions. They were able to share those last special moments together which served as positive memories for everyone. My Lord is a mysterious miracle God. I told my cousin that the Holy Spirit had put in my heart to tell him and his mom that God will continue to do miracles if they continue to testify. He will do exceedingly and abundantly beyond anything that we could imagine. We must including myself tell of His works and that is why I'm writing this book to let others know that there is an alternative to whatever they may be going through.

Now let's look at the order and see how God is a "deepie!" I cancelled out on going to my nephew's graduation ahead of time and then he got in the accident and then my Uncle Henry passes which causes his siblings to fly overseas to be at his bedside but they are really there to physically comfort him in his transcendence. In addition to that due to "the Holy Ghost timing" they will be there to assist his lovely wife and arrange as well as be there for the funeral. I understand at my Uncle's bedside one brother cradled his head while another touched his heart, a sister held his hand while the others just sang songs and his wife said her goodbyes by telling him how much she loved him and enjoyed the years they had spent together. His siblings told him it was okay to close his eyes and to go home to Jesus and their mother. Now my sister who seems to be softening up over the years told them before they left to tell my Uncle to go towards the light. And that's exactly what he did.

Now I was or let's just say to be blunt and truthful, somewhat disappointed in God. And I felt guilty for feeling disappointed because He has done so much for me and my family. You know right down to writing this book the enemy tried to not let the hard drive connect or let me save that which I wrote. Yes there's power in the name of Jesus I personally believe and respect many religions and all cultures but FOR ME JESUS IS MY KEY and all I can say is DON'T KNOCK IT UNTIL YOU TRY IT.

It is our duty to show our fellow human beings that there is an alternative to what we can see and touch for there is so much more. Like the song says "My Lord is better than life!" After all it begins and ends with a song. So we must ask ourselves the question of how the melody will be arranged to the lyrics of our lives! Um not bad Holy Spirit, good analogy!

SOMETIMES THE WRONG STOP IS THE RIGHT STOP

Yesterday I was on the train and missed my stop. The computer voice on the train said one name but my spirit was telling me to look and it was not my usual stop but He told me to get off. Now I just want to say from jump that this would be the last time that I would see this husband alive! In the past I tried to tell the Lord that this would be my last time, and feel guilty for breaking my promise when I got high. I would be doing well and then out of nowhere I would feel this inner sick feeling in my stomach to go and get high with this secret respected infamous couple. Well it had been years and since this is the train stop I would get off to go and get high I became anxious and asked the Lord to cover me with His precious blood. I didn't know if this couple were still using or not for they lived right in that easy access neighborhood. I was just being obedient by trusting my partner, Mr. Holy Spirit and His guidance. Reluctantly I went to the house and their son remembered me and was happy to see me. I always treated him with respect and would tell everyone to keep it down because he was sleeping while we were getting high!

Well he was excited and called his parents and when we saw one another after all those years we just couldn't stop smiling. They invited me in and they now had a nice kitchen, a much cleaner house and you could feel peace. The wife looked like another person and they told me how one day they just looked at each other after getting high and said, "We have to stop this" and they did. I told them how I had truly accepted Jesus Christ as my personal savoir and they said join the club. The husband was still smoking cigarettes but was delivered from heroin, crack and cocaine, so to just be smoking cigarettes, you know Jesus is for real! The wife told me how she kept a crack bag for a year just to see how strong she was. But you know what it's not about her it is about who lives inside of her. She eventually got rid of it but as she says she is not a religious fanatic but has a strong personal relationship with Jesus and a whole lot of willpower by His strength.

We all thanked God for now being in the world of the living. We can now walk outdoors in the daylight with our heads held high, no feelings of guilt or shame. For the first time ever I was able to leave that house feeling good about being alive. Now although the devil may be extremely powerful don't get it twisted, the name of Jesus and walking in your calling is even more powerful! So let's get to stepping!

FAIR-WEATHER FRIENDS

Many who were in my life and have since which been removed. There is only the few that remain that were unconditional. I remember one who I helped tremendously transition from a shelter to finding performing gigs and I would pay them to help me go to the hospital. I once heard them saying to someone, "Go and ask money bags she will give it to you!"

I awoke this morning to a rendition of Silver and Gold, "Silver and Gold, I'd rather have Jesus than Silver and Gold. No fame or fortune or riches untold I'd rather have Jesus than Silver and Gold." As I lay in bed and meditated a little I thought about going to see the doctor later and if my girlfriends would show up to the movies. This may all seem trivial considering what I've been through but not REALLY.

When I look over the past decade of my life my friends that I considered true were often tied to me by through music, doing a news story, going to parties or sex. That's the sum of it. I clearly remember this guy I considered a friend for twenty years but realized that I was only a business friend when I no longer could bring him acts, or pay for artists or lend him money. I realized this the day another long term music associate of mine (notice my new terminology gosh I'm so proud of positive change) told me that his wife had just had another baby. I knew him before his wife, I remember when they got hitched and knew the entire family but was dead wrong about our relationship I was merely a convenience. When his brother needed a place I was there, when our work needed copyrights I paid as I also did for the new leads and song placements. When his younger brother would call me on the phone for hours late at night for advice I was there. And my ex could see all of the users that were around me when I had the record label but I couldn't when so called Christian rap artists needed money for their album I was there. When a young man needed thousands to start his dream company I bought shares. When they wanted to start a magazine or have something edited or travel I was there. I am still learning who my friends are.

The revelation that I jotted down from one of the many sermons I'll mention from my Bishop G is this. "We don't own ourselves, therefore we don't own anyone else, our character represents who we are and if we are new creatures in Christ than starting from this very moment I need to look at what the Bible says about being friends and ask God to choose them for me" just as He choose my husband. And when you think about it what type of friends did Jesus have? Pretty devoted were those disciples huh but even they turned their backs, look at how Peter denied knowing Him and Judas sold Him out and had greeted him with a kiss. Talk about shady! Yep and remember my partner, Mr. Holy Spirit is helping me write this! Therefore who are we not to face all kinds of deception and betrayals? You know one of the most painful feelings a human can face is rejection and that is something that I clearly have a battle with rejection and abandonment. I was watching Joyce Meyer and she was saying to her television viewers how when you do things differently people treat you different and some will disappear. This brought to my mind the example of when I stopped living my alternative lifestyle. It was never really the sex but my emotional ties. My heart was attached and some may call it soul ties. For me love was love. But I personally submitted my total self to God's will. And no I'm far from perfect, let's get that straight but I strive daily and learn from the lessons placed before me!

It makes you wonder why are our lives cultish? If you are no longer connected to something you no longer are included. As a result people tend not to be themselves but go along with the flow in fear of being left alone. I remember years ago "getting stoned" with my at that time season buddies and I wanted to try this experiment so I passed this candy down the line and asked what color it was when it started out. So the candy started out being red but it ended up being yellow. Why? Because one person had seen it as yellow so the rest followed suit. That is called Group Think!

When we reached the campus for Howard's Homecoming weekend I said to my fellow weed heads, "You know you all must be high because there is no way this candy is yellow. Hello look at it, it's red!" Point taken it was either group think or some strong weed.

THE WORD IS HIGHER THAN THE WEED OR RUM

I'm recapping on how I attended this church with my former partner and was really into it. Looking back I feel I was placed there feel to meet certain individuals that have had grave impacts in my life and also formed lifetime friendships. Man that is where I seemed to flourish in Christ but at the same time I was getting sucked deeper and deeper into my addiction. Yep sounds strange but true. One night after service I had friends over as I often did and my partner at the time had this black rum that was 150% proof and there was this couple there and one guy kept drinking it. All of a sudden a friend of mine my ace boom coon decided to break out the Bible. You had some people upstairs "toking" on that weed and here we were downstairs reading the Word. Well all of a sudden that same guy who was a Pastor's son and he and his partner had just been baptized earlier began falling to the floor and foaming at the mouth. I thought it was a seizure since I had them on occasion but no he fell out not from the rum but from me and my friend throwing the Word at him and asking him all kinds of questions!

Now imagine the scene you have people upstairs in the bathroom getting "zooted" and we are downstairs preaching while this brother is steadily trying to get his drink on. Then when he fell out from the Word his voice changed! OMG

Well didn't that just put a damper on the party he started talking in this deep strange voice saying all these things to us. One of them I remember was telling my partner that she didn't really love me and she was so frightened that she was stuck to the couch and couldn't get her legs down. The moment he called out to her for help she was shaking like a leaf. Then he started saying to my friend 'And else for you out there every night shaking that ass in the club.' That brother whomever he was just started revealing truths all over the place so his lover started crying and screaming his name saying, "Somebody help me" and we all started praying.

I called my Mother at some ridiculous hour and asked her what should we do and everyone was at my Mom's back and call as I had her on speaker phone. Then out of nowhere we all in unison just started screaming "Hallelujah, Hallelujah is the highest Praise" and we shouted it to the tips of our lungs like we were at the NFL football playoffs. It was only then that the guy came back to himself and got up off the floor. My poor ex lover, she didn't know what hit her and truthfully none of us did. I only learned later that Hallelujah really is the highest praise and what we had just witnessed was a part of a demon cleansing! We exorcised him with the Word and the chanting of the highest praise. I always said these moments and pages in my life should be on screen and they will one day. Needless to say we all were forever touched by that moment. And guess what, the friend who started the Bible thumping and was out there shaking her booty at the same time is now a respected Minister. Peep that, and I don't think she shares that testimony with too many people.

SPIRIT OF SUICIDE WAS HEAVY ON THAT TRAIN RIDE

Last evening we were on the subway when this guy was moving his hand and body strangely. To be honest I thought he was doing something sexual like masturbating because he wasn't facing us so all we could see was his arm and body motions. Then he went outside and stood between the connecting cars. This professional stylish mild mannered lady started freaking out asking the passengers to help stop the guy from going back into the unsafe outside cart attachment. Apparently there had been people jumping in front of trains and this lady could foresee that without ever knowing this report. I mean she pressed buttons and fear was written across her face, not to mention she held her hand over her heart. I pleaded the blood of Jesus repeated in my head and my Filipino sister did the same and we remained calm. I guess now thinking about it this resembled a modern reenactment of when the disciples were in the midst of the storm on the sea while Jesus was sleeping calmly. All around us was chaos but we remained secure in talking to our Father inwardly not shouting or Bible thumping! One young lady asked why the woman was so afraid and we were able to explain how this woman has the gift of sight and that we all have gifts. The girl in amazement told as about how she had experienced that gift when she was in another city visiting a church and this lady came up to her and told her all about herself. This was her second time witnessing the Spirit of the Lord. In the end they removed the man from the train and we saw him later begging someone for a cigarette. Apparently when he was on the outer cart he told a passenger who pulled him back at the request of the lady with the foresight that he just wanted to go outside and smoke a cigarette. However he was twitching, moving erratically and thank God for that obedient lady! When we disembarked the train I held her hand and said it's all about Jesus and she nodded in agreement.

My spiritual sister and I had told the other few passengers that this lady wasn't over reacting but truly had the gift off sight and I even said boldly to the others "You see it don't you, you see what is going to happen!" and thank God she acted on it. Too often we know things as well but we do not act on them. We all have internal gifts ready to be used for such spiritual warfare because that is what this was on that train. The spirit of suicide that she saw was and is real especially during this season of recession and economic hardship. We reminded them to thank Jesus for the memory of saving a life rather than the forever thought of watching someone die.

As I'm writing my partner, Mr. Holy Spirit is reminding me that even in my personal life I have to become more active with the armor God has given me and start to activate. My friends and I often talk about some of us being superpowers and like in the cartoons and movies we must join forces to fight evil and the powers of darkness. There is more to the unseen than there is to the seen. Just because we cannot visibly see something doesn't mean it is not there. We cannot see the air but it is there. Let us not be ignorant but awaken to what is. Like that cartoon used to say" Wonder Twins activate, but now its Super powers Activate" this is not the time to grow weary!

PLEADING THE BLOOD OF JESUS IS POWERFUL WHEN YOU BELIEVE!

Finding this house as our home was a difficult situation, and then so called friends weren't coming through so it made it worse. It was as if they didn't care and truthfully some didn't. We kept on getting the same news from a so called loyal bank that the funds are not there and then I heard the song "It is already done, waiting for an answer so don't give up" the song was recorded in 1997 by the Heritage X Choir off the album 'We Just Want to Give Thanks' and here we were in 2008. I felt that song was specifically for me and I said, "Thank you Jesus for the glory." After that out of nowhere the license and inspection guy out of nowhere came through. Our past tenant was being evicted so out of spite he reported the simplest of things and had violations placed on me. Here was this same inspector and he couldn't understand that I couldn't do something at a particular time because of cancer treatment. Now keep in mind there was nothing at all detrimental to the building my records can prove this.

When I explained to him my situation he was extremely callous and said, "Oh yeah I've dealt with cancer before but that appointment has to be still met on that day no exceptions!" Well here he was at the property at the same time I happened to be there and keep in mind this building is clear across town from where I live. Now he sees all the work is done like I had told him and I just happened to be in the same apartment that had reported violations looking at a heater with my repairman. Now I had the tenant's permission to be in there and my expert fix it guy thought I had arranged this meeting but I didn't God did to ease my mind. And guess what this same Inspector ended up retiring because his cancer flared back up. This is why we have to be somewhat compassionate to one another as Jesus did and don't allow them to walk over you. After all you never know we are all humanly made in our Father's image.

We all have the same body parts with unique imprints. Therefore we never know when one of those parts is going to malfunction. Like a car we can keep up on the tires so that they don't become worn or give out causing trouble. Have you ever been concentrating so much on the engine and oil, making sure the interior and the exterior of the car are in pristine condition with that shiny rustproof paint and then you're driving along and POW you've got a flat tire or your battery needs recharging or you need water because the car is overheating. Cars, houses and people are always depicting the unexpected. So never say never.

CHAPLAIN WARLOCK

I remember this man at church doing some work for me and I knew he was overcharging me but I had the money and I needed to get the job done. He broke our agreement and was pouting and shouting to be paid in cash not checks because I guess he didn't have a checking account? He would follow me and drive me to the bank. One time he drove me to my particular bank and writing this upsets me so much that I feel a seizure coming on!.

This smooth guy from my church and a Chaplain whom I prayed with for my chemo kept bothering me for money when he clearly hadn't finished the work. He told me he couldn't take checks and I waited in line at my bank looking busted without the proper ID like a drug addict trying to get $700 cash while he waited outside in his fancy car. Another time he came to my apartment building stating that he needed more money and I gave him $400. Now keep in mind that he took me to buy the materials and the deal was half up front and the other half upon completion. Then he was telling me how some lady who was a minister he had been working with had cursed him out. He also quoted scripture like a champ and bragged about the fact that he was sexually non active.

Well one day I was in the studio and he called asking for the balance of the money and I told him I would have to see if the work was completed. He said for me to trust him and he would pick me up and drive me to wherever I needed to go and I told him no thanks for I had a private 'Save Darfur screening' I had to attend. So he became his usual indignant self and demanded that he needed this money and I didn't trust him; what a nightmare! So he ended up coming to the screening and to this day I do not know if he went inside the theatre I just know that when I came out he was there looking at an escalade saying, "I shall have one of them for God said to ask Him for whatever we desire and I shall have it." I told him did he not just see the same film I did of how people are suffering in Darfur. After all he had a very nice car and said he did his share and started quoting scriptures. Alrighty Chaplain and now ordained Minister are we Christians for self gain and self proclaim with our arrogance?

We went to the apartment that night and I could just about see it for it was dark. He rushed me in and out quickly so about less than a mile down the street he asked about the money and I went to an ATM. Now in no way is this how I like to conduct business. I need records for my taxes and this whole deal with him reminded me of years prior when I had hired some "recovering" addicts to do a job or my former contractor who we fired for showing up all hours looking for $20.

Now that I think about it before I gave my life to Christ that all the workers I had were nickel and dimmers and never finished the work. The next day in the daylight I went to see the work and there were running paint streaks through the walls, it looked like a child could have painted those walls. So I called him and he showed up in a fancy valor track suit with his bluetooth headset and as usual always arguing with some female. So I said fine and got a paint brush and proceeded to paint the walls and then I and a friend who was in the other room heard him speaking loudly and haughtily on his phone saying "Well miss so you're not happy with my work and you want your money back? Is that what your saying?" Then I came into the room where he was and he turned around and when our eyes met I saw standing straight in front of me a warlock, this inhuman face. I cursed at it loudly and told him to get out of my house now. Then I started to cry because I had used the F word and how could I retreat back and hurt the Lord. I said to that warlock "I plead the blood of Jesus" and he started to run down the stairs. But I jumped up on him shouting, "Give me my keys in the name of Jesus!" And that man fled that house you hear me!

This supernatural warlock scene reminded me of the time when I was younger and this distant cousin of mine who was known to blackmail people. He would use their secrets and control their lives to get his way and have sex with them, male and female whomever he chose. Well he met me, Nevida and Annie's granddaughter and more importantly God's daughter and he kept interfering in my personal life. I wouldn't let him have sex with me so he tried to blackmail me about being in a gay relationship so I told my parents and the workplace. However he got to my friend and threatened to expose them and they were not as bold as I was.

He came to my parent's house to expose me and my Mother slapped his face because he outright said some cold derogatory crap to her face. My Mom pleaded the blood of Jesus on him and he ran up that hill squealing loudly like a pig you hear me, and we have witnesses! Here we were years later and Satan plays the game with a twist. My Husband was in this group and all he would do is sing this same Chaplain's praises and I never told him that this was the guy who ripped me off and had shown his true demonic warlock face. All my baby knew was that it was a fellow church member.

Months later my baby was worshipping the Lord and as we were all in the Spirit he began shouting the name Jesus and saying, "That's my Daddy!" (You should have seen my boo, getting his little worship on, too cute) Anyhoo this same church warlock turned around with his new fiancée and told him in front of everyone to tune it down because it was embarrassing. My babe was so hurt and those members sitting close by told him not to let anyone steal his joy. Yep that's what Mr. Satan's job was, to steal my baby's joy. The enemy knows our weaknesses and that is what he comes after. My Hubby's was his pride and mine was my integrity.

I feel he was crushed because he looked up to this masked man. I later told him that was the same man who had ripped me off and the warlock I clearly had seen. Also I told my babe prior about my cancer situation after consulting with the Holy Spirit and I'm so glad I did. This same warlock said to told him "You know she has cancer right?" If that was not a direct violation of being a Chaplain telling something I told him in confidence in prayer. A Chaplain is supposed to be someone you can confide in. And prayer well if I'm asking you to pray for my cancer situation and I'm telling you that I don't want others to know unless I tell them; well isn't that a direct violation? Who does that? Suppose I hadn't told my baby. My babe's response to that infiltrator was simply, "Yeah she told me and I want to enjoy every day with her." Pow see how the Holy Spirit is orderly!

To this day I speak to his wife and I have never told her anything. In fact I remember the day the "masked man" was looking for his next victim. I looked up and saw him on the church balcony looking and I knew she would be chosen. Out of all the women the Spirit told me it would be her. Time later their engagement was announced and still I never peeped a word and to me that's the Christ inside of me. I strongly believe that this warlock will be exposed if he doesn't turn it all over to Jesus. No matter how visible you are in the church, or being an ordained Minister or how many scriptures you can quote if you don't have the heart of Jesus? Well I'm just saying that Christ is nothing to play with. I'm telling you this is for real for I've never seen such an inhumane evil alien face.

I feel privileged as well as feeling uncomfortable sometimes when my partner, Mr. Holy Spirit orders me to get down on my knees in public. There are times when my flesh gets prideful and now when I get up of my knees and I look around and people act as if I'm a ghost and just continue on without pausing. So why would I be embarrassed really?

In the Name of Jesus I just want to be an instrument to transfer messages and I'll continue to do so by song for this is the gift that God has given me. So whether it is by film, through music or simply writing in print I will glorify and shout to the world, "Look what God has done for me!" That for me and my countless examples clearly displays that Jesus is the answer!

Again I'm reminded of years ago when my ex and I were fighting and a friend at that time called the police. While I was sitting on the stoop on a busy street in my head I was asking God what on earth have I gotten myself into this time. Another relationship where the dark side in me is fighting against a demon. Then out of NOWHERE came a white van with large bold words on the side stating "JESUS IS THE ANSWER." At that time I trusted but not completely for I hadn't fully surrendered yet. But God is too funny always showing up on time. And you know what to this day I have never seen a van since that states that, deep huh? With all these situations I realize that it was not about me getting up in front of a church and singing his praises in front of believers but becoming an instrument to reach those who are not followers to show them an alternative. I always said to my husband and friends that I just want to be an alternative lifestyle to my stepson. I want him to be able to look at my life and see a difference so when he is older he has options. Whether wrong or right he'll have options to be able to rewind his memory bank and choose what is right for him. If he encounters such evil he will know that he can find peace, joy, strength and covering in the blood of Jesus!

A Lesson in Something so Simple

Yesterday one of my Philadelphia music buddy's and I took a break to just feel and be thankful for all what God has done for us. We were on a riverside reading and talking and one of the plastic bags that I had some food in flew into the busy street. My buddy decided in his wheelchair that he didn't want to destroy nature and proceeded to wheel on his own path and said he used the Jedi mind trick to steer the bag back into our direction. After a while I realized the plastic bag we were looking at wasn't ours at all so when he wheeled in the opposite direction we saw our brown bag that had flown away. So we were both concentrating on this other plastic bag hoping for it to escape the cars that it was bouncing off. It was as if we were at some basketball game cheering for the ball to come to our side, here we were doing this with the plastic bag to come closer to the sidewalk so that my buddy could grab it. The joke is it wasn't the right bag. But the mere fact that we could take time out and focus on that bag showed me that we could take time and recognize God. God is everywhere, that's the name of a song that I wrote when very young. When I think about it my number one passion is songwriting and the fact that I have been writing for the past twenty years and still striving could only be God.

They say there is a lesson in everything and that plastic bag chase was the simple fact that in life we tend to be focusing on the wrong things, and putting all of our energy into events, people, places, and organizations that aren't our God given purpose. What our purpose is; is what we often see slipping right past us because we tend to be focused on the substitute or the familiar, trying to make it a fit when actually it isn't a fit at all and that's why the anxiety creeps in! When something is right you know it. It is almost effortless. You enjoy the defects, the malfunctions you are lost in the passion. That's how I feel for the most part about life, my family, music, film, this book. When we get high on the Lord it is effortless but so fulfilling because it's the right fit.

I've studied many religions, and have taken parts from many but when I met Jesus that was the right fit for me. No drug in the world could compare to the euphoria you feel when you fall in love with Christ. When you ask the Holy Spirit to direct your path and things seem not as planned you can rest in the assurance of knowing that the TRINITY that you believe in has your back. That's right the Father (GOD), Son (JESUS/YESUDA) and The Holy Spirit have you in that triangle. Awesome or what! It has gotten to the point that I anoint everything in my house right down to my computer parts and my dog because I want us all to be covered in the anointing of the Holy Spirit.

I remember when I was young I had this dream and it was so beautiful and my spirit was so excited and free and when I awoke I knew that I wanted to get saved. So I called an uncle in law of mine who had a lot of rank in our church, the Salvation Army, he was a Major. I was so excited that I told him about my dream and I just wanted to get saved right then. Well Lord rest his soul, he told me countless stories of how through him this person and that person got saved and by the end of the conversation I had lost the desire, that wonderful feeling and I basically said thank you Uncle and I didn't surrender my life at that time.

You see the enemy is so slick that he used my uncle at that particular time to make it all about him and because my uncle was let's face it very conceited he used that weakness as a strength to steer me clearly away from the Lord. Now I'm not blaming my uncle because the Holy Spirit is still training me to recognize the enemy and believe me he never ever gets tired! His entire purpose is to steal, kill, destroy, confuse, deceive, manipulate and whatever he can use to steer you away from peace. Jesus after all is the Prince of Peace.

Having reviewed various beliefs I always tell people if I were a monk in Tibet and died would I go to hell. For it says in our Basic

Instructions Before Leaving Earth that "in my Father's house there are many mansions." Just sayin . . .

Now I love the Dali Lama and every other peace being that walks the face of this earth from Mother to Teresa to Princess Diana but I'm drawn to monks. So much so that I was to a point if I just thought hard enough about them they would show up, seriously I remember being in a women empowerment meeting downtown and I thought of the whole monk thing and what it must be like and when I left the building and bam there across the street were these two monks who I probably scared by running over to them and telling them that I had so much respect for them. Another time I was in Atlanta's airport between flights and talking to my love of the time and we got into the whole monk conversation and I was saying that I had visited a church in Canada and they had incorporated some Buddhism principles with Christianity and that I was reading this book and many of the practices were working. Soon after two monks appeared before me and I went and talked to them. I mean it got so bad that my sister brought me this enlightenment DVD of the Dali Lama and some friends of hers said, "You actually think your sister would like that?" And she responded, "Most definitely!" Now my sister and I over the years have only talked on a deep level in spurts so in the natural how could she know that? The answer simply is because she knows my spirit and therefore she knows me. As a result I could have nobody but my sister as my maid of honor in my wedding. And I was hers in her wedding. And today due to my spirit of peace, compassion and human rights I assist Tibetans in our region as they continue the fight for possession of their country and their people's basic human rights right down to preserving their language and culture. From jump I told the President of TAP that I'm a keep it real Christian! I represent Jesus wherever I go.

GOD'S GOT YOUR BACK KIND OF LOVE

Last night I was in Bible study and we had guest speakers and one of the things they touched on was abortion and the unbelievable number of unborn babies whose voices are snuffed out for our own selfish reasons. Our church had done a survey and about 30 percent said that they had either had an abortion or advised someone to. And immediately my mind went back to when my sister got pregnant in her last year of high school. She was afraid to tell my Dad, man I have to smile because I can just see his face and him not speaking to anyone for days. Well before that me and a friend were the only persons she told and I had advised her to have an abortion. I had it all planned I would pay for it and stand beside her. I felt I was doing the right thing but she decided not to and I'm telling you I'm so glad she did. You know how it says in the Bible that this too shall pass well so true. Dad started speaking to us again, my sister went to a tutorial school and my Grandmother at the time knew she was pregnant all the while. She was prophetic like that! I'm so glad my sister didn't take my advice and have the abortion for she gave me my heart, my oldest nephew and Godson. He was raised by my parents and my sister was able to go to college. I was like another Mommy to him and he would call me that. I remember him walking for the first time in my School House Lane apartment, gosh time has flown!

As years marched on I had a full hysterectomy at a young age because my endometriosis had spread. I used to have these intense menstrual periods and be in so much pain. One time I produced this musical workshop and I couldn't even stand up. I would have two periods a month and sometimes I would bleed for ten days at a time and lose clots on a regular. It was so bad that I would wear three pairs of underwear and something my sister and I invented called stocking pants which was the stockings being cut to serve as underwear which would hold everything neatly. Doctors had me on herbs, all kinds of stuff but the pain seemed to get worse even though the bleeding eased up. A Lady who I call Aunt Jackie and is the wife of our former Premier Sir John Swan convinced me to try a new gynecologist and I did. I credit her as the instrument God used to beckon me to get out of my comfort zone of being in pain and seek change that would save my life. Thanks Lady Jacqueline Swan! As a result I happened to go to a cousin of mine who had a new practice and I was glad to support my sister-girl. Now keep in mind if my play Aunt hadn't convinced me I would have never left my gynecologist because I was very loyal to this man for I was under his care for years. I even had my womb scraped and the bleeding had eased so I felt as though he was the 'jimmy jam.' However it was while under my cousin's care Doctor Woods and she told me the next time I was to go overseas for my brain tumor treatment I should have them check out my cervix. She said she found a spot on my cervix and I was like what now. Brain tumor and now this, oh please! Anyhoo I went away to my overseas hospital and casually saw a doctor as my cousin suggested. Well almost immediately this doctor made a few calls and the next thing I know I'm in a room with my legs in stirrups with this ultra ray laser doing its thing. I thought I was okay cause the pain had even eased a bit but when they sat me down to talk I was not ready. Woe . . . The doctor told me that I needed surgery immediately and I said I'm buying a house and have to meet with realtors, all kinds of inspectors. I was on my grind for who has time for surgery.

I called my Mom and explained the situation. To this day I don't know what was on that scribbled note from my cousin the gynecologist but it prompted this American doctor to move immediately and I don't know exactly what they saw but it must have been pretty bad. She had told me that they would have to remove my left ovary and part of my right. Makes sense why the bleeding eased up the ovaries were literally taken over by my condition and when I looked it up in the medical books it showed tumors with hair and teeth growing on the ovaries, it almost like little alien creatures! I was in a fog. The doctor had informed me that I could still get pregnant with a bit of my ovary in tact so I was ready to do this.

Now when I told some close family members about the possibility of me not having children they said well it's not like you plan on having some anyway just look at the life you are living. Now that hurt! Just because I was in an alternative lifestyle did not mean that I didn't want to be a mother. I later learned that I had endometrial cancer that had spilled over and to save the rest of my lower parts they removed everything. They did not want it moving to my vagina. So here I was with brain cancer and endometrial cancer all at the same time. Wow God you are so good!

When I went back home I was still under the assumption that I could still get pregnant later so I planned with my parents to travel for the surgery. Well the joke was on me for years ago when I did get pregnant I would do everything I could to abort the fetus. I took motherhood for granted and drank laxatives as well as riding the worst roller coaster rides. I figured if I could ALWAYS have a baby in my time! I took this one laxative that people back home would take large doses of just to get rid of the baby. One time I miscarried and talk about the biggest ugly clot. And there were other moments of pregnancy but we won't go there! I used to tell my friends if you just look at me I'll get pregnant. So here I was several years later thinking I was going to have a partial hysterectomy and then I awoke to nothing, nada! After that operation I was so sore that I had to be in a wheelchair and couldn't do anything for over six weeks. My Dad would bring me food and only twice did my ex partner at that time help me clean up. When I returned to my cousin the gynecologist I asked her did I still have the spot on my cervix and she said, "What spot? I don't know how to tell you this LA but you have no cervix as a matter of fact no womb, no ovaries, no fallopian tubes, nothing!"

All gone I was an empty barrel. And then came all the motherly feelings of wanting to bear a child and I couldn't. Last night when I was in Bible study the Holy Spirit reminded me that I have been pregnant a few times but let's just say that I gave up the opportunity to be a parent. When I look at my life and having that opportunity taken away from me is one of my greatest regrets. But you know what? Only God knows! It's funny because we all know that God has control but how many of us sincerely believe that? If we look over our lives and start connecting the dots than we can see how God really does have our backs. After all He didn't have to save me with the cancer spill did He?

END? IT'S NEVER THAT SIMPLE WHEN YOU WALK WITH JESUS

Well you know I have been away from writing for a month and part of the reason was not just that I have so many experiences and things to share but also my computer was giving me problems with my book drive, each time I went to write it shut off so it turned me off . . . but this morning I woke up with a song in my heart "Gone too soon." And I prayed and said out loud "Ok God work with me" and here I am. So much has happened over the past month. The project that only the Lord himself could give me I'm seeing unveil. I was on the shore in Atlantic City a few years ago and God gave me the entire outline for a Legends of the Arts Awards, I even penned a song to it but each time I would go home my meetings were few and far between so I just took my money and booked our City Hall.

I approached Government heads and I was told there wasn't enough money in the budget well I ended up coming back to Bermuda unexpectedly and again this is how the Holy Spirit operates once you give Him free reign over your life. I was at a bank with my Mother and I saw a particular Government official leaving whom I had discussed the project with several times and I ran after him. We spoke and he never mentioned anything and I told him I took his advice and would not put my energy into my birth country anymore because people were either stealing ideas or just so unappreciative. I've always helped my country and the desire and strong passion could come from none other than the Holy Spirit for I wasn't paid for these things from a monetary point of view.

Later I spoke with a friend and she told me to go and surprise her mother so when I did this her mother informed me that she was performing and showing me the flyer of a small award ceremony and well immediately my eyes focused on who was being honored and who it was being sponsored by and coincidentally it was that same Cultural Minister! So I went to the offices demanding an answer and later made a private phone call and was told that they had made a commitment to a certain group a year ago and it was no big thing for this was on a small scale and how they wanted to honor these legends, now tell me was that not my proposal? But you see I just said thank you for honoring these people before they close their eyes.

Later I was informed that not many people came and neither did some of the honorees. I visited with one whom I always do when I go home and I asked her why she didn't attend and maybe it had something to do with it being genuine from the heart. The story gets deeper right up to when I was told who was involved and I made a phone call and it was to an ex boyfriends fathers house where we discussed old times and he told me he was being honored. That following Sunday I attended church with a cousin of mine where another cousin was Pastor I had heard so many great reports of outreach. Guess who was there the same ex's father and his entire family. Getting back to the original award show concept a former client and friend Hubert Smith Sr. and I met constantly with several officials and it was on my sick bed that his family decided to have the show and I was told by guess who, the same lady who let me know about this one and as a matter of fact she said something like, "LA you should be used to them stealing your ideas by now didn't the same thing happen before?"

I look at life as lessons until learned. Different faces, different spaces but the same game! And believe you me I have to look at life this way as nothing more than the interconnection of dots. I get on my knees and ask the Holy Spirit to guide my path and to order my footsteps and ask the Lord for protection by his Angels in the name of Jesus and this is my daily prayer. Ironically the other day in downtown Philadelphia I was on my knees and for the life of me could not get up! My entire body had clenched up and I asked God in the name of Jesus to let me up. Funny since I had said prior to myself that I hadn't had an episode of my body getting cramped into a huge Charlie horse from the lupus for some time. But here I was experiencing this in public. I look at it as the enemy's way of trying to stop me from praying in public and now I make sure there is something to hold by; a tree, a rail, a branch, a twig or something . . . Lord help me Jesus!!!! That experience wasn't too cute and luckily I was in front of some intoxicated gentleman who just looked at me as if I was a figment of their imagination.

THINNING THEM OUT

The Holy Spirit woke me up one morning and said you are going to create your own music tracks and that is something that is virtually unheard of in the industry but I was blessed to find this software from Europe and my brain must have absorbed all of those countless hours of being in the studio . . . **with the Lord all things are possible right?** Just like I'm typing this and as soon as I mentioned the aforementioned statement the computer went into bold because "God isn't a joke!" The moment I gave Jesus reign over my life I've been fighting off demons left and right some of my spiritual family who've witnessed it tease me about me slaying witches. I don't know . . . I just know that God is in control . . . . Right down to different friends in my life I watch and hear them talk about tangling with the devil and how all things and people are potential opportunities including myself. I mean it hurts and I talked to my sweetie who is not interested in the industry but has seen how people can be and I'm telling you I have to go into prayer and ask the Lord to please have my back on some things even when my solar plexus and center or the core of my being don't feel right. I ask God to cover me in the blood of Jesus because I now know when it's coming at me. I was in church the day after July 4th and the eve prior I was with some friends and witnessed hundreds of young black people walking aimlessly in mob form and at that moment I connected another dot on my life's woven journey.

At my church they said raise your hand if you've lost a love one and in my mind I said thank God I don't have to. Now every week they do this so the members can flock around you for prayer. I never say this but I just know that someone is always dying or get sick in my family to the point that sometimes you don't even want to share it for people may think you are saying it for attention . . . Well the truth is my cousin's wife had died a few days before but I wasn't that close to them and I contacted my cousin to make sure his immediate family was supportive.

While in church a lady next to us said that her sister had died suddenly and I remember the Holy Spirit having me say repeatedly, "We must trust Jesus and thank him. Even in death we must trust Him! Now I knew my Mom had called me at 9:18 a.m. long distance from her cell so I tried to call her back and left a message that my service starts at 9:30 a.m.

The entire time I was repeating about trusting in death, my spirit was informed for my cousin had been killed in New York shot to death over a cell phone conversation. He was with his brother and a friend and this intoxicated man thought that he was talking to his girlfriend but everyone told the guy it wasn't about her but the person on the other end of the phone. They walked away and the guy who accused him of talking to his girl was embarrassed in my book for making such a scene and therefore came around in front of his girlfriend and just shot my cousin to death right there in public. I said to myself here we go again less than a year ago my partner in age and first cousin was shot to death in front of his kids over a television, and years prior to that another first cousin of mine was shot in the head but survived the million to one chance. All male, all closely related.

You know I was telling a realtor friend of mine and his response was nonchalant stating that oh that happens a lot in your family. Excuse me but what type of crap is that like we ask for it. Just like when my music partner talked about how nothing like that would ever happen to him because he wouldn't put himself in situations. And what situations could that be that justifies you steering down the barrel of a gun! So I WAS HAVING A DIFFICULT TIME seeing why the Holy Spirit had me reaffirming to trust Jesus even in death because even in death we see the light. In these murders I got to see people who I thought were friends I got to see them for who they really are and how they really feel about me. That's why I know without a doubt that God is going to bless me like in my visions to bless others in His name and that is why He's thinning my circle down to a pinch of family and friends.

You know the Holy Spirit when He's leading you and driving your car it all becomes so clear. Like Michael Jackson's song says, "it doesn't matter if your black or white," at the end of the day God doesn't see color, gender or culture but hearts and if I can leave this world having touched hearts and assisted in healing by letting the world know who Jesus truly is and can be in our lives than I know I've served my purpose. Now I don't discriminate anyone but try to understand. I may chose not to be around certain spirits but God is love and that is all we are here to do is spread that love in its purest form.

IT'S ALL ABOUT LISTENING AND BEING OBEDIENT!

Now that I've taken care of some things but the last thing I want to share with you today is my most recent prophetic experiences. Firstly when I was on the plane I started to think to myself of all the times I fly I just take for granted that nothing is going to happen. While flying I began thinking about how my Great Aunt Eva Fox was in a plane crash and never flew again. The subject started I believe by a passenger telling me that he wouldn't want to crash in water and I thought that was weird since we were over nothing but water . . . Anyhoo I'm on this plane returning to the US and I have these thoughts and in the midst of them I hear, "Get your anointed oil." Well my oil was in my carry on up top in the overhead bins so I had to get out of my comfort zone and go to the overhead while passengers were still getting on the plane. Then I heard get down and pray so for the first time in my life I got on my knees between the seats and again I was out of my comfort zone and I prayed for protection. When we were about to take off speeding down the runway bam the pilot hit the brakes and lights were flashing that the cockpit door was still open. Imagine if we were in the sky and that happened! It took another 45 minutes before we could leave the runway because they had to ensure that everything was safe. While some may take these things for granted but the Holy Spirit having me anoint and pray just prior to this discovery was no coincidence! Trust and believe.

Later I'm at the Newark airport having walked my feet off to find the gate to catch this small 20 seat passenger commuter plane and then I find out that they changed the gate. I watched this girl coming and saying that the gate was changed and left with another passenger. I remained at the initial gate like everyone else because it seemed so 'random.' About 30 minutes later I saw people starting to leave so I asked where they were going and they said someplace else so I got up rushed to see the screen and sure enough they had changed the gate number just as the girl had announced. Just thinking about it who is to say she wasn't an Angel because trust and believe she disappeared so quickly and was definitely not on our plane. Now where I had to go to was believe me not that close and I was breaking my neck to get to the gate because now I went from having all the time in the world to running late. As I was rushing through the airport I saw a television screen with Michael Jackson's face on it and began to keep walking but something had me peak back and I saw the words hospitalized. Now let's look at God's timing if the Holy Spirit hadn't beckoned me to leave I would have missed my plane and I wouldn't have seen the image of Michael on the screen at that particular time. As I rushed off I heard something say, "Oh he's dead" and I said, "Lord why would I think that?" And then I was prompted to start praying for his family. I couldn't wait to arrive in that final airport in Philadelphia where I called Bermuda for my Mother but my Dad answered and I told him what I just experienced and if it was unfortunately true remember that I had told him what I felt without any media knowledge. Next I receive a text from a music source saying Michael died of a stroke.

Well to me that was my confirmation so I sent out the text to others. Then I called my Hubby and he said, "Well honey with you it's probably true but here on CNN they are reporting that he is still alive." Then I felt bad for forwarding the texts saying he was dead and asking for everyone to pray for his family. Others were adamant with me saying that he was dead when the media stated that he was alive. Therefore I sent another text to everyone saying they revived him but to keep his family in prayer. Now that was supernatural because how would I know anything about them trying to revive him when absolutely nothing had been released! My family in Bermuda said they hadn't received any news of his death. Later I girl told me that I told her of his death several minutes before it was released by the international world press . . . Many wanted to know how I knew and others dismissed it saying well you said they revived him afterwards remember? Well I also saw the time 2:26 PM in my mind and it wasn't until days later that I read he passed around that time. I told my Bishop what occurred and he didn't respond. I told my neurologist who suggested that I must be disturbed by these things since I was telling her and maybe it was the intense emotion and had to do with my remaining cancer cells launched in my brain. Well all I know is that the voice of God is real you bet your boots and if I ever questioned myself about this "knowing" gift well here was a day of less than 24 hours of self proclamation of proof. After all they used to call me psychic and a good witch but all I know that since Jesus is my personal Savior and the ruler of my life, all these things from plays to songs to films are directed by Him . . .

There is no questioning about higher power or higher self for these recent experiences confirmed it for me. Then I watched his memorial and the Holy Spirit was present as they lifted up the name of Jesus that is M J's ultimate purpose to let millions who were watching know that Jesus is real, the Holy Spirit can reveal and the love of our gracious Lord abounds without limitations and it defies discrimination. Now was that not the confirmation of the former affirmation "even in death trust him" and he showed up to the masses all in one day at one appointed time to show the world who is Lord. I even heard singer Mariah say thank you Jesus.

As I'm writing it is being revealed that Jesus wants to become a fixation within our culture and no longer a shameful thing. I can't wait to see what the Holy Spirit has in store for my cousins funeral in New York I'll be sure to let you know . . . until then remain blessed and continue to walk in the Spirit in Jesus name and I pray protection and blessings over every reader at this time Lord. I speak life where there is no life and I speak hope when there is no way out. I speak freedom where there is so much bondage. In the name of Jesus Christ, Lord cover every reader with your son's precious blood from the crown of their heads to the very souls of their feet. Lord even in the midst of reading this I' m asking you to show up and show out and show the world that it is not about religion but a personal one on one with you . . .

OUR GOD IS LIMITLESS

Well the concert was incredible there was a count of 15,000 people 11 acts and six hours of jamming for Christ. I'm talking from 5 p.m. to 11 p.m. I mean you could feel the Holy Ghost wave from old to young with a mix of cultures there was that even flow of love. My Hubby said, "We were all rejoicing with the one common denominator, Jesus Christ." He often shouts in the spirit "That's my Daddy!" My baby's too cute. I needed that memory to trigger the goodness of Christ in the midst of life's continuous storms. You know yesterday morning I awoke to a strange feeling in my tummy. I couldn't describe it but I felt midway between nausea and anxiety. I could feel a shift in the spiritual atmosphere and just knew something bad was happening. So like my Mom had taught me when I felt the unexplainable to ask the Lord to protect my family, friends and myself with the blood of Jesus. Later before my babe left for work and did his morning covering prayer for us and I told him how I was feeling. I told him I felt sad, a sense of lost and didn't know why.

Well soon after he left I went on my laptop while in bed to post something on my face book page. I continued with my morning routine but then something told me to jump back on my laptop. Now I usually use the laptop from my bed and I had already gotten up to start my day but my partner the Holy Spirit had pressed on me to get back on face book. Yup he even works through the social media. I tried to pull up our Ministry site "Keepin it Real 4 Christ" and it was gone. I tried and tried and then I felt sicker. Now with all the confusion one of our members had sent me a text a few nights prior that he wasn't coming back to my house to anymore meetings. Now I had sent out the usual invites for the same time, same day of the week and I hadn't heard from him since the showdown.

Let's call it more precisely the spiritual battle. I guess I was like David and didn't back down from his Goliath syndrome so he found other ways to get at me. He called my house names and I still responded by saying "I'm sorry you feel that way but my house is anointed." Then I wished him all the best and still maintained my composure. The other night after my meeting with the others my Hubby told me to change the passwords but I said everybody deserves the benefit of the doubt and I would wait and told the other members that if he does do something rash it would reveal who he is inside. And guess what when the Ministry disappeared from face book he admitted to another what he did. He didn't have the decency to say he wanted to be removed, was leaving or anything. He just made the decision to make a dictator move. I was crushed and cried out to God but thanked him for showing me and protecting me with His comforter my partner, the Holy Spirit. I keep mentioning Him because I am so grateful and there are no words or deeds that I can do that could ever measure what He has done in my life. Again all I can say is, **"Lord I'm so grateful."**

Later I still felt that something wasn't quite right. My Hubby and I have been looking forward to this one day trip for quite some time to see my cousin but I was prompted by my partner to make a call. And there it was my cousin telling me that she and her husband had to cancel the trip. I was blown away and later as the music resonated from the car stereo while my precious stepson had his head peering out through the sunroof, tears came streaming down my eyes as I listened to the song "Lord I thank you." And that I did and called my spiritual sister and she immediately said, "What's wrong, you okay?" I told her the story and she was going through her own battle as well. But don't get it twisted I told her how I felt God was so awesome in preparing me for every disappointment.

Oh I forgot to tell you that two days leading up to the day of I had uncanny experiences with thinking of people then calling them and finding out that they were very sick, or just got out of the hospital or was experiencing a crisis at the exact moment I contacted them. Deep huh . . . I don't know God is moving me from seeing to feeling things . . . . I mean I first felt others pain with the death of Michael Jackson when I knew he was dead and felt and prayed for his family the minute I saw him on that airport television screen talking and it his death wasn't even publicly announced yet. I just felt this sadness come over me and said, "Oh no Lord what about his family" and just prayed for them at 2:25pm on June 25th, 2009. And to seal the deal I called my Father and told him what I felt and my Hubby and sent out texts. And up until this day there are those that can't figure out how I knew thirteen minutes before the AP press announced it and I was flying between New Jersey and Philly. Throughout this book I have to keep reminding us all that with God there are no boundaries for He is limitless!

You know this is truly a limitless journey for God is limitless and never ceases to amaze us. Since we are created in His image we too are limitless and can experience His greatness just as long as we seek Him and channel His face. I mean last night while in the bathroom I prayed for my nephew's soul and that he would come to recognize that the Bible is not a fairy tale book as he's been calling it but truly the book of Basic Instructions Before Leaving the Earth. We have to get it right we aren't perfect but our faith has to be as Hezekiah Walker's song says, "Faithful, for faithful is our God!"

LORD I CRAVE YOUR PRESENCE

Well it's been weeks since I've gotten back to writing or some may call it journaling but it's all about God's timing. I'm being led by my partner, the Holy Spirit to make music, work on His web and produce. Now in the interim my personal life has had its roller coaster ride. But during the storms I prayed without ceasing, and hey I even attended three church services back to back last Sunday. You talk about dragging God around, man I was holding His hand and pleading for a touch. I know He is always there but sometimes we can't feel that presence. You know the one that makes your heart jump, your head spin, or the one where our whole spirit just wants to jump out of our skeletal shells. This is what I longed for just as my former functional drug addicted body craved when triggered. You know I have to walk in my deliverance it's a daily choice to hold on. You all just don't know how much I love my best friend, my deliverer, my conqueror, my Lord and Savior. I can now feel demonic spirits when they walk pass, enter the house or even come against my flesh but I shout out in the name of Jesus and literally like Benita Washington's song "Hold On" says "Just hold on . . ." Like Bishop Hezekiah Walker's song says "God favored me."

I was advised my one of my spiritual genuine mentors to read the book of James. And honestly I started to read it, highlight it, study it and swallow it. You see many times we chew on a message or a passage but do we swallow it do we absorb it into our bodies so that it can begin working within our lives and that's what the book of James is doing in my life. It maybe the smaller book but it is so powerful. And the Holy Spirit reminded me that even in the small things God will show Himself in the most magnifying ways. I prayed with someone and they told me that God will show up and I just kept turning to Psalms 46:10 "Be still and know that I'm God."

There have been certain situations where I know it's nobody but my Father. As the saying goes "bring you to your knees" well that isn't just a saying it's my reality!

COVER ME HAS NEW MEANING

Psalms 17
Pray fearlessly that we should be bold.

You know this morning I got up early and after an evening of open honest communication with my husband the Holy Spirit awoken me to deal with a few fears. One of my fears is speaking to 20 to 25 medical students about how and why the doctors have me written down as a medical miracle. This will be the first time that I'll be in a setting where I get to minister professionally to the medical world. So I awaked to Ephesians 6:19-20 where it says "Pray also for me that whenever I open my mouth, words may be given to me so that I will fearlessly make known the mystery of the Gospel, for which I am an ambassador in chains. Pray that I may declare it fearlessly, as I should." This opportunity came with a set of many rules including that I can't be videotaped or say anything religious. My doctor in the department that is hosting this is from Eastern Europe and he will tell you that he did not believe that there was a God or that there was something more out there until he met my body which God has used as an instrument to showcase His realness.

That's the key I need to find a way to do this. My partner, the Holy Spirit just reminded me that He will show me what to write down, what to bring to the classes, what illustrations to supply in order to successfully illustrate to them that being a medical miracle goes beyond man's medicine. That without being preachy or breaking the rules that Jesus is all alive and well and there is a story to tell and be told in me. I have said to God time and time again that I want to be an instrument of praise, that He can use me however He wants for I belong to Him. And my friends that is the key as well when you die to self the more you will be able to edify your spirit man. Now "edify" and only that word could have come from my partner, the Lord. I'm looking up the word in my study Bible rather than getting out of my bed and going to my office to get a dictionary because lets face it I'm feeling too comfortable unless my partner tells me to do so. Therefore by looking in the back of this particular Bible which I love the New International Version (NIV) life application study Bible this is what my partner had me turn to Christian Worker's Resource under "Plan."

I looked at the definition and the questions that it presented that would help me with applying God's plan. There were three questions 1. What does God want us to do with what we have learned? 2. What steps will get me to that goal? 3. What should be my first step, how should I get started? You see these are the questions that I have in my subconscious and God knows this and this is Him answering the questions that I haven't even voiced because He knows our hearts, you feel me? This is precisely why we call it the Living Word because it is the only religion that has the active power of the Holy Spirit. It goes beyond practicing principles or reciting phrases, it is light, and it is life and without saying now this is the situation so what should I do? Okay it says I should pray or gather amongst counsel. It is real you all, it is light for in darkness we are lost. It is a switch that only turns on not out of principle or steps that are followed, but by power, a supernatural energy that cannot be explained in the natural!

I once heard a Bishop say at this smaller church that the Holy Spirit is the electricity.

We may not see it but we sure can feel it. And getting back to my case and point about preparing for tomorrows class where there are specific rules and boundaries that I must adhere to; as it clearly states with words jumping of the pages that I need to explain my case calmly and confidently. Write out my points beforehand so I won't go off on tangents and get upset but will carefully explain my position. For there is a big difference in knowing and doing and teaching and showing.

THE MEDICAL FACTS

While I'm participating in a study on Rheumatic illnesses let's concentrate on the facts. The medical world loves facts. My facts are that in November 1999 I had brain surgery that removed 80% of a cancerous oligodendroglomia and this left me with 20% of an inoperable cancerous tumor lodged in the left lobe of my brain. On November 11th, 1999 they delivered the news that I had brain cancer. I only recently discovered that my "oligo" apparently accounts for only 2% of all brain tumors and they are thoroughly researching for a cure.

I had to follow certain procedures such as the clinical trials of medications. Some anti seizure medications such as Tegretol left my entire body in a severe red rash and had it not been for the University of Penn on staff social assistant I would be dead. The rash indicated that I was being poisoned when my former Bermuda doctors had told me to keep taking the medication. You see after what I consider a successful surgery at the Lahey Clinic in Boston my friends suggested that I go to University of Penn hospital since I was familiar with the area and that they were one of the best facilities in the country focusing on research as well as advanced teaching. We all know teaching hospitals are places that allow for experiments or what we term trials. So what I did was have my physician in Boston transfer my screens to HUP. At that time HUP had scanners and equipment that Boston didn't so it was clear that this was a divine move.

In addition my assigned neurologist Dr. Amy Pruitt speaks throughout the country so I've been truly blessed. I only recently learned that she was from Boston and knew my brain surgeon beforehand. Look at the order of God! I returned to Bermuda but that is where I could have died because **some** doctors there aren't on top of their game; and maybe it's the fact that no one really sues them. I traveled between the two countries because at that time Bermuda did not have any MRI machines so as a newspaper columnist I was able to help lobby for that. It was also a time when the new trial drugs were so expensive and insurance in Bermuda didn't want to cover them. I remember neurontin costing me $500 for a month's supply. And let's not talk about shopping for insurance, I was turned down with some executives having the nerve to tell me that I was such a high risk and I responded with I intend to live. Well that was over a decade ago and some of those companies have folded and some of those same executives have passed on from guess what, cancer! In this world you just never know what you might get served on your plate so be ready for anything and everything.

It was also at a time when there was no oral chemo and since I was diagnosed with an inoperable tumor that was deep. I had to have faith in God and my doctors that they would develop something that would prolong my life; some procedure that would be available if I ever needed it. The fact that it has been over a decade and I'm here talking to you today is a miracle. Let me give you some more background so you can see how it all ties together and the reason as to why I am termed a medical miracle! Since I was diagnosed there have been so many who were diagnosed with brain tumors, and systemic lupus and most of them have passed on. I've always been sickly from day one and I do mean from my first day on this planet. I remember being in a protective bubble for my severe asthma and they had to bring me my school work in the hospital. Then at a young age before turning five I had an enlarged spleen, heart problems and even polyps when I was two. Without going too deep I even had some hair on my privates as a toddler. I've had problems with my menstrual cycle my entire life and tried everything back home including holistic. I remember one time doing a musical conference and the pains were so severe that I couldn't even walk or stand for that matter but the show had to go on. I would bleed so much that I would wear 2 tampons, 2 pads and 2 pairs of underwear. I called it the 2 for 2 technique. While at HUP Doctor C B was my assigned gynecologist and she told me how I could have the operation and still get pregnant with one ovary since I was still young. Unfortunately because I had gone undiagnosed with such severe endometriosis for so long, the result was severe cancer and they didn't want it spreading to my reproductive organs so they had to remove it all. I awoke to thinking I could still get pregnant because they had informed me about the one ovary and I held on to that hope! When I awoke I remember thinking I was dead and had crossed over because there looking down at me was this bright white angelic figure. But it was actually someone from my former church who happened to be a white woman, my angel Gail. I still didn't know I was on a cancer ward until I had them wheel me around the other side so that I could thank the nurses and it was there that I saw the chemo drips set up. I was devastated! My natural self felt like curling up and dying but the God inside of me said, "You must fight to live for me so that others around the planet will experience freedom and peace through me. This is your assignment!"

They say God will give you NO more than you can bear. After the surgery because of no estrogen and to ease the menopause and slow the aging process I was administered pills that had synthetic components to counteract the aforementioned. I believe it was a certain hormone pill were the side effects were blood clots, uterine bleeding and breast cancer just to name a few. After taking those for a while something told me to stop. When I went to my new doctor in Bermuda Dr. Fiona Ross, she had insight and suggested that I go for a mammogram and it revealed two masses. As a result I had to have a biopsy. It was extremely painful. I remember there was a long tube where they extracted flesh and then they inserted a titanium chip. Later when they went to look for the masses they could only find one which became smaller. To this day I still have my chip in my left breast.

Then I went through a stage in 2005 where my joints would crack and it started in my arms and thumb. We thought it was carpel tunnel and of course they said they would have to cut my hand. Around the same time I couldn't walk without my joints being in intense pain. It felt as though my knees had bones rubbing against each other. I was like "God please I just came from the wheelchair to walker to maneuvering to find a way to put on my own underwear.

You know the hell I've been through with the brain surgery and hysterectomy drama. I don't know if I can handle something else! Is this another trial?"

Soon after I was going through it with so much pain in my joints I took a bone density test and guest what? I was diagnosed with osteoporosis. No surprise since I stopped taking those hormone pills. And to this day all I take is calcium and the small amounts of vitamin D and plenty of greens. I remember just trying to walk in New York with family and each step was unbearable. Then it got so bad that often I couldn't walk so I would crawl and take all these pain killers and my doctors tested me and it wasn't related at all to my remainder brain tumor so I was relieved with that news! Then one day I was waving goodbye to some friends across the street. Well when I went to put my arm down it was in a locked position so I quickly transferred my bag from my other arm and played it off. Can you imagine when I think back all I can do is laugh because it was something straight out of a comedy flick. If I hadn't lived it I wouldn't believe that this much medical drama could happen to one human being. I felt like saying, "Okay Lord can you skip over me for a change?" When I got home I had to rub my arm with my other hand. I try to look at the humor in life and I can see why they call it a trip. Early mornings I could just about get out of bed and I crawled so much that my dog thought I was playing with him. I thought with the pain in my feet that it was heel spurs and arthritis so I started taking anti inflammatory for arthritis and I sometimes wear custom feet pads. This eased my pain and I sought out some holistic medicine guys in Old City. I had sound therapy and a special fruits diet.

When I returned to Bermuda my Aunt Es took me to her holistic Doctor Alma who does Reiki back home and she worked on my hand and it stopped me from having surgery. She cracked my open my third eye and cleared the toxins out of my body. So much so that when I went to drink some juice I could feel it traveling throughout my veins.

Well My Aunt had previously set up a dinner party for me at the Lobster Pot Restaurant while I was visiting home because she knew that was I true Bermy and that we just live for sea food. Especially me, I mean scallops and Bermuda lobster are my favorites. But earlier that day Doctor Alma told me that if I didn't wish to be in pain like that anymore I would have to cut back on the shell food and I would have to stop eating lobster period because of the high iodine content. That night my willpower was put to the test and my Aunt Es in support decided to eat fish with me while we watched the others with their scrumptious Bermuda lobsters. I'm telling you all you haven't had a lobster until you've tried a sweet Bermuda lobster yum. It's the best, I could taste it right now and I haven't had any since 2005.

I don't like raining on people's parades so to speak. I remember talking business on my cell phone while I was getting my feet molded for castes due to my Lupus related foot condition of plantar facetious but the people on the other end would have never known. Why would I want to inflict my burdens on them. I was just happy and fortunate to be in the knowing of my challenges because the not knowing is what destroys our spirits!

I answered God's call and realize that my attitude towards my personal health challenges often depicts my emotional outcome. It's about me looking deep within and saying well I accept such and such but this is how I'm going to deal with it.

The other day I got down on my knees in a public bathroom and begged for God to help me and intervene and then I prayed for Him to cover me with the precious blood of Jesus. "Lord I love you so much and I know one thing for sure is that you did not bring me this far to leave me. Lord I love you for who you are to me and not for what I think I should be in your eyes. I love you for just holding me in the midnight hour and I love you for never forsaking me. Jesus you have always been true to me and the love that I have for you is like none other. I mean when fair-weathered friends turned their backs and money ran out or when I no longer was in the limelight you Lord never ever dropped the ball. Lord you carried me when others let me down you and my precious dog, well you know the deal. When my cousin stole my chemo money or when tenants played me while I was ill. You Lord never have forsaken me, you have been so loyal to me. So much so that I honestly don't know what I would do without you. Lord you were and are there in my darkest and brightest moments.

You Lord have remained consistent throughout and it was I that cheated on you but you never cheated on me. You have loved me unconditionally and as I write this tonight all I can say is, Yes Lord, yes to Your will. I'm humbly yours; use me for what you created me for. Lord Jesus I answered the call and now I'm just asking that you direct me Holy Spirit as to how I should go. I'm your bride first and foremost. Thank you Lord for just being beside me always and I will defend your name forever. Jesus you are my Lord and Savior and I am forever grateful to you. I just want to be a better person for your Kingdom Lord. I am grateful for the real estate, I'm grateful for my health, thank you for making me a responsible human being. One that is compassionate, thank you for removing people from my path that meant me no good, thank you for making me empathic and not going through life on a free ride. I know that you will guide me through these waves and ease my pain in my heart."

My plea is that I leave a legacy that reflects you Lord Jesus as being the transformer, the ultimate unconditional friend in our lives. You know it's funny how the Holy Spirit works for I just asked for a passage to put in this chapter and I was led to Psalms 10 which I didn't realize was noted as "A Song of Confidence in God's Triumph over Evil." Thank you Father Selah. Therefore I'm going to get off the computer and go and quietly worship. I will leave you with this though, when people make statements such as, "Oh that's just how they all are or we all go through or that's just how it is!" We must not accept that because we are God's children and He does not want us to go through confusion. He is not the author of confusion or deceit. He is compassion, empathy and love. Just remember that we serve a God of truth and He is peace always. Remember that unity is who our Lord and Savior Jesus is . . . lets never get that twisted . . . .

"Lord I trust that you will continue to assist me with my bills . . . we can never put our faith in men because we all are fallible but you Lord who I serve are not a man that you should lie. Thank you Jesus, oh you are so deserving of our love and praises always . . . The more I go through I truly realize that I live for you! I desire to show this planet that you are the way, the truth and the light and by sharing my journey. I hope someone will be touched by your presence and see and feel your light!"

Sharing Testimonies with Medical Students

Last week I had the opportunity to speak before twenty five University medical students and the preparation was quite draining but I was able to hold the Lord's hand as I had to relive some not so fantastic moments. I was able to deliver my testimony in front of the students that only God could have chosen. They had moved me from one classroom to another saying that it couldn't be in the classroom I was originally assigned to because one of the presenters, another patient wasn't comfortable because it was too cold. I saw this only as an act of God since the first Professor seemed to have a face of stone and if you ask me her room was the colder room in spirit that is. I met some great people and later had lunch with one lady who suffered from one of my same illnesses, systemic lupus. The Holy Spirit had prepared me to bring props, pictures and my pills as well as speaking about my diet. The others didn't and one presenter mentioned how she didn't think of that and they had done auditoriums prior. Well I didn't think of it myself the Holy Spirit did! I had asked for prayer from Pastor Dion so that the Holy Spirit could take over the situation since I had been told that I couldn't do or mention x y z especially Jesus.

My biggest concern was how could I possibly give my account without mentioning my greatest physician Jesus. The only name I could say when I lose my speech . . . Well I sent out texts and asked for prayer. I live by Proverbs 3:5-6 literally and I truly believe that if you trust the Lord with all your heart earnestly and acknowledge him in all your ways He will direct your path and that is exactly what He did. Right there in front of those medical students in a full classroom I sang His praises without Bible thumping of course but I let them know that there is something bigger out there and for me that is God. I let them know how **the name Jesus alone is so powerful** that faith in Him and the Trinity will set you free. I gave them my daily accounts and history as their Professor asked me questions and later the students. I allowed my partner to guide me and asked Him like I did for my wedding ceremony that I desired for God to show up and show out. And true to form He did! I ended or should I say we ended by piggy backing off the other presenter's question as to why they chose to be doctors.

One said to help the poor and I asked them all with boldness was it for the status, the money what? I let them know that I had a sister in law who is a dentist and family that were doctors. After all my Great-Great Grandfather was a respected doctor and the Gynecologist who discovered the spot on my cervix is a cousin. I let them know how the eastern medicine and herbs work alongside the western and this led to a discussion on one herb that is now used for patients with rheumatic illnesses and the Professor was more than happy to express her knowledge on that topic! I let them know that by me having a variety of illnesses doctors cannot be isolated or have the God complex and that my Bermudian doctors both traditional (Dr.Ross) and holistic (Dr.Alma) work hand in hand with my American doctors (Dr.Pruitt and Dr. Derminov).

We presented several near death examples where all facts pointed to my demise but the local doctors were on the phone with my overseas doctors and they figured it all out collectively. We let them know first firsthand and illustrated the truth by showing them the props and pictures. As a result these students had their own conclusions about what type of doctors they intended to be. The choice is theirs to make and we, my partner Mr. Holy Spirit and I warned them that there is that power bug out there so be weary! I congratulated them for choosing the medical path and to remember that God is in charge and they have been chosen to be gifted to help make change in people's lives which is the greatest gift of all. In closing I gave them my usual adapted quote which is, "Be that change and make those changes that you wish to see on this planet." I told them as Gandhi said, "You have to be that change."

Wow we got through it and it feels good to have planted positive seeds. Yeah!

NOT MY BABY!

Now these are my G (God) reports that I send out via texts to people that I feel genuinely care. It is like twittering. Well it is the close of the year and Christmas Eve to be precise and a "friend" asked me late last night was my dog ok and she was praying for him. So I said, "I anoint him everyday" as he actually pushed his head under my arm while I was wrapping gifts! Earlier he had tried to get me of his side of the couch. Now how cute is that?

An hour ago I awoke to my baby fighting for his life. His body was on fire and all his legs were clenched, his mouth was opened with his tongue going in the back of his mouth. So I cried out to God, "Please don't take him from me this Christmas morning." I called the 'friend' who had the foresight and I awakened my Husband to help me pray over my baby.

I cried out to Jesus to protect my family with the blood of Christ. The Holy Spirit had me pouring anointed oil over his lifeless body as I cried and held him in my arms. I took the oil and started taking pulling on his ears for the fever and demanding that the demonic forces leave his body. Then while still in my pajamas I took him in front of the house and placed him in the snow and cried out in tongues against all demonic strongholds to leave my family, my neighborhood and called names only the Holy Spirit could have given me! Then miraculously my baby started running and I just anointed the entire house including my Husband's head. After praying with the lady on the speaker phone when I went outside, he went back to snoring. Therefore I'm pleased to say I'm now lying on the floor next to a peacefully sleeping pug. "My friends, **Jesus is real**, you all rebuke every demonic stronghold and we declare victory in the name of Jesus because without prayer this Christmas morning could have been quite different. So give thanks in every moment enjoy the last single digit Christmas . . . ."

REFLECTION PRAISE

I'm listening to the praise XM station listening to Whitney Houston's song "I Look to You" and for the first time I can feel the lyrics "for when the melodies are gone "the sweetness isn't there and it is during these times that God is molding our characters for the trials that will strengthen us! We worked on her album for two years back and forth but hey it wasn't meant to be.

Right now I'm looking forward to tomorrow's first "Reflection Gathering . . . ." Now let me tell you something about this specific gathering. It came to me in a dream so I sent out invites via texts and prayed at the end of the day for the right people to be present. One of the guys my trainer and wedding caterer who I spoke to the night prior had said he was definitely swinging through but never made it so I figured something came up because I prayed about who to invite and then gave the lists to my "Daddy" and said, "Well whoever you want to be here will be present." My trainer had to go into the hospital and on New Year's Eve which was the next night he had to have surgery so flow with me and you will see the setup!

This is the text that all of the attendees received. *"Thank you for fellowshipping with the Keepin It Real family. We enjoyed having u at r first Reflection Praise Gatherin this is a Divine Appt n it will grow bcauz this is truly a Kingdom Movement!! Now go n get ur praise on."*

Months later my trainer fought a good fight but passed from colon cancer. He was granted his desire and had the opportunity to minister to numerous people from his bedside.

SONGS IMPARTED
4 SPIRITUAL WARFARE

I'm here at a peaceful resort with my family and "Lord Reveal" is the title of the song I was given. I can clearly recall how it was imparted to me, in the midst of a spiritual storm. We were at a spiritual retreat and while we were eating at a rustic restaurant I heard the melody so clearly. So I began writing the lyrics on a piece of brown paper bag. This was the Lord saving me from emotional confusion that was going on with someone close to me. I could feel the energy shift and didn't know what it was at the time so my spirit was crying out even though I appeared okay on the outside on the inside I was seriously crying out silently to the Lord, "Please help me for I can't deal with them." As I wrote the song this lady who is termed a Prophetess leaned over and said keep this paper for it will be worth something one day so I tore it off and kept it. I give all credit to my partner, Mr. Holy Spirit who has taught me how to compose music and would awaken me just to create. He taught me how to film, edit, direct and most of all how to keep my sanity when many evil spirits surround me. It has been a constant battle and I thank all of my prayer partners, warriors, ministers and prophets who were there and those that remain. It was these people that God used to keep me from insanity and I'm just so grateful for we have the victory!

I recall waking up New Year's morning 2012, it was a Sunday and I could hear every lyric, every melody when I awoke to "Hallelujah we exalt thee; you are worthy to be praised!" I was so excited I recorded it on my phone and then sang it to my cousin David. Later I was given just short verses from one of my life saving books, Psalms. Hence I checked in with my partner and we decided to title it "New Year Psalms." Now God knew what I was going to go through, (dah He is God). I hadn't formally recorded and arranged it yet because I had to go to another court hearing for that neighbor thief. For once he showed up with his sons who smiled at me and I smiled at them and said, "You all know what time it is!" When I went to use the bathroom I passed through this long hallway with tons of police seated in two lines on each side. It was there were the neighbor thief appeared like a huge demon vomiting from his lips these words "You want to take me to court hey, you want to go this far well watch what me and my lawyers are going to do to you. Yeah that's right I'm going to sue you for all the work I did on that so and so Property of yours!"

I responded, "How could you say that? You stole from me and only painted one room with our paint! And you offered to do that." My heart was pounding and I felt my blood pressure rise. As he walked boldly down the hallway in front of the cops he turned around and said this. "Yeah and else for your weak so and so cancer, I don't want to hear that so and so!" Now remember this was the neighbor I defended when the neighborhood complained about him being on "Megan's List" (law for registering sex offenders) and living directly across the street from a new high school that was being built. He told me he was changed and belonged to this church on 60th Street and was delivered. So as a good Christian I befriended him. It was after the fact that I discovered once again I was up against Lucifer's helpers. But I'll tell you this when he threatened me in that court hallway and I felt like dying inside you know what the Lord bought before me . . . . the song "Hallelujah, we exalt thee, you are worthy to be praised." That imparted worship tune from New Year's morning.

I went into that bathroom and cried my head off and got on my knees and just started dialing all of my prayer partners and I couldn't get in contact with anyone. Then I dialed my parents and my Dad said my Mom wasn't home and I shouted, "Daddy I need you to pray with me now before I have to go back in." He said, "Well your Mother is not hereand what's your number?" All I could do was cry and say, "Lord I need you right here the bathroom and I told her to excuse me but I have to talk to God because only He can save me. I got up off my knees, wiped my eyes, fixed my face, put on my lipstick and walked out of that bathroom with Holy Ghost boldness. When I returned to the hallway there was demon Teflon. We will refer to him as Teflon since nothing in the Philadelphia Judicial system seems to stick to him despite factual tangible proof. Everyone seems to be afraid of this bully. I called my neighbor and prayer partner Ms. Renee who prayed with me and we just started reciting scriptures out loud. I was able to all of a sudden reach my husband who told me not to fear for that was of the enemy and that is what he plays on so I said in front of that lined hallway of police that the God I serve will neither leave me nor forsake me and I entered that courtroom with confidence, minus all fear! Like the song "Poetic Night" says "the fear of the Lord that is wisdom. Where can wisdom be found because it sure doesn't come from human understanding. God understands the way to it and He understands where it dwells." So I rest in that "the fear of the Lord is Wisdom and to shun evil is understanding!" Job 28 "Come Holy Spirit my partner activate right here, right now!" My Dad ended up praying with me and then I felt at peace. There was a woman present in the bathroom and I told her that I had to turn to both of my Fathers, my earthly and my Heavenly.

As I'm writing this the case is still going on but I tell you this much God showed up and showed out where the Judge had to issue a stay away order against him despite the fact that every policemen who was there denied hearing anything . . . deep huh! Was that a conversation in the supernatural because he was extremely loud. I put my trust in the Lord just like my Dad whose organs are ill and he believes so much and will tell you that God has him covered. I can tell you that this is a most fulfilling moment and memory that I have with my earthly Father.

This is a live example of Romans 8:28 "Whatever is meant for bad will turn out for the good of those that love the Lord." I later went and formally recorded the song "Hallelujah we exalt thee, you are worthy to be praised, we magnify your name!

When things seem to be getting rough, it's only you that we can trust." The rest of the words we wrote there along with the arrangement. The music and the first draft was so powerful that the engineer was visibly effected.

The case is still going on but I tell you this much God showed up and showed out where the Judge had to issue a stay away order against him despite the fact that every policemen who was there denied hearing anything . . . deep huh! Was that conversation Teflon and I had in the supernatural because he was extremely loud.

Well I sang boldly in the studio with Franz that afternoon. There is such intensity with the lyrics from Psalms 18:17 "You rescued me from my enemies and my foes that were stronger." It was an anointed moment and I hope this inspires someone for in all things and situations you can find your rescuer, your Savior, just seek within. He is there waiting for you to grab onto His extended hand! The song was written for me and you to walk in that knowing with assurance! When they nailed Him to the cross and pierced his side that is our surety.

Breaking the Silence about a Mangled Judicial System

Well the trial ended before it even got started. All I could do is awake this morning to feeling like it was all just a bad dream. For nine months of my life I fought to get back what was rightfully mine. The so called good neighbor who we found out had overtaken our other neighbor's property and was on bail for forging a state trooper's signature at a check cashing place and had stolen a bunch of people's deposit monies. Yes I know I'm sounding like a broken record but it's a record that continues to be played and no one is changing it. What is going on with our Judicial system and who is this DS guy really? After all he gets away with paper murder. *He was taken to court several times but never convicted. In addition he is a registered sex offender and there is no proximity law in Philadelphia like other states were you have to live a certain distance from a school. This man bulldozed himself into a house of a senior directly across the street where a remodeled high school was being built.*

Neighbors talked about it but living right beside him we had no clue what we were in for. Well at least I didn't! I wanted to prove to the neighborhood that people can change through the Lord. Let's refer to the "neighbor who bulldozed his way into the neighborhood "Teflon." He even took down the fence, removed my trees without permission and had three pit bulls harassing the neighbors. But of course nothing happened after being reported. Let's not forget the fact that he would bring home intoxicated boys and disturb the neighbors with loud parties and screams of people begging for their lives. Still nothing!

There were numerous court cases were the tenants would show up as witnesses and Teflon wouldn't. I tried to drop the case because I had empathy for my witnesses' jobs but the District Attorney's office said a firm "no" that once the judge moved it to trial it was now their case. They listened as Teflon ranted and raved on his cell phone about how he was going to sue me for all the money he lost in parking when he was the one who stole from me. He once said loudly "How dare you take me to court!"

Yesterday morning I talked to God and got all my prayer warriors on board both near and far and went to court. A strange feeling of not caring anymore came over me while me and my partner, Mr. Holy Spirit waited in what appeared to be a disorganized circus as Teflon sat behind me with his son and for the first time his "church" mother. Also for the first time he didn't appear arrogant but more child like. Seated beside me was a girl who was complaining that they keep bringing her back for bags of weed that she admitted belonged to her two years ago. On the other side sat a grandmother with her three young grand children seated amongst drug dealers and thieves. There was a whole lot of cussing and utter confusion and they were there for having a basketball going into a neighbor's yard which caused a fight between the two mothers. Anyhoo the "weed" girl was telling me how her family member took over a house and signed fake leases and is living large by scamming people. As she stated, "The system gets all extra over a little weed but they can let people like my cousins get off for scamming innocent people. It's not fair!" I told her what my situation was and that God was in control. I also said that I had a feeling that I wasn't going to win the case in this courtroom because it is much bigger than this!

Soon after my partner prompted me to go and check my voicemail since I didn't see any of the witnesses. I remembered overhearing Teflon tell his sons last time not to worry for he would only be there three more times. Now the DA was telling me to be strong because he had to have his lawyer present or he would be served. Just to think each time we were lied to by the DA and told fake encouragement lines as, "Yes he and his lawyer are criminals and you just have to keep showing up and not to give up!"

I checked my voicemail and like clockwork there it was the new assistant DA who had been assigned to me saying that even though I was served a subpoena to come ;I didn't need to come only Teflon and his attorney had to show up. How shady! I left her a message stating that I had already cleared my day and that this was short notice since she called very late the evening prior and I was already here after traveling by bus and train. When I returned to the court room it was like something out of a movie! If I wasn't there physically I wouldn't believe it.

Earlier that morning I took two "Awake" magazines from the Jehovah Witnesses at the subway station. I asked the Lord which one should I read and I noticed that one of them talked about injustice and how sometimes God allows it for a bigger picture. So from that moment a seed had been planted and I said, "Well Lord what are you trying to tell me?" Therefore when I lost the case and NOTHING was ever introduced I knew how it played out but no one was prepared for the way it all went down; not even Teflon. Here's the scene:

My Assistant DA never showed up and neither did the witnesses because they got the call from her the day before. The female Judge then asked Teflon if his counselor was present and he said "No your honor." She asked if he could afford another attorney and he said yes he could. Then the second round came when his name was called and she stated again "Is your counsel present?" and he said "No your honor." Then she asked for his attorney's name. He gave it (remember they were mentioned as criminals by the previous Assistant DA and her associates in front of witnesses). Once the name was given it all moved into a fast pace, a call was made from his attorney who still never showed up physically and we don't know what was said but the judge turned around and said everything is discharged. Teflon just stood there and said, "Huh?" The Judge repeated, "All charges have been dropped." The court screamed in unison, "WHAT?" Teflon then asked would he get all of his money back from parking and bail and get this they said yes! Now remember I'm still out a couple of thousand dollars. Well I had on a hat and had never signed in so I stood up with Holy Spirit boldness and sternly said "You mean he steals my money and he walks, well it's not over so I hope you watch every channel!" Right after my outburst the Judge said to Teflon to leave before she changed her mind and the criminals in the court all shouted at Teflon "Go, Go just leave!" You would have thought we were at a Philadelphia Eagles football game. He looked in disbelief and when we were outside the courtroom he had the audacity to say to me, "God is good" and I replied, "He sure is and He will take care of me." Then went to get on the same elevator and I got on. It was half empty but had some police, lawyers and civilians on it. I said to him "What you can't get on, you mean your conscience won't let you on. But I thought you didn't do anything and that is why they let you off?"

Now my partner and I are preparing for the next phase and that is exposure. You see the press wrote an article and contacted me but I didn't want to interfere with the trial, yeah right what trial! Also the television stations would love this report of abuse of the law or should we say above the law. Teflon and his crew were right they are above the city's law but never above God's. Like I said earlier as we waited for the Judge, to "weed" girl and "basketball" granny that Teflon may get off in this court room but what God has planned on the outside is so much more. I told them and I know his mother heard me that this is to save the next boy from being molested or the next senior from having their home stolen from them. However God showed me that although I may never get the money back, it was never about that, it was about saving the next victim. You see if Teflon had been stopped along the way he wouldn't have become so smug in his behavior and all those that assisted along the way all these years will be exposed for God doesn't do anything halfway. Stay tuned as the journey continues and thank you for reading my spin cycle for truly my book is my story, it is my life's journey!

DON'T GET IT TWISTED THE BATTLE CONTINUES

You see just when I thought I got it, there comes the demons of confusion, destruction and health busters I call them. However when you recognize them and feel them in the pit of your core, your being, you can call on the name above all names, "**Jesus**" quietly or loudly and ask for discernment at all times. You know the greatest trick that the enemy ever tried was to convince you that he didn't exist. As I write this I must ask for Godly wisdom so as not to expose my private family life. Let's just say there are certain gates and the enemy knows how to attack them or better yet attach himself to them. I had to get on my knees and cry out once again to my Lord and Savior. It never ceases but the battle gets easier to fight when you can see your enemies. And many times humans don't even know that they are being used. We ourselves must individually guard ourselves and stay covered with the blood of Jesus at all times. All I could think about was that scripture "Because of His love we will not be consumed, for His compassions never fail" Lamentations 3:22 and actually follow through with the Scripture 1Thessalonians 5:17 "Pray without ceasing."

We must love and rely on the Lord in and out of season, there are no breaks and we can not go by our fluctuating feelings. This thing is real and we are at war so just accept it and put on your armor. **There is more in the invisible realms than the visible.** I'm still in court fighting the neighbor that stole my rent and deposit money and is on $20,000 bail from a previous case. Theft by Deception they termed it. This same man has been allowed to steal my neighbor's house by illegally moving in and bullying them. As a senior the owners father cannot afford a lawyer so they are just letting DS do whatever he feels. In fact I'm number 13 as far as him being tried for the same exact cases and getting off; but the Lord I serve pays His debts in another way and will take my revenge. I have to believe that for He didn't save my life for such evil. My partner and I have faced demons before and this one comes with a story that will expose much more. Hey even with the Distort Attorney who were pretending to be on our side, the case still must be proved even though they have the proof and he doesn't show up in court time after time! This is to wear us down so we can give up and lose our case. Trust and believe DS and his lawyer know the game so well. I'm in the midst of this as we speak but I ask for God to strengthen me, under gird me and go before me **for my trust and hope is not in men, or the system but the Lord. The Lord who appoints, never disappoints, who positions and calls you to take a stand!** Sounds familiar? But I know that I am overcome by the words of my testimony so all of these circumstances in my life are just that my testimony to proclaim His glorious works in my life. I often say to my partner, Mr. Holy Spirit that this book will never be finished and it won't because my life like yours is a limitless journey where the pages will continue to turn! Like the song says **"Answer the Call!"**

MY TRUE FRIENDS WEN AND ANDY ANSWER MY CALLS

Last night on my way home I sat in the car and talked for hours to one of my best friends Wendell and we discussed finishing up my book. He said if anybody should write a book about all the coincidences in their life should be me. We laughed, reminisced and even started singing some of the first songs that we wrote decades ago. He said if anyone didn't know that these things were true they would believe they were the greatest fictional stories but this is my life. I consider my friend Wen the '**discusser**' and my other best friend Andy is the '**reasoner.**' They both have experienced up close my tangled intertwined set of events and divine connections that only now I get it since walking with my partner, Mr. Holy Spirit! I want to take this time and say thank you for being there over the decades and being consistent fixtures in my life's journey. So many have come and go or wanted this or that but you guys have been positioned in my life without 'rhyme or reason.' And as our song states "our love is in and out of season babe . . ." I love you guys I truly do!

Andy and his bass

MY D WITH YOU THE LAUGHTER BALANCES OUT THE TEARS!

Now I have to shed tears as I watch my beloved Diego go blind and become feeble. I hurt as a parent since he was my cancer dog that I got because once diagnosed they tell you to get a pet to keep you focused on something other than your illness. I for some reason wanted a pug and it had nothing to do with the pug in the Men In Black movie. Now the first litter died so I asked to remain on the list and wanted the most feisty one. I clearly remember when something had me look in a newspaper while at my now deceased adopted godfather's house. I looked for pugs and there it was and the gentleman said, "Do you know where you are calling?" I replied, "No I just felt led to call this number that I saw with pugs." He said this is Amish and Mennonite country. Now I could have called any other number but I was obedient to the Spirit. Wow as I'm writing this I realize my baby was a Christian from the start. They brought him to me by train at age three months in a small box and their little daughter cried. I couldn't believe here were these people dressed in clothes that at the time I had only seen on the Harrison Ford movie "Witness."

It is funny thinking back for I had named him while at the office I was working at in Bermuda and his middle name was from a co worker of mine. She took me and my former female partner's nicknames and created LaBoo, yep "Diego LaBoo." My partner had named him Diego after the famous South American soccer player.

Diego has been with me so long that people ask me is he still alive and I would shoot back sternly of course that he's only in his eleventh year and they can live up until fifteen and beyond. But in my heart I know Diego wouldn't live long enough to move back to Bermuda with us. My Husband would always say, "Yes he is and don't say that!" Diego has been through all of my transitions from drugs to being married to his first parent to now my hubby and stepson. From residing in the city condo to my escape penthouse (views of life) apartment to an actual house with his own little yard. We are so close that when I was going through chemo he would know I was sick before I did. He started acting frantic and then I would become nauseous and crawl on the floor to the bathroom. Hey he's been through it all so now he needs to hang in there and see the upswing of what God is about to do. D as I affectionately call him has fought numerous attacks and this last one was a bit much. I've cried so much and have been sleeping on the floor with him. That's my baby who I put winter clothes on and of course he has his own wardrobe. We would have birthday parties for him and invite other dogs.

Once we even entered this Halloween dog costume party and invited other pugs and they ended up winning over our baby, we were livid! After all our baby was the cutest in his count Dracula outfit . . . I would say "Yo D you wear it well!" I would have to say living in the city were some exciting times for my baby. I remember getting lost in Center City when I first moved there and I was holding him in my arms and these people came up to me and said, "How cute" and then when I moved the blanket they jumped back. He was even on the set of a famous movie and the crew fell in love with him. It's true once you fall in love with a pug it's all over.

I remember my ex getting into an argument at a boating place because this extra skinny lady said that my D was the ugliest dog she had ever seen. "Are you kidding me my baby is very handsome for his breed" I yelled. I recall one time and the only time really that these former tenants of ours had a pug puppy and were excited to show him to us and Diego decided to pee on the baby pugs head, now talk about awkward moments. What was that? I mean whose child would do such a thing? Well we corrected D but they decided to stop speaking to us anyway.

I recently told a friend of mine that last month we were at the vet's for his annual shots and he had a clean bill of heath other than being eight pounds overweight which they said was a bit much for his heart. Also those hoofs he has for nails that he wouldn't let them cut and tried to bite them. But he won't be biting anyone now with his off balance and twisted neck self; he's probably begging us to cut them so he can at least balance himself and walk better. I have to make jokes so the laughter balances out the tears. I mean I could write a book just dedicated to D because we went through so much. Other than God in the past eleven years he has been my confident and best friend. Someone I could hold, sniff, and cuddle with no matter what? I guess that's why they term dogs as being man's best friend. Yep like chucky till the end. Everyone from Celebes to Bishops, Pastors and people of every color and persuasion have met my baby. I mean there was my flamboyant masseuse who had to massage the both of us because Diego would get on that table and not move. We had the East Indians, Asians, Puerto Ricans, Bermudians, and Jamaicans and how could I forget his paid transgender babysitters who later turned on me. Who knew? But I bet you Diego did! He has many secrets right down to the greatest love betrayal of my life that God turned into my greatest blessing!

WHEN YOU'RE TIRED OF KNOCKING GOD HAS A PLAN

Well my extended family so much has happened since we connected last year, December. The Holy Spirit directed me to a job and it seemed like my dream job but then it was sales and I went through a month of back and forth and never getting paid! I would travel there and catch the bus, then the subway, then walk fourteen blocks. Sometimes I did this three times a day and get there early but as time went on I noticed I was the only one showing up from my class of ten. I know I trust in God but my body became weary and then I was told to show up and the person who was in charge wouldn't. Even after doing tasks and taking it to the limit and meeting with people I released it all and had faith. After not feeling well and experiencing the same symptoms that landed me in the hospital years ago with fluid around my heart and in my left lung I decided to lay in today and work on my TV project. Still working I know, even typing this some would consider working. But during my month at my dream job I have spoken with many believers and given them hope.

One lady broke out speaking in tongues. Others I recognized the God in them and when I told them that they gave me the thumbs up! I say this to say that I don't know what plans God has for me I can only rely on my partner's direction and continually seek His face. I know the gifts God has given me and the visions but this not getting paid stuff and continuously asking is a bit much. I'll go in this evening because I said I would and promised many young people. I feel like I'm there for the reason of integrity. I read that scripture this morning in Psalms, let me look for it . . . Here it is Psalms 25:21 "May integrity and uprightness protect me because my hope is in you." And that is how I honestly feel but I'm human and I'm not going to lie to you, this test is wearing me down because of expectations.

In the midst of the storms you my Lord are there. Right now in my life there is so much circling of unsettled waters. I'm still in court with that man who blatantly stole my tenant's deposit monies with no remorse. But standing before the District Attorney's office and judges before Christmas and having the case drag on until after the New Year has had its toll on me and again this is my lesson in faith. There are those in the industry that have asked me to do certain things and each time I deliver but still don't see anything concrete, again these are my tests in faith. My body broke down around Christmas but I still came to "work' and sat with a lady who God used me to give hope.

In the midst of my personal life drama which I threw up in the air to God and said, "Lord catch this because I can't take it anymore." I was tired of crying, I was tired of having people pray with me not knowing who were witches and warlocks and I say this to say that not everyone we go to in prayer is of God. Some may seem pretty close but I've learned that if your 'gut" tells you otherwise than you take it to God yourself and ask for revelation. I mean it got to the point that when certain people asked how family members were including my dog and said they were praying, every time "bam bam" something bad would happen like clockwork. And I'm talking serious unexplainable things in the natural like my dog barking hysterically at what in the natural eye looked like nothing and then he would start gasping for breath like someone was choking him! It got to the point that we started bleeding the blood of Jesus silently and eventually they started revealing themselves. I'm just saying . . . . if it looks like a duck but acts like a frog then just maybe it is; no matter how much we want it to be different. Yeah I'm ministering to myself because I'm always running into quacking ducks.

Acceptance is the key and time reveals all. I remember my beloved Debarge family song "Time will Reveal" and yep it surely does. I've learned that seeking God's wisdom and asking for his grace and mercy to reflect in who you are is more important than any meditation, men's expectations or words. My partner of this book, Mr. Holy Spirit brings me back to that deep dream where I jumped and it said in red **"You are now a Servant of Jesus"** so why do I get disappointed or surprised when friends and family or people period are swishy washy. My trust shouldn't be in them in the first place for it needs to be in my Lord and who, what . . . my Savior? That's the key term Savior, it does not say so and so it says "Jesus, the Son of the Living God."

Check this out in the midst of all of what's going on God is still working out His plan. The key is that it is His plan not our plan. Sometimes we say if we had the chance we may do things differently but then we would miss out on key pieces in our lives. Like my Tibet experience. It's no secret for those that are close to me know that Tibet is a country I've always felt connected to and I've always said that before I transcend I have to visit Tibet. Once when I was in Canada I had sincere conversations with people from their neighbor country Nepal where many Tibetans have escaped to. I felt drawn to these two shirts which had writings on them and the opposite symbol of what "Hitler" used to represent hate. In the natural I did not know why I was so drawn to this symbol. In the natural I did not realize that the swastika symbol was universal. In various ancient cultures the inverted symbol meant many various things.

The shirts I was told by the Nepal owners represented noble love and when I wore them into the clubs several persons would greet me with respect saying that I had the courage to wear them. These were symbols that many Westerners had no clue of the meaning other than the inverted version of it. Some would say why are you wearing that and I would explain it to them that it originally meant something positive. Interesting huh? I guess Adolf Hitler researched the symbols before he turned them around to mean the exact opposite. That's the enemy for you, always twisting things.

GOD PLACES AND DISPLACES

Did I mention that about a month ago I found my dream job. After asking my partner what should I do and I spotted an ad and said I would apply if I saw it again. Well I did and had my cousin pray with me. I got a message to attend an interview and when I tried to change it because I had another meeting scheduled I was told that this was urgent and I may not be able to reschedule. So I stepped outside of my box of being so accommodating and rescheduled my meeting and attended the interview. I was excited at first and called only my immediate family and told my Mom to keep it hushed. Soon after that I went to my cousin's play in New York and sought out some talent.

When I returned home I continued to pound the pavement leaving home for eleven hour days and walking fourteen blocks three times a day and sometimes more. Because of my conditions and the 3500mg of meds I take a day I had to take a nap for at least an hour which meant traveling to another side of the city by train and then walking. I did this for two weeks straight and then my body started to break down. I began having break through seizures and I remember one evening I went in for my additional four hour run and I could hardly talk so I had my Hubby pray with me and he said, "Babe are you sure this is worth it? I replied, "Yes I have to give my all and if it doesn't pan out than I know that God has something lined up but at least I will know I gave it my everything." I went in that evening and later had to interview two clients and one was grueling with all the extra questions and the other started breaking out speaking in tongues and called me a prophetess and that she could see me with nations. Now you know I wasn't prepared for that! However when I look back I ask the question as to why is it that we break our necks to go to work but when it comes to having a relationship with God we slack off? And I feel so much better and as I'm writing this because I know without a doubt that I gave that talent/model agency my all. I gave up public holidays, my birthday celebration and all in the name of commitment to a job where I never got tangible payment. What I did receive was payment into myself and I was able to speak life into individuals in the name of the Lord.

As of last night I went in and explained my situation and they explained their sales rules and because I see people as creations and not dollars I couldn't do it. When I see talent and believe me I have always been surrounded by talented individuals approaching me across the globe from South Africa to England. Even on family trips I would drag my family through the mountains just to go to a radio station to promote someone's music. I did that for free but it was so internally rewarding. I don't know what that means but as for right now I need to go to Florida and spend it with my family and reflect and seek God's guidance. As I'm writing this I was thinking what does all this mean, the TV shows, radio etc and then I heard Dottie People's song 'Let Jesus Lead You." And you know what that is the best advice!

TIRED OF THE SPIRITS? THAN FIGHT

Well I just have to share this. I was on the train the other day and this lady who resembled a top fashion model kept walking on the heels of another passenger and it got to the point that the passenger said, "Can you please stop walking on my heels I've asked you twice before." Well the fashion look alike that was high as a kite started saying, "Oh yeah you want to fight let's bring it" and started taking her clothes off. The passenger said "I asked you nicely" and all I saw was a flash of something. The fashion look alike reached into her purse and the passenger who was behind kept talking and I told her boldly to hush and rebuke. I said sternly, "Rebuke it" because I was in the middle and all I saw was me getting mistakenly tazed or worse shot. I started rebuking and pleading the blood and then the train operator escorted the model want a be fighter and her friend off the train.

Recently I've had a new battle with spirits in my house and especially my bedroom. Last year when I returned from visiting my family I experienced something so out of the ordinary. I was sleeping one afternoon and I felt something touching me in my sleep and massaging my shoulders and I enjoyed it truthfully and then it started to touch my nibbles on my breasts and I awoke to severe coldness in a biting motion. I clearly saw between the two realms a huge slivery bluish grayish rip moray disappearing.

Last night before I went to bed there was this pungent odor and I went all over the room trying to find where it was coming from. I even had the window opened full blast and I couldn't get rid of the smell. As a result I sprayed vacuum foam and air freshener but still the odor crept through. So I went to sleep and had a strange feeling like butterflies and I had to ask God to cover me with the blood of Jesus. I suddenly got up and looked over at my Diego and he was foaming and looking in the air with his body stiffened. I started crying out to God. "Lord I m tired of these spirits get them out of this house in the name of Jesus" and I anointed my dog's feet and his body and just started speaking in tongues. Again I said," Lord don't take my child" and I had the faith of a mustard seed to trust and know that only God could break it. I kept bleeding the blood of Jesus over him and like the Bible says demons flee at the sound of the name above all names, that being the son of God JESUS. Well this is my truth because I've experienced the power, the real deal. And get this the pungent odor vanished!

The night prior I was at some event and a lead singer of a group I represent was there and she said I have been going through something and I want to know who is this Jesus that you talk about and turn to? I told her, "He is the Son of God and while you cannot tangibly feel him or touch Him you know He is there you can feel His presence. Just as we may not be able to grab a hold of the air but yet we know it is there. I guess you can just say the presence of Jesus is mystical!" Then I immediately awoke to this message posted on our former blog cast "keepinitrealchristians.net" where a military person did a sermon entitled "Just who is this Jesus?" Then they made us remove it after they had given us permission to post it. But either way I'm telling you it was electrifying because you could feel it in your veins, your heart and soul; you could relate. Everyone is entitled to believe whatever they want but for me Jesus is like Coke a Cola, the real thing! Maybe one day they will let us repost it.

THE END IS THE BEGINNING

As we approach the end of the year so many things are propelling me forward that it could be nobody but the Lord. Let me start by saying I applied for this job after praying with God that I had this desire to do more with my talents and no longer did I want to be giving away my gifts for free. I can't explain it but there was this whole shifting thing going on. As a result my partner had me restructure my resume and I just put it out into the universe as some would term it but for me I just gave it to God. The result was some clients being referred to me and after several meetings we decided to go with each other and sign a one year contract. It was a project that is a challenge because it was out of my comfort zone but not out of my range. In April I had signed with a band that was also out of my comfort zone but I prayed and God made a way and truly directed my path. I asked for a new family in my creative life. I prayed that He would remove the thorns from my life and replenish it with those that He wanted me to show my light to and He has.

It's been a year of losses, replacements and new additions. At this stage right now I'm happy with my marriage, my family, my church family, my spiritual friends, my clients and just overall favored. I balance it all with the guidance of my partner, Mr. Holy Spirit. It has been a year of trials, tribulations and restoration but most of all the building of character.

Just now they started playing my song "Hosanna" by Kirk Franklin on Music Choice so I had to jump out of bed, put the laptop down and start worshipping. Out of all the music genres worship is my thing, that's the music that touches my soul, my core, my very being. And my partner just brought it to my attention that I was made to worship.

It's funny that song "Hosanna" I will forever remember because I was invited by some friends to attend the hearing impaired church one Sunday and they were playing this song when I was arguing on the phone with my husband outside. Now looking back what on earth were we arguing about? I can't even remember so anyhow imagine the visual I'm arguing with the cell to my ear and my hubby starts going on after a weekend of hell now that I do remember! I began to allow myself to get sucked in with the negative energy and I'm going there trust and believe but still I'm pressing on to my friend's church. In the midst of all the chaos it was like the heavens opened up and I started hearing voices singing "Hosanna, Hosanna" and I realized where I was and started walking then breaking my neck to get inside literally; I could have been leaping(smile) with my phone still on and my husband still ranting. I went into the church and started worshiping with the cell on and I know those spirits heard the worship and me singing to the top of my lungs! Funny how God said, "Ok you two enough is enough "and like the verse says in Psalms 18:16 "He reached down from on high and drew me out of the deep waters" and that my friends is what He did all year and throughout my life but I just wasn't actively aware of it.

Now on Christmas day I started to experience the cancer feelings similar to what I experienced four years prior when I quit the chemo. This time I knew to start talking to Him and I now had scriptures I could recite as well as knowing how to listen to the Holy Spirit and follow His guidance. The result was me remaining calm when the attacks came and I experienced about five that day. In the past I tried to resist and the result was a full blown grand-mal seizure. I kept calm and recited scriptures repeatedly like Philippians 4:13 "I can do all things through Christ that strengthens me" and Philippines 4:19 "God will supply All my needs through the glorious riches of Christ Jesus." Psalms 18:17 "You rescued me from my powerful enemy and my foes who were stronger." Psalms 18:32 "God arms me with strength and makes my way safe." Jeremiah 1:8 "Do not be afraid of them, for I am with you and will rescue you." Jeremiah 1:19 "They will fight against you but will not overcome you, for I am with you and will rescue you." Then I struggled against the spiritual warfare and added Lord you are my rock and my redeemer!

Periodically I recited these scriptures in my head even while talking at Christmas dinner and then when I returned home I had an attack and my husband thought I was walking off from him but I explained calmly later when I came back to myself that I was fighting another seizure. It was then that I asked my partner what to do and I took extra Phenytoin/Dilantin and drank some pure apple cider vinegar which wasn't the greatest taste. OMG! Anyhoo I could feel the release coming from my brain and all this fluid and mucous started coming out. The next morning I got up and wrote my two papers and attended my Monday morning meeting and check this I was the only one in my class that showed up. Now tell me God isn't good! Can I get an Amen on that one ... hello!

RECEIVING IS A RESULT OF BELIEVING

I feel so thankful, grateful and blessed to say that my Lord and Savior is Jesus Christ! I was just talking to my hubby on the phone and we were discussing the order of God and how we can clearly see it. I grew up always fighting for my passions but now we see the order and believe me it's so true for when they say your steps are ordered well they aren't kidding. When you learn the verse from Proverbs 3: 5, 6 "Trust in the Lord with all your heart. Acknowledge Him in all thy ways and He will direct your path." I'm so excited about the news that I just called a friend of mine. She called me back upset thinking something was wrong and said I scared the mess out of her because no one calls her six in the morning and said, "LA what's wrong" and I told her we are going to be aired on cable starting this Thanksgiving and then for nine weeks. Then I called my other actress friend who was a part of it and she said the same thing, "What's wrong LA?"

Well this feeling of accomplishment is so intense that I had to share it with those in my circle. I'm so excited but I know the feeling is only temporary for I went from early yesterday morning saying I can't do anything right to relying heavily on the Holy Spirit and this is the result. My show, the one that my partner prompted me to go forth with from beginning to end; from the title to the format, to the contestants, to judges, to hosts, to team, to venue. God is good and that isn't just a cliché. I asked for my partner's guidance in every step. Right down to the computer programs used I would say, "Ok Holy Spirit what do you want me to use?" Lead me, guide me along the way isn't just lyrics to a song but true application. When I look back over my life I've always relied on God for my shows and so this was natural. Lord thank you for always being there. We will continue to "Rock it Clean Live."

HEALING HEARTS/HEALING SOULS

As I've gotten older I realize that my life is full of stories not of shame or game but given to me to proclaim. Um . . . . partner this seems like another song, should I take a break and write it in my song book? Give me minute readers . . .

Okay I'm back you know it's funny because the more I travel along this journey I realize that nothing is by chance. Everything consists of grains of truth and the more I strive I know that just me being alive to write this is living proof. I once said to my Asian church that if you don't believe in God just look at me. I consider it a privilege to be walking and talking so writing, singing, composing and producing are God's toppings. I like to refer to them as sprinkles from God; you know the ones my stepson likes, the rainbow sprinkles. I look at life through rose colored glasses because God has sprinkled every one of us with that gift called special.

The gifts He has imparted us with have that name special and I refuse to let anyone or anything block me from receiving or utilizing what my Father has given me. My partner once gave me a song as I waited in a Canadian airport amidst so much negative energy that I started to feel sick and then that gift that He planted in me said, "Oh no!" That special gift imparted into me wrote an entire song with a melody called "Meant to Be" with one of the lines stating "Even prior to your conception you were born with a purpose because you are meant to be." So by George, when they come at your neck hold on and just keep your hand in His. All of this will fade but the love of God never fades, it never discourages, it never abandons, it never makes you angry for as in one of my favorite scriptures it says in Lam. 3:22 "Because of His great love we will not be consumed for His compassions never fail." That scripture is alive in that when others try and crush your dreams or break your spirit no matter how much your emotions will get to you, you NEED to know that God's love will not let you be consumed.

Jesus has you and will carry you. I thank God and last night I went to bed wanting badly in my heart to attend this fire Kirk Franklin concert but no one wanted to go. I just knew that I would go alone if I had to because I needed to. You know how that song says shattered but not broken well it's real baby. In the midst of my sorrow God allowed a friend of mine to call and say they heard some promotional package and did I still want to go. You see I planted that seed by calling her and others and asking them to go to this concert with me but peeps were not feeling it. God knew I was going and my partner's job was to prepare me in the midst of my storm to move forward and rise above the enemy! I went from a few days ago of feeling a sense of accomplishment to now one of defeat but I know that spirit and it's called jealousy and emotional abuse! This spirit was so familiar that years ago I wrote a song about it. My husband makes a joke and says that I'm like that man that says, "Hey you know I wrote a song about it." Yeah I guess that's part of my gifting, writing about all sorts of things. I guess I'm a life songwriter.

TODAY IS THE DAY 2 REMEMBER

Today is the only time in history that there will be an 11/11/11 which marks my twelfth year of surviving with this brain cancer. Apart from occasional setbacks which I note as distractions I'm remaining here for a reason and I am so grateful. I do not take any day for granted and especially not Remembrance Day. My Aunt Eleanor reminded me that so much has happened to our family on

November 11th. My first cousin was shot in the head and survived with a chance of one in a million. He lost his side vision and there are fragments of the bullet still lodged in his head but other than having a few occasional seizures which are under control he is okay. And he lived to bring a beautiful daughter into this world. Tell me that wasn't God and his Angels!

Also on this day twelve years ago I was diagnosed with brain cancer. The tests revealed that I had a huge mass on my brain and the doctor asked me whether I wanted it out through my nose or to open up my brain. I thought about it for five minutes shed a few tears and answered go in through my brain. It was already a shock that that they told me I had a brain tumor since the doctors back home didn't know. Some thought I had a stroke, others felt due to my prior cocaine use I had damaged myself; which I did don't get it twisted. Not to mention my primary doctor was treating me for epilepsy. It's funny when I look back; because I love to dance every time I was in a club with flashing lights I would close my eyes. I was told that the flashing neon lights would trigger my epilepsy but all the while there was this entity that attached itself to my brain.

I can recall the day that I bashed my head continuously against a radiator because the person I was getting high with looked like a monkey. They actually left me in that condition can you imagine? I did have a family member who knew from my mouth how bad my habit was becoming and I knew I could confide in him because he couldn't talk due to his speech being lost as a result of a severe stroke, therefore I knew he wouldn't tell anyone. Yeah I experienced firsthand the deep sincere pure love of someone who I attended musical events with and would spend hours just fascinated as to how he could build new attachments to the homestead or fix things. I guess that's where I get that restoration bug from whether it being people or buildings, there I am with my hammer and nails to fix things. Well the one I couldn't fix on my own was me!

That family member was my buddy, my Grandpa Joell who I last saw on this planet earth after a cocaine binge. My pants were soiled in blood because I was so busy getting high and was too paranoid to move to clean up myself. I told him I was sorry and would seek help and he put his arms around me and I told him I loved him. I went back to college overseas and got better. But occasionally I got caught up and the result was me bashing my head one night and getting so high and disoriented to the point that I couldn't board that plane the next morning. That's right I missed my buddy, my Grandpa Joell's funeral and it has taken years for me to forgive myself. However a few months later I was able to redeem myself when my Grandmother got ill. I dropped out of school and moved back home to work and I would visit her every day in the hospital. She died six months after my Grandpa. My Mom and her siblings lost both of their parents months apart. That was some year we lost a total of twelve family members. A decade later I didn't want to leave them due to the guilt and shame.

Getting back to November 11th, 1999 I had the operation and came through. The surgeon said they could only get 80% and the remainder was like a piece of bad meat that was inoperable and was cancerous. In my heart I already knew but my parents were sad. That was the new day of the rest of my life. I'm so thankful that I had to take a break from this computer and go and get my worship on. I will continually sing His praises in my mouth.

I vow to never judge or be a Bible thumper but be a living testament of His wondrous works!

Lord Continue to Dress Me

I have been having serious dreams of being taken for granted and I'm so tired. Yesterday was the ultimate and I know it's time to be compensated for it. But I'm rushing to take a quick nap before I head out . . . Well I'm back and let me tell you those dreams were warning signs for a dreamed of tapeworms which at first I thought were snakes and I called this friend of mine up and she said she felt these worms moving in her intestines that same night. The deception and being taken for granted piece just played itself out with everything from a so called friend accusing me of cheating with her husband who was also friendly with my hubby. I had prayed seriously about God protecting me and every morning I do my best to read the prayer of Jabez and then I ask my partner to show me where I should read, what do I open myself up to or what is it that He wants me to learn. Then I close with the armor and suit myself up with Ephesians 6:10. Yep because every day is a battle out here so we must remain suited.

And you know it's funny because last week the band I work with had a weekend of media publicity. Just a week ago after our TV shoot we were at the subway station at the World Trade Center former site and was talking about God and His beauty and awesomeness for at least two hours. I mean it was just a blessing. Before the shoot I asked that we hold hands; and we prayed with a group that consisted of Muslim, and Buddhist. I the Christian gave the prayer and religions just didn't matter because we are one. I mentioned this beautiful experience to someone and they told me, "Oh no you shouldn't be praying with them as a Christian." I sternly replied, "Hello what? I called the prayer and they all know I'm a keep it real Christian and since when did Jesus stop hanging or praying with those that the "churches" of that time thought were unworthy." We all serve a limitless God and that is where I'm coming from. I'm not "churchin" this thing, I'm living with light and my ultimate response was "Are we not the salt of the earth?" Hello . . . .

Last night I was feeding the homeless or as a friend of mine says "the city's residents." It was raining on and off and I had my hoodie on. I was wondering why this man passed me a snack bag but I put it aside and just went on handing out the plastic bags I had bought with me and then this nice lady came up to me and said you know we have some women's clothing over there so I said "Oh Madame I'm not homeless" and pulled my hoodie off to show my entire head. She started apologizing over and over and then the tall Preacher man said he assumed I was because I was handing bags out with another resident. I told them hey we all could be homeless it's only by Gods grace that I'm not and laughed. But seriously I have such a connection with them, I don't know I'm comfortable with them discussing life and how they see the beauty in it rather than hearing about money and possessions all the time, that gets on my nerves.

I could see why Jesus snuck away and Buddha and Mohamed gave up their worldly possessions because it's just about being one. I will leave this segment with this story of how my little group gave out clothes and life testimonies at this women and children's shelter. There was an associate of mine who was in the shelter that I had given a few new wigs and clothes and encouragement. Well one day I was going through it and she came by the house and collected some stuff and was all dressed up. I assumed she was dressed to make herself feel better. She invited me to the shelter and I remained in my sweats but when I got there I was greeted with all this press media and the Mayor was leaving and we exchanged pleasantries. I felt uncomfortable because when I looked around all the residents of the shelter were dressed up so I definitely felt under dressed. I spoke to some of the residents and they acted like they didn't know me because I wasn't dressed up enough I guess. Funny isn't it. I did feel some way about that though, I was saying the nerve of you but you know what if that is where people's heads are! After all I thought my husband was homeless but still obeyed my partner, the Holy Spirit and approached him with words of encouragement. At the end of the day it really doesn't matter. We are all human beings, the one species on this planet that hasn't figured out how to survive together yet.

When I was living in the gay life and fighting for just causes I never really felt accepted. Then when I made the choice to change partners some of those same gay friends of mine turned their backs on me but like I told them I'm the same person just a better me spiritually. It's funny because when I was married to a woman and going to church I told God that I desired someone who worshiped Him and when I decided to stop being with women and go back and try having relationships with men, that desire was still there!

I used to plead, "Lord I want someone I can worship with" and it didn't happen overnight but He gave me my wish.

However I had to get naked before Him and allow Him to dress me. I couldn't keep putting on winter jackets in the midst of summer . . . you feel me? And every now and then in various areas of my life I'll try and put on what I want but who knows the weather better He or me. I remember a line from a song that my Bermudian writing partner and I wrote "Our love is in and out of season without rhyme or reason" and that is what we should strive for, a real spiritual love. My WIT counselor reminded me yesterday; "We are spiritual beings having human experiences." Therefore "Lord as I go forward today and ask what should I wear, please dress me so that I may weather any storm that comes my way, let me always remember to pray. Good morning Lord and you readers have a blessed day!"

CAN'T STOP THE FLOW OF GOD

Its funny years ago I had a Holy union with another woman because in my heart I knew that fornicating was wrong and I just wanted to be faithful to the one I loved. You see when I was diagnosed with cancer I said whoever I'm with at that time I will marry. Wrong or indifferent, male or female it didn't matter and I strongly believed Christ first but second was my focus on getting married. I have always set the bar low regarding myself worth and even today I continuously go to counseling to assist with those deep rooted issues which are traced to my childhood. You see everything stems from the beginning just as we stem from our Creator. I love the Lord with every cell of my being and deep down I guess I always have and I realize this more and more as I turn the pages of my life's path. I recognize that there are good and evil, those with open hearts, those with selfish motives, those who judge and those who accept and let's just sum it up to say humans are human. I grew up in a mixed world and stemmed from a mixed ethnic family so

I knew from early that there was no real difference underneath our skin but the one thing that has kept us connected is that we are one. That's right no matter how you cut it, try to separate it, at the end of the day we are all created the same, we are born the same, we ALL speak the same baby language, we have the same basic wants and needs such as food, clothing and shelter. We all seek some form of acceptance, laugh, cry, bleed the same color blood and transcend when our spirits leave our bodies.

We go through all the same emotions and desire love as we are connected to this greater existence. That greater power we have given many names but I call Him God Jehovah and I believe in His only Son that walked this planet and His name is Jesus or Yeshua. I can feel the presence of the helper, the administrator, the guide, the internal instinct that comes alive the more you rely and acknowledge its existence and I call this the Holy Spirit or the Holy Ghost because you can't see it but you can feel it, you can experience it. I believe there are more questions than we can answer but based on my personal experience I know without a doubt in my life that there is the Trinity the Father, Son, and Holy Spirit. My partner in writing to you all, the one who gives me boldness to disclose certain things and guidance is my numero uno, my guide, the one I call Mr. Holy Spirit.

As I go through this life I see that we are more connected than we are apart. We may be separated by language, tradition, belief and custom but that is about it. No matter how you cut it we are more alike than different and every nation, every society from the lost ages of time has always sought a higher existence, a higher something to believe in and through studies of indigenous cultures there was always other life forms but this should be no surprise no matter how we try to deny it. Just because we can't understand something doesn't mean that it doesn't exist. Hello Hollywood was trying to tell you this for years but never the less we can rely on the BIBLE. The most translated book on the planet. Some say it stands for Basic Instructions Before Leaving Earth.

Yesterday I experienced an outpouring of the Holy Spirit at a church gathering and it was no ordinary church gathering. This was the celebration of an anniversary of a church that was founded by a man that answered a call of God. This gathering consisted of blacks, whites, Asians, Hispanics, gays, straights, bisexuals, transgender, young, old, distinguished, wealthy, poor and some Muslims and you know what they were all there for one purpose and that was to give glory and honor to God. You could feel the hair on your arms stand up when they called on the name Jesus. People started just letting themselves go and praising the Lord and dancing like David did because of the joy in their hearts. It was amazing but also a reminder that Christ reigns no matter how we try to downplay it and separate it; we need to leave the judging to Him. As recent as yesterday I was speaking with my Muslim artist and she was telling me about the celebration of "the EID" which was based upon Abraham sacrificing his son Ishmael (Isaac). While I was talking on the phone to her I was walking from the Ben Franklin Parkway to the Uptown in North Philly and all of a sudden I heard some Inspirational songs coming from a church. I told her I sometimes do this and I went in, got my spirit fed and left and continued walking. I had to get to those children, I felt an urgency. I ended up sharing my testimony with a young man and it was on time for his mother was being prepared for brain cancer. In addition to this the next Sunday morning there was a guest speaker from South Africa and guess what he spoke on? The same story of Abraham and Isaac. I called my Muslim sister and said, "What are the chances of that; you being Muslim and then my Christian church delivers that same message?" Both of us said, "Look at the Spirit of God!" And who showed up to my walk, the Muslim not my fellow Christian sisters. Not One!

When people see me they don't know the full story; for this book could not hold all that is, all the connection points God has placed throughout my life. Some have gone on to become movie stars, major recording artists, Prime Ministers, legendary songwriters, actors, major Hollywood producers, senators and the list of earthly accolades continues. But I realize that none of this could have happened if it were not in God's bigger plan. It will be interesting to see how His plan unfolds in not just my life but yours as well!

WAKE UP WITH A GOOD GIGGLE

Despite the storms in my life I had this dream last night about my friend Carol Ann who I grew up with and we were at this gathering and she was telling my sister and I how her hair used to be down to her knees. We were rolling with laughter saying that we didn't remember that and we have known her for all of her life. She turned and said using my full name "Oh this is before you met me I was nine." And my sister and I fell out laughing and as I'm writing this I'm remembering all those who make me laugh and have been constants in my life; whether it be for a season, a reason or a lifetime. At this particular time of course 'Satina' is doing their thing and my hubby and I have to see the detectives about the neighbor stealing the rent money, I mean who does that really? And no we aren't laughing about that but I'm sure as time goes on we will find a giggle in that as well. For the most part I try and find humor in everything for example I was telling my Aunt who has a peculiar lung disease about an oxygen story. Now here she is facing a serious reality but we found a giggle in it. Check this, I told her that carrying around oxygen has never stopped anyone from living. We laughed about another cousin who carried that tank everywhere and I do mean everywhere! I told her about a friend of mine who carried a tank and was driving me around while I was relocating. One day I was telling him to hurry across the street because his chord was going to get run over by a car and he said to me "Come on LA you know me by now I've got this! And I said, "You would want to move before the chord strangles you when it's run over by a car. And no sweetheart God's got this!" I relayed this story to my Aunt who has to see a specialist from abroad today because of her condition, she got the point.

When I look back over my life and the people that God has placed in my life I can see all the reasons people who have been in and out of my life due to oxygen. Even when I was getting high I had oxygen tankers around me and I would say "Oh no I'm not getting high with you, that thing might blow up!" But they got high with someone else anyhow. Here I was trying to save us when in reality the drugs were killing us anyway. Another giggle that came to my mind was when I was living back home and I thought I lost my trusty purse. My friend Andy rode his bike all the way from Shelly Bay to Parsons Road and then we thought we saw my Mom's car and we signaled it to stop. We rode up on the car and he poked his head in the window shouting, "Where's the purse!" When we looked back it wasn't even my mom's car. Can you imagine our first car jacking? Well we rode back to the church and there was my purse sitting on the porch and no one touched it and that in itself was an act of God! Firstly for the people not reacting to us negatively because they were so stunned and we said, "Wrong car sorry" and rode off. Secondly for my purse being safe in that area. Therefore the lesson here is like the movie to live, love, laugh and of course pray. For when the chips are down you can giggle as you pick them up!

FULL CIRCLE

When I look back over my life I can see how there was a common thread or theme. So many times it included the same lessons or activities just in different settings over various stages of my life. When I was young I used to be in and out of the hospital from day one so being quote on quote ill I was being trained for. Those arrows that the enemy would throw at me I was already trained in weapons 1, 2 and 4.

God knows it all, staged it all so He knew I would be juggling a few major illnesses before my ultimate breakthrough. Now when I was a girl I was raised in the church and hung out at youth group, had sleep-over's, my first boyfriends were in the church, my exposure to writing a play, directing, producing and standing up for the masses. I once stood up and told the people in the church not to judge us youngsters because we are reflections of their past actions and everyone gagged but latter said yep she spoke the truth. But it wasn't me it was the authority of the Holy Spirit in me that allowed me to stand boldly. Later it came out that there was a lot of shadiness going on within the church and one time we all found our beloved leader on top of another member and it was devastating for us kids. Now that I'm an adult my life has run full circle and I desire to do those same things and I'm experiencing similar stuff but this time I'm equipped.

You see what I went through as a child has prepared me as an adult. I'm not running away from my church home. As a matter of fact in service yesterday we had an interactive session and the Holy Spirit once again had me rise up and state that God brought me here and that I will not be leaving until He tells me to do so. So many have been run off my by the iron clad fisted minority but God had prepared me as a child to withstand the attacks of the adversary right within the church. As a matter of fact as we approach the end times we need to stand firm within the Lord. When all else fails we must stand. We must ask for Holy Spirit direction and guidance and ordering of our steps. I am constantly reminded in circumstances that many are called but few are chosen. I remember that four o'clock in the morning call to my mother when a spirit within me said "Mom I sold my soul for your life" and I remember her saying get a Bible and there amongst my coke head friends was a Bible and she said just open it and wherever your finger falls read it. Now check the scene, a bunch of us young and high on cocaine with several grams spread out all over the place while I'm reading the Word. Can you see the seed? When I randomly opened that Bible I turned to "before you were born, you were chosen!" Well if that wasn't enough to knock the earthly high out of you. Here it is decades later and I remember, even in my altered state. And as I'm writing I'm looking at God's hand outstretched over my life. Every morning I listen to my Mom's advice and I read the Prayer of Jabez 1Chron. 4:10 and I believe. As I'm writing this my husband and I are in the midst of a true battle of deceit and I have no other choice but to trust in God's plan.

My neighbor who the others on the block told me he was on Megan's list as a registered sex offender and had robbed the couple of the house next door as well as some state trooper of more than $20,000. I asked where the proof was and they could only show me the Megan's list. Therefore I looked at him as innocent until proven guilty and his past was his past. I mean hey many of us had colorful ones, your reading about some of mine! I asked myself not my partner questions as to why did the lady who was quite smart just blog about it online and why would he be living across the street from the school. All these whys . . . plus he was a friendly neighbor, my husband said too good to be true and he kept his yard so immaculate.

I knew that when I was going through some personal issues I prayed to God to send me someone to help me and the neighbor came along. He said he could rent the apartments from his site. I told him I already had ads online and my husband and I had done 98% of the work completed. I told him if he could find me some tenants I would give him half a month's rent for a finder's fee and we shook hands. Time went by and the next thing I know he had tenants in the property long before I signed any leases or received deposits. The first apartment he came through after only ten days so I let him do the second apartment and this time I had my realtor go to show it as well but there was someone already there. I also met with a lady who wanted to take a second look and she told me she saw an air conditioner in the window.

Here we are almost a month later and nothing and on top of that he had the nerve to collect rent from the first apartment and now is dangling our money of over two thousand dollars over our heads. He texts us, calls and says he's bringing the money and then turns around and shouts abruptly that he has bills to pay. He's a mess; can you imagine he's paying his bills with our rightful monies? I told him enough is enough and I've turned him over to the Lord. I told him I forgave him and you know what, I now have peace. Yes I'm angry at how he has had the audacity to treat us with the attitude of you'll get your money when I have it attitude. Are you serious you stole from us point blank but I sternly gave him a deadline and I will be going to press charges! However in the midst of all of that financial drama, I had to go get my brain tumor checked so stress is something I do not need and when they put the contrast into my small veins it was so painful that all I could do was to recite scriptures to keep my mind. Isaiah 26:3 Keep your mind on Him, trust in Him and He will give you perfect peace and that He does. Like I told the neighbor in a text that in his life he had to come across me because I would be the one to be used by Christ to make an impact. So whatever God has planed I know I'll be protected for I have peace in knowing that and I just asked Him to direct my path as to how to deal with our overdue bills. I'm not telling you anything I don't know our church always says "Prove me Lord" not that He has to but I'm telling you as the pages turn in my life I know that I know that I know that God is my strength, a present help, a provider . . . He is my Jehovah Jirah. For instance I just got my MRI results and I'm in my twelfth year with a grade 2 brain tumor diagnosis and it's steady. I'm here to tell you to fight for the position that God has ordained you, the position of His purpose NO MATTER WHAT!!!!

Ok PRAISE REPORT . . . here it is three hours after writing the aforementioned and I know I have to pay these utilities for the property but we don't have enough money since the "thief" neighbor is holding it from us. But I asked my partner, Mr. Holy Spirit to place in order what He wants me to do and immediately after that request I hear "go and call these companies but stall." Well I looked for my energy bill and there was God's favor. It was a quarter of what I thought we owed on that statement. I called in the payment and paid the extra fee of less than four dollars and I'm telling you I started writing out checks for the other utility companies like a robot, one after the other. A little something here, there and everywhere. All I can say to anyone reading this is that if you just trust Him no matter what you're going through He will favor you. Yes we may complain, have a brief pity party and holler and scream but like a child just knows that Daddy has you. Now I must call my mom overseas but I just thought I would share this with you . . . to show you that FAITH truly is confidence in GOD!!!

GOLDEN TEARS

I can't sleep and instead of counting sheep I recite scriptures of peace and my friends it works!

There is this thing in my spirit, my soul that is so Mother Teresa like that I just want to save the world. That is my call for missionary work and as I told this Rabbi the other night while in a meeting I feel that is one of my calls to assist the community. I find myself crying when I think of the children who touched my life in Guyana and I know I touched their lives as well for many are still in contact with me years later, still holding onto the hope that I will return. The beautiful thing is that it isn't about money but genuine love. I have this one Indian student that every time I think of her she writes me and she has Jesus engraved in her heart even though she married a Hindu.

Look all I'm saying is that my essence as I once answered in church one day is HOPE. I cry these golden tears because I can't believe that another human who appeared so delivered and truthful can blatantly steal from another human. Someone next door and I do mean literally, we have #20 and he stays in #18. That neighbor who the block hated because of his past label as a sex offender, I wanted to give him hope! I'm crying because I messed up by allowing him into our lives but more so I'm trying to figure out how I will pay these bills. Right now my mom is getting my vacant property ready overseas so there is no income there and I feel responsible. We have lost income here due to according to police terms, theft by deception and all I want to do is give back to those who have taken care of me. My Father may have to have an operation, my Parents and Aunts are getting older and I feel that I'm a burden. So self pity is creeping in and all I can do is cry out to the Lord.

Finally yesterday my husband and I pressed charges against the so called good neighbor that stole our rent and deposit monies. I know for me personally it is time that I learn my lesson in people but on the other hand it had to go this way. We found out last night that he is on $20000 bail for a current fraud case and if I knew this the question is would I have given him a second chance? And the answer is probably yes because of my "savior' mentality but as my counselor said to me I cannot save the world. She boldly stated that if you look up the name Jesus in the dictionary you would not see my face. As I look back over my life I can see the correlation and as Quincy Jones and BeBe Winans song says "Everything Must Change" including the good sections of me.

My partner just turned me to a Psalms and my eyes fell upon the name Vindicator. I really need to seek divine wisdom and discernment and not accept or do ANYTHING without seeking my partner, Mr. Holy Spirit's approval first and ask for confirmation. Despite the pains in my head I feel better for I know that the victory is ours I just need to learn how not to walk in my eyesight and start depending on my Savior for He will show me hindsight for at the end of the day He has the Master plan and all of these mishaps are apart of my unfolding story. I accept the fact that if we have no tests there can't be any testimonies!

IT'S ALL LAID OUT

It's funny how I'm always saying that life is lessons repeated until learned and trust and believe the more I go through I'm learning to live my life this way. When you view life from this perspective you realize just how awesome God is and you can feel a sense of relief and can just breathe. Now I've had family members murdered and another who actually did the murder and coming from this angle you look at both sides. I say this to say that when our neighbor tried to rip my husband and I off by stealing our tenants rent and deposit monies we could have snapped and everything in our being went there trust and believe. I trusted the neighbor to find the tenants and do what he said he could do with the background checks and leases. He ended up moving in tenants without our knowledge and taking their money from them and acting as if he outright owned the property. He has a silver tongue and when he couldn't come clean with the money or the leases on time it got heated! My husband and I have similar thought patterns in that we can talk street amongst ourselves but when it came to actions I noticed that I went straight to my prayer warriors, my parents while my hubby went to the other side where he was used to, street style if you know what I'm saying! That neighbor should be happy I'm a praying wife. You see the closer you walk and talk with God you learn to start putting His words into action.

My partner reminded me that I had to stop saying fleshly street things with my husband and teach him how to pray it through and how to turn to God in prayer. Over the years I've learned that there is no greater source of power than the Creator of everything. Men have limitations and are fallible and sometimes we wander through this life like pilgrims feeling that people can't protect us from anything; and that is why we have to turn it over, like the song says "Turn it Over to Jesus." The Word says weeping comes for the night but joy comes in the morning. We have to go through our weeping periods in order to appreciate our joy periods. We have to behave like the song He gave me "Praise Him through the Circumstance."

This morning we woke up with to the mountain of the lying stealing get away neighbor who remains in view but does not and will not obstruct our perspective. This neighbor was shun by everybody on the block because of his past that was printed on the internet and I let him know from the door that I was a keep it real Christian and that I believe in second chances. Oh well he got off 13times from the Philly courts due to his supposed connections but I have to trust and believe that my God has it all laid out!

Just maybe the neighbor had to go through the court scene to realize that the only person he is fooling is himself and he needs to fully surrender. My hubby needed to see how my approach is that of relying on God verses the streets. "At the end of the day" (my great quote from former Senator Jerome Dill) we all have to <u>go through</u> in order to <u>get to</u> our destinations. I have to put my trust in God for peace especially since tomorrow morning I go for my brain tests to look at the cancer activity. Our health is our wealth and in the midst of this entire episode one of my long-term friends made the decision yesterday with his family to pull the plug on his mother's life support. So while my husband and I awoke to the theft situation my friend awoke to wondering if his mother is still alive. Sort of puts it all into perspective doesn't it? Our lives are laid out but it's the decisions that we make that can deter our course for the most part.

IN A TWINKLING

The past six weeks have taken their toll. You know how you have a strange feeling come over you and then a bunch of racing thoughts well that is what has been happening to me. My chest has been feeling full of fluid, my heart sometimes hurts and then my eyesight. OMG as they say today; it has gone from nearly perfect to fuzzy. I want to go to the doctors but the bills are so high and the apartment remains vacant. My personal life has been in shambles to the point where I can't even ask for a ride to visit people. I don't know what mood is going to greet me or meet me so I've gone into a shell. I never wanted to have this as my new life but just as sure as the earth is revolving God never told us that we wouldn't face trials. He does assure us that He will never leave us nor forsake us and when I look back over my life I can clearly see His fingerprints. If I don't know anything what I do know is that He has my back and has kept me alive to share my story whether it is through word, song or deed. Just not sure about the order but I do know that we have to trust Him because like the Minister said at my uncles funeral yesterday, God is in control. I think during the past two months I wanted to believe and knew this in spirit but to apply it to my trials was another story.

In a twinkling of an eye when you accept Jesus Christ as your personal Savior it's a decision that you will never regret. Now it will alter the course of your life's direction to hope of eternal friendship, hope of a life beyond this one that we can't comprehend. As I write this I'm listening to the highest praise "Hallelujah You're Worthy" by Brooklyn Tabernacle Choir and I'm telling you tears of joy are streaming because yesterday I heard at the home going service how my uncle was saved and even though I didn't get to physically say goodbye I felt his presence. Now because I was going through personal problems I wanted to take my husband to meet him, so he could see where I spent a large portion of my life around laughter and love. I always had this invisible sync up with my Uncle and felt him so I called. I did not know in the natural that he had just gotten out of the hospital so when I called my play brother he informed me how Uncle Don almost died and had went code blue but God saw to it once again that he would live. Anyhoo I spoke directly to Uncle Don and we chatted about memories and he called me Leslie and asked me how is this, how is that and when was he going to see me? I didn't have the heart to say that I've tried but was shut down time and time again. Therefore we planned for my bro to pick me up the following week. I cancelled everything and was looking forward to that day. We spoke throughout that Wednesday June 29th and I waited for my bro to get here.

Uncle Don said doesn't your husband have a car and I said I'm not asking him to take me anywhere and didn't have the heart to tell him that during the past two years I had repeatedly asked him. Anyhoo I said I would wait for Brian and hours went by to the point where I started to give up and then something was saying to call him and I did and his Godson Rick was there who I hadn't spoken to in years. So Uncle Don and I spoke and he said again how he really wanted to see me. I cracked a lame joke and he said "Leslie I love you" and I told him the same and said well lets meet next week and I said, "Are you sure that's okay" and he answered "Yes." Well he passed the next day and the lesson for the rest of my life is that when your spirit tells you something don't let anyone stop you from doing what you should. There is no excuse as to why I allowed another to block me, that is the second time in my life this has occurred. I'm telling you it doesn't feel good.

This man walked me down the aisle for my first union; this is the house where I hung out with my best friend Nate from young. This is where they threw me my first adult surprise birthday party, where I had my reception and the list goes on and on. This is where I accidentally set his bed on fire from my cigarette. This is where I would talk to my Bermudian friend Keith who later I repeatedly tried to reach and would get a strange voice which I knew wasn't him. But did I press the issue? No I went back home to Bermuda and the moment I stepped on a plane I was informed by my same Uncle Don that he mysteriously died and that is another story.

The question is if I had so many great memories there why would I stay away? Look I'm telling you to learn from me for that saying is true never put off today that call or just a simple follow up. I guess that is why I fight so hard through the pain but the older I get I'm becoming redefined in a twinkling of an eye!

THE RELEASE OF KEITH

Earlier I spoke of my friend Keith and for years I carried so much guilt of just knowing that I played such an intricate part in his journey and death. You see I used to hang out with Keith in our lovely Bermuda. We would double date in the most magnificent places, I mean just breath taking water views and exquisite dining. Looking back they were some of the best times of my life. Well Keith wanted to go away to school and I told him about Philadelphia. Never knowing in the natural that a decision I helped him make would end his life. I wasn't going to include this in my book but I prayed about it and trust and believe sought guidance from my partner, Mr. Holy Spirit. The answer to my question was how could I not include it; I owe it to Keith and myself.

We would visit and discuss possible schools and living arrangements in Philly and he trusted my judgment. I told him I knew of a friend of a friend who was left a huge house by his deceased parents and he might be able to stay there until he got settled. Well check this:

He went away to study at a University in Philadelphia and while at the student lounge looking at a postings board for a place to stay all of a sudden this guy walks up and places a post of "Roommate needed" etc. The guy just happened to be the friend of a friend I was telling him about. What are those chances?

Anyhoo he moves in and everything is great. I visit with my Uncle Don for a while and Keith and I talked but never got the chance to link up physically. I connected him with my Uncle and his friends and all was well. I left and came back to Philly and every time I called for him he wasn't around (pre-cell days). I called so much that eventually when I did get him it wasn't his voice. After a few times of getting the fake voice I knew something was up and told my Uncle to look out for him and headed back to Bermuda.

One day while I was out at the Princess hotel about to go and get my hair done the front desk told me that there was a phone call for me. I was wondering how they knew I was there but one of my relatives had tracked me down. My Uncle Don called to tell me they had just found Keith dead. I was with a girlfriend and I instantly fell to the floor hysterically in tears. That was the first time that I experienced shock.

Within days a friend of Keith and I flew out to get his body but to his surprise and everyone else's the housemate had already made arrangements to have him flown back without an autopsy. As a result Keith and the friend passed each other in mid air. While the friend was flying to Philly Keith's body was flying to Bermuda. What are the chances of that? There was NO autopsy because the housemate told the distraught family that he had taken care of everything. He was studying to be a doctor and was "well connected." I know firsthand that he had tried to come onto Keith several times and Keith dismissed his advances. Now the day of the alleged suicide Keith was on the porch smoking a cigarette in a great mood with another neighbor and told them he had to go back into the house to check on his laundry and he never returned. It was stated that all of the towels were freshly folded and later that evening in the middle of the laundry room with a clean towel around his neck there was Keith hanging from the ceiling. The housemate got Keith's address book and started calling people back home. He consoled them and then flew to Bermuda. When he arrived he looked just like Keith even with his mannerisms and started to talk like him. Well naturally Keith's family took to him but something didn't sit right with me, my Philly friends or my close cousin. He befriended all of Keith's friends and tried to become close to them by saying, "Keith would want this" and with some he made moves on. Hours before the funeral the housemate went swimming at Clearwater Beach and was splashing in the water like a child saying, "I can't believe Keith gave all this up to move to Philly, this island is so beautiful can't we just skip the funeral?"

The night before at the viewing we noticed Keith's hands and his knuckles had bruises on them like he had been in a fight with someone. They weren't just on one hand but both almost as if they had been in a fist position for punching. I have several witnesses who saw this as well. After the funeral the housemate continued to return to Bermuda and even looked into relocating there. He would stay with different friends or associates of Keith's and each time would try and become closer with them and certain siblings; it was almost as if he had taken over Keith's identity. This of course has never been investigated but in my heart I know that Keith would want this to be told. Thanks for allowing me to break free of this mystery which many of you can figure out that it is no mystery at all. This segment of my life resembles one of those lifetime movies and my cousin. We sometimes go there with that which must not be said!

CHOICES THAT MAKE YOU SAY 'AH'

Grace and mercy are exactly what I need from my Heavenly Father to get me through. It's been almost two weeks since I wrote to you all but as usual it's been a whirlwind. It is almost as if God is deleting people, showing me things and presenting me with choices at a neck breaking speed. I think of people and things and they magically appear or I feel things so strongly in my gut that once revealed it could only be the Divine. Yesterday I was so sad and disappointed that I cried hard and it has been one thing after another and in that order one after another.

I had these artists that focused on themselves with one never acknowledging me but I realize that was just a sign but God taught me how to watch and separate. This one artist never had money to pay me because I didn't put myself out there like that. I always do things freely because there was something inside of me that just made me present myself as a freewill offering. I always had a desire to help others and when I had money I had the burning desire to give it away to the wrong people. When I used drugs I would give them away and then listen to them talk about how much of a fool I was and a sucker. They would say stuff like, "Yeah look at her now we used all of hers and she things she's going to get ours well she is getting nothing." It was almost as if I wasn't there when they would talk. I used to get upset but then I realized that they were saving my life and many of them have died. All those that stole money from me or my possessions are no longer on this planet and have died of overdoes or illnesses or strange accidents. This one guy we took in to work on one of the buildings and we paid him $600 cash for his weeks work as well as paying for whatever supplies he requested. Well he didn't want to pay us $25 a week and instead stole from us, did drugs on the premises and would stash the bags in the walls.

Yep money wasn't a factor but the game was the same. This guy would go home broke and tell his wife we hadn't paid him and his lies caught up with him and she kicked him out so he had to leave the country and go back home. Well let me show you how the scripture in the presence of mine enemies works. I was at this acquaintance house with my Mom and Rosie and forgot my video camera was on. As I walked through I couldn't believe that this guy's house was constructed like the inside of a jail cell. I guess since he spent half of his life in jails in Cuba, America and Bermuda this style was of comfort to him. There was a picture on his wall that I recognized of the guy who had worked for us in Philadelphia, it was a picture of his beautiful son and I said does so and so live here and he said yes. This man went from owning a top of the line truck and living in an exclusive area on the East Coast to sleeping on a concrete floor with a few belongings and a picture of his son. Now he had a great view because the property was overlooking the turquoise water, but can you imagine? Then he was riding a scooter and working extra hard just to take care of his now exploded drug habit. I asked my mom to go to the job site so I could tell him off but God blocked it. No sooner did I get on that plane to return to Philly did I hear that he was riding his bike and went to light a cigarette and the unthinkable happened right out of an action movie. When he looked up there was a truck in front of him with cement blocks and one fell on top of his head when he ran into the back of it because he wasn't paying attention and was too busy lighting up when it had stopped. The cement blocks crushed his head. I couldn't even feel sorry for the thief and I know that is not Jesus like but I've got to work on that. My Mom always said that God doesn't pay in debts.

You know my whole life my Lord has been just that my Savior. I've been in buildings and felt a bust was coming and would tell everyone in the house to get it together but they would pay me no mind and then the door would be slammed down. One girl was so arrogant and I heard soon after that her heart froze from all the cocaine. Then there was the nice guy, my buddy O who I let drive my car and he got shot. Or the guy who was so pompous with his drug self and went and sold fake $5 bags and one of the customers turned around and shot him dead. The list goes on and on.

I recall getting high and seeing this dealers girlfriend looking down on us and then when GOD himself cleaned me up I went back to visit some people and there was the old lady who had a stroke but was still getting high and told me to leave because I was too good for all of this but she let me pray with her. However in the in the other room was that same dealers girlfriend now strung out and my heart sank as tears rolled down my cheeks. Another lady came to me for prayer that she would get clean because she was just about to get her children back. I was a living testimony for I went from buying drugs to share with them because I was always a sharer don't get it twisted; to getting high with them to being a witness for Christ. I think about them and pray for them for they were a part of my story. Sometimes I would revisit areas just to take a glimpse of my past to recognize where He has brought me today. God is truly awesome, thank you Jesus for saving me and always looking out for me! I truly believe because my heart didn't become selfish that is why I was saved and allowed to get back into my body.

I can recall being in this building and there were just lines and lines of people of all ages getting high and I remember saying to myself back then that this was something out of a movie. I mean I could get high but sit back and just observe. When I look over my life that same selfless spirit has caused me heartache from the job market, to my love life to my spiritual life. You see it's only now that I realize as the pages of my life turn that this people pleasing spirit is definitely not the way to go. I could still be giving but not at the expense of God's creation and transformation. He chose me and my best way to serve Him is to learn the lesson. My best gift back to Him is to finally graduate. You know how proud your parents are when you graduate well the same goes for our Creator. And by George I'm finally getting it Lord. You present the choices of the paths and it is up to us to be guided by the light for I believe in Psalms 119:105 where it says that "the Word is a lamp to my feet and a light for my path" so I'm finally switching on my flashlight and walking with my partner, Mr. Holy Spirit. Sorry about that Lord I know you must look at me and say will she ever get it. So my decision to the person who wants to take advantage of me tomorrow is NO I cannot and like my UK friend Crystal says, "I'm not able!" People, places and things will forever present themselves in different wrappings as gifts but the Holy Spirit will let you know we just have to allow him to guide us. He is a gentleman and will always give us a choice and it is up to us to make that "Ah" choice! To end this chapter I'm listening to "Thank You" by 33 miles. Thank You for everything, it doesn't matter what tomorrow brings and I have to remember that Lord you are always on time.

WHERE I START
IS WHERE I FINISH

As I get closer to my conclusion of this first book I become boggled with so many things and projects that aren't completed, so even writing is difficult. *I realize that it's a spirit of fear so in the name of Jesus right now I rebuke this spirit of* fear of not finishing in the name above all names my Lord and Savior Jesus Christ. I recognize that I'm in a time of change. Change of circumstances, change of friends, and change of situations and in order to reach that change I have to plunge and take a leap of faith. I talk about it and have exercised it but right now at this very moment I am my own worst blocker and many times we are just that blockers. We get caught up in the drama so we need to make that change. As I'm writing I'm listening to Jimmy Hicks/The Voices of Integrity song "Blessed like that . . . The devil doesn't like it because you're blessed like that . . . ." That's right we are blessed like that so as you read this look at that blocker in your life that's keeping you from the other side and say Devil step aside because I'm on assignment! So here it goes . . . There are so many stories or should I say examples of how my partner has never left me.

The other day I was at the airport leaving Florida with my parents and their flight was just over an hour earlier so as we said our "see you later." I remained sitting at their gate all comfortable. I had spoken briefly with a woman from Brazil and she was telling me how she adopted these kids from Africa and said how they really are her children and check on her. She went on to say how proud she was of their accomplishments and we hugged at the end and I said, "God bless you." The way how she held me I knew I was in the presence of a human angel. I felt great and starting getting back into my book where God was responding to my questions since I hadn't brought a Bible with me. The book was by Psalmist Judy Jacobs called "Don't Miss Your Moment." As I was reading away and relaxing; all of a sudden I heard "Go to Your Gate." I looked at my ticket and it said another flight number. I had assumed since we were all using the same airlines and going to the same destination just at different times, I thought it would be the same gate right? Well no I was wrong I had to walk to a different section with a different gate. Check this; it was 8:40a.m. When I arrived they were calling the last group of people to board my flight which was set to depart at 9 a.m.

I made it just on time and when I look back I've always had these supernatural airport moments from me mentioning monks and they would appear, to me feeling Michael Jackson's death fifteen minutes before it was announced. I believe airports have special positions in my life for transferring messages. So with regards to me just making my plane again I know that this is how God wants me to look at my life. I may think I'm traveling like everyone else but once I'm in tune with my partner, Mr. Holy Spirit and allow Him to truly guide me, I will be aware of the fact that just because I'm using the same carrier doesn't always mean I'm at the right gate. However if I allow myself to be obedient and adhere to His voice and follow His instructions He will get me to my destination. So you know what, I no longer feel how I felt when I began to write this book for this is a message for me that needed to unfold just as it is for someone reading these words. "Thank you Lord you are so awesome and I'm willing to be positioned at whatever Gate you place me at."

Bruised but Not Broken

What's on my heart foremost is that I have a funeral tomorrow of someone who was such a part of my life. For two decades this gentleman played the role of father, Godfather, uncle and most of all friend. His birthday was the day before mine but we of course were decades apart. Even writing this I can't stop 'balling' my head off. He walked me down the aisle in my first Holy union. Yep this man has been a part of my journey and I didn't get the chance to say goodbye physically but we did chat before he died. You know his passing made me look at my own life and how truthfully at this moment I feel like a ping pong ball but as of yesterday my mentality has changed. Like I told someone that was very concerned about me that I'm no longer on the playing board.

You know some things in life you want to be on the playing board for like music and film but due to the numerous bumps and bruises I've taken myself off the board. I realize I'm living in my extension with this brain cancer thing and I'm sitting and watching who is who in my life. It's almost like watching the story unfold and people showing their true selves. Sometimes it's painful but I have to be still and let the story unfold by itself and that includes every aspect of my life. I'm learning to become more intimate with my partner, Mr. the Holy Spirit. He knows everything about me and can push me to keep going when I feel like giving up! However God reminds me that He is love in its completeness and that I was created to love. Just as I finished proofing the majority of the manuscript I checked my voicemail and there was a Prophet M who left a message about a little boy he had prayed over with a brain tumor. God used him as a vessel to heal the child and then he said if I have a prayer request then call for he sees God favoring my health and finances, so you know I called in. Therefore despite the bruises just listening to the voice of God reminds me that I'm worth the effort and no matter how many bruises my spirit encounters it is not easily broken!

I trust that this book has enlightened, encouraged and empowered you for we are imperfect beings living in a microwave chaotic world of darkness trying to do our best by seeking that which is right, your light in the Heavenly Father. If any reader out there has not discovered what it is like to have the assurance of a personal navigator over their life but wants to or even to experience a closer walk and encounter with the Holy Spirit please repeat these words:

Lord I come to you for strength, guidance and protection over all the corners of my life's journey. Jesus I want to develop a personal relationship with you. One that goes beyond the church walls! One whereby the Holy Spirit will become my director, my comforter and friend. I commit my ways to you, I submit my pride and I want you Lord Jesus to come into my heart and become my personal Savior. For Lord I need you as I breathe you.

Thank you for taking the time to ride along my Holy Spirit led Limitless Journey!

with deceased Coretta Scott King

Race for Hope Team LA walkers

Grammy Cert Dec 2012 (2)

with Ny on radio show

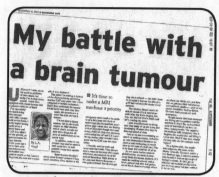

Article one day prior to surgery

A Poetic Night pic by Walter Brown

at Mixing Board

Creating n Producing in the Studio

Race 4 Hope Brain Tumor Walk
Philadelphia 2012, 1 week exactly b4
my 13th year n God still has me here
2 showcase His Power n Glory